LABYRINTH

An International Journal for Philosophy,
Value Theory and Sociocultural Hermeneutics

Printed ISSN 2410-4817
Online ISSN 1561-8927

Vol. 19, No. 1, Autumn 2017

THE HERETICAL PERSPECTIVES OF JAN PATOČKA (1907-1977)

Guest Editor: Dr. Ludger Hagedorn

Editor-in-Chief:
Prof. Dr. Yvanka B. Raynova

Managing Editor:
Dr. Susanne Moser

Advisory Board:

Prof. Dr. Seyla Benhabib (Boston), Prof. Dr. Debra Bergoffen (Fairfax), Prof. Dr. Peter Caws (Washington), Prof. Dr. Lester Embree (Florida), Prof. Dr. Reinhold Esterbauer (Graz), Prof. Dr. Nancy Fraser (New York), Dr. Ludger Hagedorn (Wien), Prof. Dr. Alison M. Jaggar (Boulder), Prof. Dr. Domenico Jervolino (Roma/Napoli), Prof. Dr. Andrzej M. Kaniowski (Łódź), Prof. Dr. Alexis Klimov † (Trois-Rivières), Prof. Dr. François Laruelle (Paris), Prof. Dr. Hedwig Meyer Wilmes (Nijmegen), Prof. Dr. Herta Nagl-Docekal (Wien), Prof. Dr. Elit Nikolov (Sofia), Prof. Dr. Sonja Rinofner-Kreidl (Graz), Prof. Dr. Hans-Walter Ruckenbauer (Graz), Prof. Dr. Ronald E. Santoni (Granville), Prof. Dr. Anne-Françoise Schmid (Paris), Prof. Dr. Hans-Reiner Sepp (Prague), Prof. Dr. Helmuth Vetter (Wien), Dr. Brigitte Weisshaupt (Zürich), Prof. Dr. Kurt Weisshaupt † (Zürich), Prof. Dr. Andrzej Wierciński, Prof. Dr. Richard Wisser (Mainz)

Axia Academic Publishers

Bibliographische Information der Deutschen Nationalbibliothek:
Die Deutsche Nationalbibliothek verzeichnet diese Publikation in der Deutschen Nationalbibliographie, detaillierte bibliographische Daten sind im Internet unter http://dnb.dnb.de aufrufbar.

Die wissenschaftliche und redaktionelle Arbeit wurde von der Kulturabteilung der Stadt Wien – Wissenschafts- und Forschungsförderung unterstützt.

Labyrinth: An International Journal for Philosophy, Value Theory and Sociocultural Hermeneutics is a serial publication of the Institut für Axiologische Forschungen / Institute for Axiological Research, Vienna – www.iaf.ac.at
For more information, please visit the Journal's homepage:
www.labyrinth.axiapublishers.com

© 2017 Axia Academic Publishers
Vienna
All Rights Reserved
Journal & Cover © 1999 Institut für Axiologische Forschungen
Printed in Germany

ISSN 2410-4817 / ISBN 978-3-903068-23-0

www.axiapublishers.com

LABYRINTH, Vol. 19, No. 1, Autumn 2017

THE HERETICAL PERSPECTIVES OF JAN PATOČKA (1907-1977)

Table of Contents

EDITORIAL

Ludger Hagedorn (Wien)
Editorial — 5

FROM THE ARCHIVES: A LECTURE GIVEN IN HISTORICALLY CHARGED TIMES

Jan Patočka (Prag)
Die Funktion der Literatur in der Gesellschaft (1968) — 12

AN ICONIC TEXT RETRANSLATED AND RECONSIDERED

Jan Patočka (Prague)
On the Matters of the Plastic People of the Universe and DG 307 — 23

Jozef Majernik (Chicago)
Jan Patočka's Reversal of Dostoevsky and Charter 77 — 26

THE HERETICAL PERSPECTIVES OF JAN PATOČKA

Ludger Hagedorn (Wien)
Die "unermessliche Leichtigkeit und Zerbrechlichkeit des menschlichen Faktums." Jan Patočka und die Krise des Humanismus — 46

Ovidiu Stanciu (Paris)
Subjectivité et projet. La critique patočkienne du concept heideggérien de "projet de possibilités" — 63

Jan Frei (Prag)
Zerstreuung, Verschliessung, Hingabe. Zur Figur des Transzendierens bei Jan Patočka — 79

Jason Alvis (Vienna)
"Scum of the Earth": Patočka, Atonement, and Waste   102

Christian Sternad (Leuven)
Max Scheler and Jan Patočka on the First World War   120

Martin Kočí (Prague)
The Experiment of Night: Jan Patočka on War, and a Christianity to Come   138

Philippe Merlier (Limoges)
Patočka, the meaning of the post-European spirit and its direction   156

DISCUSSION

Susanne Moser (Wien)
Political Correctness oder Tugendterror?   166

INTERVIEW

Klaus Nellen, Jakub Homolka (Wien)
Patočka ist gestorben. Wir müssen etwas tun!"   180

BOOK REVIEW

Susanne Moser (Wien)
Jan Assmann: Totale Religion. Ursprünge und Formen puritanischer Verschärfung   191

EDITORIAL

This first issue of the Journal *Labyrinth* in 2017 is dedicated to the philosophy of Jan Patočka. It commemorates not only the 110th anniversary of his birth (* 1.6.1907 in Turnov in Bohemia) but also the 40th anniversary of his tragic death in 1977. In that year, Patočka became one of the first spokespersons of the civil rights movement *Charter 77* – an engagement marked by confrontation with the communist regime, which ultimately cost him his life. Weakened by poor health conditions, Patočka died in the aftermath of a police interrogation on March 13th, 1977.

The issue's title *The Heretical Perspectives of Jan Patočka (1907-1977)* invokes this double commemoration and alludes to his most famous and most heartily debated book, *Heretical Essays in the Philosophy of History* (Patočka 1996). These essays, written towards the end of his life, in some sense can be seen as the culmination of his inquiries and long-term aspirations in the philosophy of history. Yet, it is by no means unequivocal why the author deemed these six essays to be "heretical."

Since they address the philosophy of history, the obvious explanation would be that the essays are considered heretical in regard to the most influential theories of historical evolution and lawful progress, such as in Marx' famous and often referenced "iron laws" of history. Patočka's break not only with the Marxist view of history is all-too obvious when he bluntly expresses his disbelief in the ideas of socialism, of progress, of democratic spontaneity, of independence and freedom – all of which, according to his considerations in the 6th essay, don't achieve their full meaning in themselves, but only in relation to an inner shaking and upheaval of human existence. For those who have gone through this existential upheaval and learned to overcome the admiration of mere force and to relinquish the objectifying calculation of human life, Patočka instead envisions a new solidarity – his famous and abundantly quoted "solidarity of the shaken", a solidarity even of the enemies despite all their contradiction and conflict. It is not difficult to discern the "heresy" of these assumptions in regards to all philosophical claims made about the laws of history and their universal validity. Written in Communist Czechoslovakia in the 1970's, the prototypical Marxist understanding of history seems to be the foremost target of this critique, yet Hegel's historical idealism assuming a natural progress of world history following the dictates of reason is evidently the main philosophical opponent. And, from a different angle, Patočka's existential view of history certainly also undermines philosophies of evolutionism such as Comte's "religion of positivism" with its three periods of a theological stage, a metaphysical stage, and ultimately the positive or scientific stage that is meant to offer stable (eternal) solutions for the social questions of humankind.

However, while such distancing from the main currents of philosophy of history is evident, it is also true that, in the foremost meaning of the word, heresy is always an attitude towards and within "one's own church." In this sense, it is especially Patočka's extensive processing of Husserl's and Heidegger's philosophy that is of interest. Although both of them are not *philosophers of history* in the eminent sense, Patočka dedicates in-depth analyses to them. This is in keeping with his overall philosophical venture which always tries to live up to both of their approaches and carefully ponders the complementary and mutually elucidating character of their thought.

As throughout his oeuvre, also in the *Heretical Essays* Patočka expresses great admiration for Edmund Husserl and his attempt to base life on insight, reason and responsibility. Yet it also is clear that Husserl's idea of a teleological nexus of European history is too much of an idealizing assumption that he is not willing to share. In that regard, as Patočka holds at one point, Husserl's phenomenology is even more reminiscent of the absolute character of Hegel's philosophy than of enlightenment rationalism. Conversely, Patočka often is critical of Heidegger's ontology for its lack of "phenomenological provability." Yet in regards to the philosophy of history, it is precisely Heidegger's approach that, for Patočka, recommends itself as a starting point, since it is eminently "historical" – its inherent historicity deriving from the fact of being built not on any kind of disinterested spectator, but on every human being's interest in one's own destiny and in the history of Being. Therefore, as Patočka holds, Heidegger's philosophy – in contrast to Husserl's – takes its "departure from freedom and responsibility already in being human, not only in thought" (Patočka 1996, 51).

While this preference regarding the starting point of his philosophy of history is clear, the appropriation of Heidegger is nonetheless, and blatantly so, carried by a heretical attitude. One could characterize it as a double heresy. Firstly, there is the *heresy of Heidegger's philosophy*, i.e. his apparent turning away from the philosophical tradition. Obviously, Patočka is fully aware of this and even lends his own twist to it. Writing about the novelty of Heidegger's approach, he at one point holds: "Freedom is not an aspect of human nature but rather means that Being itself is finite, that it lives in the shaking of all naïve 'certainties'..." (Patočka 1996, 49). The breaking not only with Husserl, but also with any subject-based philosophy is evident, yet by describing this move as an existential "shaking" and loss of "certainty", Patočka immediately gives it his own (Socratic) shift. This proves to the second kind of *heresy*, which is pitted directly *against Heidegger*. While Heidegger's diagnosis of Western philosophy is that of a "forgetfulness of Being" (Seinsvergessenheit), which makes him want to revive the very early sources of pre-Socratic philosophy, for Patočka it is precisely the Socratic impulse that serves as the guideline for his philosophy of history. In this sense, the overall venture of his *Heretical Essays*, namely to give an account of European history along the lines of Socratic questioning and the "care for the soul," is an undertaking that, from its very beginning, is heretical to Heidegger's basic idea.

Finally, and as a third explanation for the "heresy" of these essays, one has to refer to the context from which the word itself derives. First and foremost, *heresy* obviously means heterodoxy in terms of religion. For Patočka it is a heresy in regards to Christianity – and once again one could distinguish a double meaning: firstly an important aspect of his thought that stresses the *heresy of Christianity*, i.e. its potential to serve as a resuscitating source amidst the patterns of Greek "metaphysical" thought, and secondly it is a distinctive line in his philosophy that is *heretical towards Christianity* itself, clearly questioning its basic assumptions and its ongoing meaning in what Patočka declares to be a *post-Christian epoch*.

The attempts to rethink Christianity, or to unfold its "unthought" potentials, represent a continuous effort of his philosophy. They are led by the endeavor to exhaust philosophically Christianity's heritage for the contemporary world, or, more pertinently, for the future. In this sense, Christianity for him is (and always will be) a Christianity to come. Its real shape is still in the process of emerging: some kind of "Christianity" after the end of Christianity, understood as an organizing principle for political and societal order. Accordingly, also the repeated talk of a "post-Christian" epoch entails a double meaning: it (still) articulates a strong inclination to Christian ideas, yet in a setting that transcends or exceeds the limits of its religious connotation. "Christianity unthought" then would indicate a kind of heretical adaption: the maintenance of a certain core of Christianity even after its suspension, and through its suspension. It is the signal for an investigation into what is left of the Christian spirit without being confessional or credulous.

Regarding its role in the history of ideas, Christianity for Patočka is characterized by one central trait that has strong (anti-)philosophical implications: the truth for which the soul struggles is not the truth of intuition but rather the truth of its own destiny. This led – as Patočka puts it – to an "abysmal deepening of the soul" and makes Christianity "thus far the greatest, unsurpassed but also un-thought-through human outreach" (Patočka 1996, 108). The chief difference appears to be that it is only with the arrival of Christianity that the inmost content of the soul is revealed, namely the struggle for its own destiny, bound up with eternal responsibility. One could hold that Patočka's whole conception of history is driven by the conviction that precisely this heritage is (or rather: should be) an irreplaceable component of the European history of ideas. Derrida, in his reading of Patočka, calls it the "Christian mystery" or the "Christian secret." The marginalization, repression, suppression of this secret would exactly be what Patočka understands not only as the post-Christian, but simultaneously as the post-historical epoch. History is the history of responsibility, and every attempt at its totalizing appropriation forces responsibility out of history, turning it into post-history.

The heresy of Jan Patočka's thought thus can be understood in manifold ways. Derrida nicely sums it up, when writing:

> What is implicit yet explosive in Patočka's text can be extended in a radical way, for it is heretical with respect to Christianity and a certain Heideggerianism but also with respect to all the important European discourses. Taken to its extreme, the text seems to suggest that Europe will not be what it must be until it becomes fully Christian (…) (Derrida 1995, 29).

This might suffice as a little motivation why the editors decided to put this issue under the title of "heresy". The articles collected in it cover the wide range of Patočka's thought and interests. Under the first rubric, *From the Archives* we are happy to publish a lecture in German that so far was hardly accessible to readers. It was presented in the history-charged year of 1968 just after the suppression of the Prague Spring at the Protestant Academy of Hofgeismar in Germany. The author starts his lecture on "The Function of Literature for Society" with the sweeping remark that literature, or better to say *belles lettres*, is at the "heart" of all intellectual endeavors and in the center of the intellectual world. Literature – Patočka says quoting the contemporary German writer Heinrich Böll – is the search for "a habitable language in a habitable land." (Böll 1979, 53) Moreover, it seems that the dual criticism he formulates, a criticism of communism as well as of capitalism, carries a lot of the spirit of Prague Spring that was so abruptly suppressed less than a month before this lecture was given.

Also the second rubric is opened with an original text by Patočka, and indeed an iconic piece of his. Written in late 1976, it was the first article that he conceived in his new role as a spokesperson of the civil rights movement *Charter 77*. Entitled "On the Matters of The Plastic People of the Universe and DG 307," it is a writing of public defense for some underground musicians of the two eponymous rock bands who had been arrested for political reasons. Yet at the same time this short piece is also a powerful reflection in which the author – as if speaking to himself – explains the reasons for his turn toward political engagement. Not of least importance, the defense entails a wonderful reversal of Dostoevsky's short story *The Dream of a Ridiculous Man*: it is not only that, as in Dostoevsky, a single human being can morally corrupt a whole planet, but also, as Patočka puts it, that the moral integrity demonstrated by some young rock musicians can ultimately change and awaken the tired consciousness of a whole society. Jozef Majernik has done a careful new translation of this crucial piece into English, which here is published for the first time. It is followed by Majernik's commentary and an insightful reading of this text as the final articulation of Patočka's "lifelong striving to live in the best possible, truthful and *clear* way", i.e. "to live the properly human life."

The third category, *Articles* is comprised of seven original contributions that highlight the wide spectrum of Patočka's versatile oeuvre. As is good practice for *Labyrinth*, articles are published in three languages: English, German, and French. Ovidiu Stanciu's "Subjectivité et projet. La critique patočkienne du concept heideggérien de *projet de possibilités*" is the sole contribution in French, yet it is also outstanding in another sense, because it represents the only reworking of a phenomenological core issue. Starting off with Patočka's critique of Heidegger, Stanciu especially examines the novel approach of his "asubjective phenomenology" and its entrenchment in corporeity. A distinctive closeness to the phenomenological mode of thought is also characteristic of Jan Frei's "Zerstreuung, Verschliessung, Hingabe", an article that analyses the different representations of "transcendence" in Patočka's philosophy. While, on a more general level, transcendence for him always means a liberation of the human being from her/his distraction between things, Frei also emphasizes the emphatic meaning of "transcendence" as a turn to the "myth of the divine man" and the key metaphor of resurrection.

As becomes evident in Frei's paper, a certain inclination towards religious topics and a language of religion is typical of Patočka's oeuvre. It seems most fitting to characterize it as post-Christian in inspiration; i.e. in the above outlined heretical sense of a reflection on the innermost meaning of Christianity precisely after the "end" of Christianity. This aspect of Patočka's thought is also a crucial point of reference for the articles by Jason W. Alvis and Martin Kočí. Alvis offers a rather novel approach by interweaving the two core motives of "solidarity" and "sacrifice." The idea of solidarity figures prominently in the *Heretical Essays* where the "solidarity of the shaken" is envisaged as the main hope and prospect for mankind to overcome its war-like status of permanent mobilization and instrumentalizing of other human beings. Kočí characterizes this grim hope as "The Experiment of Night" and describes it as Patočka's somewhat paradoxical attempt to give a spiritual response to the discontents of modernity and its destructive energies. Similarly, Alvis invokes the power of sacrifice (or self-sacrifice) to counteract these tendencies and, as a biblical comparison, recalls St. Paul's famous prompt to the Corinthians to become "The Scum of the Earth."

The topic of war and its disconcerting handling in the sixth and final of the *Heretical Essays* is also at the center of Christian Sternad's contribution. It is one of the significant merits of his article that this topic is traced back to Max Scheler and his "war philosophy." This influence has hardly ever been recognized. Sternad convincingly outlines Scheler's engagement for the "spiritual mobilization" in the First World War and highlights a characteristic trait of his philosophy of that time that he designates as a "dangerously romantic conception of *force.*" The main assumption of Sternad's article is that it was this conception of force that underpinned Patočka's estimation of the 20th century as a "century of war" and led him to analyze it in terms of "excess" and "total mobilization."

The section of *Articles* is completed by two further contributions that tackle crucial issues of Patočka's political thinking: Philippe Merlier analyses "the meaning of the post-European spirit", and Ludger Hagedorn examines the "crisis of humanism" and its shimmering, ambivalent reflection in Patočka. While Hagedorn focuses on writings from the period of the immediate aftermath of the Second World War, Merlier highlights Patočka's "visionary texts" from the seventies. It is the great achievement of Merlier's article that on the one hand it recalls Plato's "care for the soul" as a pillar of European philosophy, but on the other hand takes Patočka's ideas as an invitation and, in fact, as an urgent call to think anew the formation of Europe and its preeminent tasks today. Hagedorn draws the reader's attention to the fact that Patočka's existential philosophy indeed debunks any "cult of the human being" and heavily questions all ideologies of evolution and progress. Yet, his thought nevertheless insists on the precious integrity of human life, a claim that paradoxically can be met in life's confrontation with its inherent weakness and fragility.

This issue also is comprised of a section for a *Book Review* and another one for *Discussion*. Susanne Moser contributed to both of them. Her intervention in the section for *discussion* is highly topical, since it addresses the ardently debated claim for political correctness in its inherent danger to install a moral and juridical system of "Tugend-Terror" (= terror of virtues). She convincingly discusses this issue along the lines of religious or quasi-religious war: on the one hand political correctness as a new kind of religious surrogate especially for academics, on the other hand political correctness as the main target of its (typically right-wing) opponents who attack it with a fervor that also bears quasi-religious connotations. Susanne Moser's *book review* tackles a further delicate issue: the interrelation between monotheism and violence. Jan Assmann has worked on this topic for many years and put forward an impressive collection of writings dedicated to this issue, most prominently his *Monotheismus und die Sprache der Gewalt* (Assmann 2006). The book reviewed by Moser – *Totale Religion. Ursprünge und Formen puritanischer Verschärfung* (Assmann 2016) – can be seen as a continuation and sharpening of the same question against the background of an alleged "return of religion" that overshadows recent debates and eagerly generates new bogeymen. It is also more than a superficial coincidence that the German title of Assmann's book immediately reminds of Hannah Arendt's *Elemente und Ursprünge totaler Herrschaft*, her masterpiece in analysis of the totalitarian political movements of the 20th century. With this parallel in mind, Moser's book review also nicely links back to her article discussing the new "terror of virtues" and the ensuing ideological war on political correctness.

Finally, the issue is concluded by an interview that Czech philosopher Jakub Homolka conducted with Klaus Nellen, founder and former head of the Patočka-Archive at the Viennese *Institute for Human Sciences* (IWM). It recalls the early days of Patočka research and the dramatic circumstances of the rescuing of his literary estate. As such, it is the perfect conclusion for an issue that is dedicated to Patočka's intellectual legacy.

Dr. Ludger Hagedorn, Institute of Human Sciences, Vienna
hagedorn[at]iwm.at

References

Assmann, Jan. *Monotheismus und die Sprache der Gewalt*. Wien: Picus Verlag, 2006.

Assmann, Jan. *Totale Religion. Ursprünge und Formen puritanischer Verschärfung*. Wien: Picus Verlag, 2016.

Böll, Heinrich. *Essayistische Schriften und Reden II. 1964 - 1972*. Köln: Kiepenheuer & Witsch, 1979.

Derrida, Jacques. *The Gift of Death*. Chicago: The University of Chicago Press, 1995.

Patočka, Jan. *Heretical Essays in the Philosophy of History*. Chicago and La Salle: Open Court, 1996.

FROM THE ARCHIVES: A LECTURE GIVEN IN HISTORICALLY CHARGED TIMES

Patočkas Essay zur Funktion der Literatur geht zurück auf einen Vortrag, den er am 21. September 1968 bei einem feierlichen Freundestreffen der Evangelischen Akademie Hofgeismar hielt. Der Vortrag wurde später in den *Berichten aus der Arbeit der Evangelischen Akademie Hofgeismar* (Nr. 5/6, Dezember 1968, 166-175) abgedruckt, blieb aber darüber hinaus unpubliziert. Eine tschechische Übersetzung erschien in: Jan Patočka *Sebrané spisy* (*Ausgewählte Werke*, Bd. 12: *Češi I*, Praha 2002, 175-187). Der mündliche Charakter des Vortragstextes wurde weitgehend beibehalten.

Der Vortrag steht in einem historisch bedeutsamen Kontext, weil er unmittelbar nach der Niederschlagung des Prager Frühlings gehalten wurde. In der hier weggelassenen einleitenden Adresse an die Zuhörer formuliert es Patočka so:

> Das Thema scheint mir für eine Zusammenkunft der Freunde nicht ungeeignet zu sein: Denn wonach sehnt sich das Herz der Freunde, worauf wartet es heimlich mitten in allen Beschäftigungen des Alltags und Festtags, als auf eine Antwort auf dasjenige, was alle gemeinsam bedrückt, die Frage der Gegenwart, der Zukunft, der Macht, der Pflichten des Geistes in unserer harten und angsterfüllten Welt? Wenn Freunde diejenigen sind, die ein gemeinsamer, über bloßer Utilität stehender Zweck vereint, was kann Freunde mehr aneinander binden, als freie Mitteilung dieser Ängste: Der ganze Mensch wird da an und ausgesprochen und fühlt sich durch Aussprache und Kommunikation, auch mitten im Streit, bestätigt und gestärkt.

Diese leicht pathetisch anmutende, aber doch auch sehr anrührende Passage gewinnt ihre ganz eigene Qualität, wenn man sie vor dem Hintergrund der politischen Ereignisse des Jahres 1968 betrachtet. Patočkas doppelte Kritik, am Kommunismus wie auch am Kapitalismus, ist getragen nicht nur vom Geist des Prager Frühlings, sondern spiegelt insgesamt sehr schön die Stimmung der 68er Zeit, wie sie etwa in Adornos oder Marcuses Kritik an der Kulturindustrie artikuliert wird. Ersichtlich ist auch sein Ansinnen, seine Reflexion in den Kontext der zeitgenössischen deutschen Literatur (Böll, Grass) zu stellen.

Speziellen Dank an Klaus Nellen, der den Vortragstext für die vorliegende Ausgabe behutsam redigiert hat.

Ludger Hagedorn

JAN PATOČKA (Prag)

Die Funktion der Literatur in der Gesellschaft (1968)

Wir fangen an mit einer scheinbar sehr entlegenen Frage: Warum sind wir eigentlich intellektuelle, denkende Menschen? Wohl weil wir urteilen, etwas über etwas auszusagen vermögen. Im Aussagen verstehen wir einander: Denn wir vermögen dasselbe über dasselbe auszusagen. Dasjenige, worüber wir uns denkend ausdrücken, wird dadurch, dass mehrere es aussagen, nicht vervielfacht. Dadurch entsteht aber erst das Problem, wie wir zu dieser Einheit kommen. Denn wir sind ja auch im Bereich desjenigen, was *vor* dem Urteilen und seinen Momenten und Bestandteilen liegt, keineswegs einfach im Besitz dessen, was wir meinen und worüber wir später denken. Wir meinen uns wahrnehmend unter Dingen, lauter mit sich identisch seienden Einheiten, zu bewegen. In der Tat gibt auch Wahrnehmung uns Sinneinheiten, keine dinglichen Einheiten. Das sieht man am besten daran, dass wahrnehmungsmäßig Gegebenes immer in Verwirrungen mit anderem steht und von diesen Verwirrungen nie ablösbar ist. Gesehenes weist auf Ungesehenes hin, gemäß einer Bekanntheitstypik, die immer weiter verweist: Äußeres weist auf Inneres, Nahes auf Fernes, und alles einzelne ist dabei eingebettet in Möglichkeiten eines "und so weiter". Nun sind die Möglichkeiten eines Anvisierens des Vorgegebenen praktisch unendlich und hängen von unseren Einstellungen und Interessen ab; wir leben ja in Verfolgung dieser Interessen, die manchmal grob und ungegliedert, manchmal höchst differenziert sind. Nun wurden unsere Interessen ursprünglich nicht durch das Hinsehen, sondern durch das Tun artikuliert: Wir sehen Dinge in Entsprechung zu dem, was wir mit ihnen vorzunehmen vermögen; die Phrasierung unserer Welt erwächst uns zunächst aus unseren praktischen Möglichkeiten, Gewohnheiten und Fertigkeiten; und da das Vorgegebene mit unseren Handlungsmöglichkeiten zusammen dasjenige ausmacht, was wir eine Situation nennen, ist die Sinnartikulation des von uns Erfahrenen eine situationsgebundene. Die Situation ist aber ursprünglich keine rein individuelle, sondern immer komplex, sie betrifft mehrere Individuen, ein Wir; die Teilnehmer spielen da die Rolle von einmal komplementären, einmal gleichrangigen Partnern; erst die gemeinsame Situation lässt den gemeinsamen Inhalt, die einheitliche Bedeutung entstehen. Die wird nachträglich mit Wortausdrücken belegt und bleibt als solche zur Verfügung, auch wenn Wahrnehmungsmäßiges nicht verfügbar ist; so wird man befähigt, Dinge zu meinen, über sie zu urteilen, über sie nachzudenken, gleich ob sie wirklich erfahren sind oder nicht, ob sie existieren oder nicht, ob dasjenige, was wir sagen, stimmt oder nicht stimmt.

Die Gemeinsamkeit des Anvisierens, der gemeinte Sinn hat also eine praktische Grundlage und ist situationsbestimmt. Die Sprache kommt aus dem Sprechen, und Sprechen ist ursprünglich situationsbedingt. Darum sind sog. okkasionelle Bedeutungen, die Personal- und Demonstrativpronomen, die Orts- und Zeitadverbien das Grundgerüst des Sprechens und der Sprache überhaupt, und es ist eine Verkehrung des Sinns, die in der griechischen Metaphysik des Dinglich-Nominalen gründet, sie Pro-Nomina und Ad-Verbien zu nennen. Die Sprache ist ursprünglich nur ein Bestandteil der Situation der Menschen und darum nicht aus sich selbst verständlich. Das hier Angedeutete betrifft jede Sprechäußerung und erstreckt sich auf alle Sprachmittel, auf Vokabular und Syntax. "Dieselben" Dinge wurden auf die verschiedenste Art und Weise anvisiert und angesprochen, und zwar in derselben Sprachgemeinschaft und desto mehr in verschiedenen Sprachgemeinschaften, welche sich wohl ursprünglich auch praktisch, in ihrer Struktur und im Fertigkeitsbereich, voneinander unterschieden. Das Artikulieren des Sinnes wird auf verschiedene Weise vorgenommen, obwohl in Hinsicht auf dasselbe Universum des Seienden, und es ist keineswegs apriori feststehend, dass jede Sinnartikulation in einer Sprache in der Artikulation einer anderen ein genaues Äquivalent finden müsste – wie ohne weiteres dort vorausgesetzt wird, wo ein Wörterbuch aufgestellt wird. Darin liegt, dass jede Übersetzung ein Umschaffen ist; die Bedeutungsstruktur kann nie adäquat wiedergegeben werden; deshalb verwenden wir z. B. beim Referieren von geistigen Zusammenhängen gern Namen der ursprünglichen Sprache, reden nicht vom griechischen Staat, sondern von der *polis*, sprechen nicht von Kraft und Auswirkung, sondern von *dynamis* und *energeia*, nicht von Prinzip oder Anfang, sondern von *arche* usw.

Aber Situationsbedingtheit bedeutet noch mehr. Die Sprache lebt, indem der vorhandene Bestand von Sprachmitteln in immer neuen, wechselnden Umständen auf die wandelbare Lage angewendet wird. Der Anwendungsbereich verschiebt sich, die Bedeutung selber lebt, das Metaphorische und Metonymische der Sprache ist etwas Wesentliches, was nicht weggedacht werden kann: Sprache kann nur auf dem Grund des Sprachlichen wachsen, sich bilden und korrigieren. So ist die Bedeutung der Sprachmittel selber, ihre Identität, nichts Bestimmtes, sondern hat einen nebligen Rand, einen Charakter des Nicht-Fixierten, des Korrigierbaren, Schwankenden. Es wird zwar dieses Schwankende oft nur als eine Mangelhaftigkeit der Zeichen aufgefasst und es werden eindeutige Tendenzen von Wort und Bedeutung verlangt; aber das setzt die Fähigkeit voraus, Bedeutungen zu unterscheiden, und diese Unterscheidungsmöglichkeit kommt erst nachträglich, muss erst aktiv hergestellt werden. Allerdings ist es ein Faktum, dass die Situationsbedingtheit der Sprache, die sie zum bloßen unselbständigen Bestandteil der menschlichen Handlungslage macht, selbst etwas Wandelbares ist und dass der Mensch verschiedene Auswege eröffnet hat, welche uns befähigen, diese Lage zu überschreiten und eine Tendenz zur Umkehr der Lage anzuzeigen. Wir versuchen sprachliche Gebilde zu erzeugen, welche aus sich selbst, abgelöst von der Einzelsituation, verständlich sind und einen geistigen Gehalt ausdrücken, welchem der Wechsel unserer Lagen nichts anzuhaben vermag. Und wir versuchen, Bedeutungen zu fixieren, die Sprache selbst bewusster und unseren geistigen Anforderungen entsprechender zu machen, z. B. der Forderung der Eindeutigkeit, der Schärfe, der Genauigkeit des Ausdrucks.

Aus sich selber verständliche, situationslos begreifliche sprachliche Gebilde können Erzählungen, Darstellungen, Berichte oder andere Außenprojektionen des innerlich Gelebten sein, die eventuell mündlich weitergegeben sich vom ersten Urheber ablösen und ein Sonderleben führen können. Dieses Sonderdasein wird dadurch bekräftigt und bestätigt, dass sie schriftlich fixiert werden. Nicht jede schriftliche Fixierung des Sprachlichen ist situationsgebunden, vielmehr besteht die Hauptanwendung der Schrift darin, der Ablösung von der Situation zu dienen. Erst nun kann die eigentliche Arbeit an der Sprache ansetzen;

denn erst in der Ablösung von der Situation hat die Sprache angefangen, ein Sonderdasein zu führen, und zwar in den Sprachwerken. Bis dahin ist sie nur Werkzeug und Wegweiser, Teil und Moment; jetzt aber ist sie in Wort- und Bedeutungseinheiten da, die einander halten und sich gegenseitig stützen, auf die man zurückkommen kann, um sie erneut zu durchlaufen. Jetzt erst kann man prüfen, ob etwas adäquat, stark, glücklich, scharf ausgedrückt ist, jetzt erst kann weitergegangen werden über das Ungefähre, Schwache, Abgedroschene hinaus. Und wenn die Ablösung von der Situation, das Überschreiten dieser Bedingtheit des Wortes einmal so fortgeschritten ist, dass es sich ganz selbständig gemacht hat von allen Einzelsituationen, kann der Versuch unternommen werden, die Welt selbst mit dem Menschen darin zum Ausdruck zu bringen, das Wort dem Seienden und seinen Bedingtheiten überzuordnen: Dadurch aber entsteht das *literarische Kunstwerk*.

Das Kunstwerk ist kein bloßer Teil der Einzelsituation des Menschen mehr, sondern es ist zugleich etwas, worin die Welt sich spiegelt und in diesem Sinne darin enthalten ist. Der Spieß wurde umgedreht, wir sind über die Lage und über uns selber hinaus. Im Sprachkunstwerk werden wir potentiell mit einem Ganzheitszusammenhang des Seienden konfrontiert, welcher vom und im Kunstwerk ausgedrückt werden kann – mit dem Weltsinn. Denn das Sprachkunstwerk referiert nicht bloß Einzelnes, spiegelt nichts Reales ab, sondern bei Gelegenheit eines als möglich dargestellten Zusammenhanges stellt es Weltkonstanten auf, welche allem Einzelnen und Zufälligen gegenüber erhalten bleiben und die Weltstruktur als ein Ganzes aufleuchten lassen. Nicht um Antigone und Philoktetes, nicht um Faust und Dmitri Karamasoff handelt es sich, sondern um den Sinnzusammenhang, in welchem die Artikulationen des Seienden stehen und der das Leben leitet, das Schicksal gestaltet und über Erfüllung und Leere, Verhängnis und Strafe entscheidet; um den Zusammenhang von Natur und Übernatur, menschlicher Freiheit und göttlicher Macht, um Mensch, Gott oder Götter, Mann, Weib, um Mitsein in Arbeit und Kampf, um Schuld, Leid und Tod. Und weil es um diesen Zusammenhang geht, kann das Ganze des Zusammenhangs genauso gut aufleuchten in einem lyrischen Gedicht wie im Epos, Roman oder Drama. Dadurch erhält nun der Einzelne auch eine Antwort auf seine persönlichen Fragen; er wird in seinem ganzen Sein beeinflusst, mit dem Weltganzen konfrontiert, das Zufällig-Wandelbare auch seines eigenen Seins wird dadurch überhöht und auf einen höheren Zusammenhang gewiesen. So ist es schon im Mythos als bloß mündlich tradiertem Sprachwerk, so nachher im literarischen Werk im eigentlichen, schriftlichen Sinne des Wortes, nur ungleich komplizierter und differenzierter, mit einer viel ausdrücklicheren Arbeit an den Sprachmitteln und ihrer kunstreichen Ausnutzung. Deshalb hat T. S. Eliot recht, wenn er sagt, der Autor eines Werkes der Einbildungskraft unternehme den Versuch, uns als Menschen in unserem ganzen Sein zu beeindrucken, ob er sich nun darüber klar ist oder nicht; und dass wir als Menschen durch ein solches Werk beeindruckt werden, ob wir wollen oder nicht.

Nun ist aber die Ablösung von der Lage, welche von einem Sprachkunstwerk bewirkt wird, nur eine Ablösung von Einzelsituationen, keineswegs von der Situation überhaupt; die Bedeutungen des Sprachwerkes wurden zwar so benutzt, dass sie nur aufeinander verweisen, einen geschlossenen Sinnzusammenhang ergeben, aber sie stammen dennoch aus dem Alltag und seinen praktischen Bezügen. Die Einzelsituationen sind nicht mehr zum Verständnis nötig, sondern das Werk steht als selbständig bedeutungsvoll da;

aber aus ihrer Gesamtheit, aus der Gesamtsituation einer Epoche sind alle Bedeutungen geschöpft. Es schöpft ja der Schöpfer des Sprachwerkes nicht aus einem Arsenal von abgezogenen reinen Gedanken, sondern aus der lebendigen Sprachtradition und Sprachwerktradition; er wendet sich auch an die Menschen, die in dieser Tradition leben, Und in ihnen erfährt das Werk erst seine Bewährung oder seine Verwerfung. Die Genialität des Schöpfers besteht darin, dass er durch seine konzentrischen und aufeinander abgestimmten Sprachmittel, durch *seine* Sprache der Mit- und Nachwelt die Einsicht in den ihm vorschwebenden Weltzusammenhang zu vermitteln vermag. Das bedeutet aber weiter: Auch er steht in einer Situation, auch er hat die Lagebedingtheit nur relativ überschritten, auch die Welt, die er im Werk niederlegte, ist seine je eigene und nur von den andern bestätigte oder teilweise bestätigte und übernommene Welt. Nicht vor, sondern in und durch diese intersubjektive Auseinandersetzung hindurch existiert die Möglichkeit, zu einer Überpersönlichkeit, zu einer Überwindung der Subjektivität zu kommen. Der reine Gedanke liegt nicht am Anfang, sondern im Fluchtpunkt dieser Auseinandersetzung; der Anfang ist die praktische, beschränkte, historisch einseitige und zufällige Situation mit ihren Bedeutungsartikulationen.

Nun könnte ich mir aber gut denken, dass jemand mich unterbricht mit der Bemerkung: Ist das alles nicht eine arge Übertreibung der Bedeutung des sprachlichen Werkes, besonders des Sprachkunstwerkes? Gibt es keine andere Möglichkeit für den Menschen, die Einzelsituation zu überschreiten und sich mit dem Ganzen des Seienden auseinanderzusetzen, als den Weg der Sprache und der Überwindung ihrer Realität? Gibt es nicht z. B. andere Künste? Gibt es nicht Philosophie, Wissenschaft? Wie steht es mit ihnen und ihrer Beziehung zum Sprachwerk? Natürlich gibt es das alles, aber ich behaupte, dass alle anderen Künste für sich nicht imstande sind, einen geistigen Gehalt im Sinne der Konfrontation mit dem Ganzen des Seienden anders darzustellen, als indem sie schon die Weltdeutung im sprachlichen Sinn, also Sprachwerk voraussetzen, auf seinem Boden sich bewegen, aus ihm heraus den Sinn ihres Tuns vollziehen; denn das Werk, das sie herstellen, wäre ohne die geistige Bedeutung ein bloßes Ding unter anderen Dingen, hätte nicht jenen Weltbezug, der ihn zum Symbol, zum Schlüssel des Ganzen macht. Das Bildwerk z. B. bedarf des Mythos, welcher es deutet und denkt; man denkt aber schließlich immer in der Sprache. Und natürlich gibt es auch andere Weisen als das Kunstwerk, um die Einzelsituation zu überschreiten: Es gibt einerseits den Dialog, die Polemik, die Konfrontation von Gesichtspunkten, Stellungnahmen, Einstellungen, den Versuch, ihre Beschränktheit und ihren Gegensatz zu überwinden und neue Ebenen des Diskurses zu eröffnen. Und es gibt den Versuch der Wissenschaft, besonders der mathematischen Naturwissenschaft, überhaupt alles Subjektive an unseren Bedeutungen auszuschalten, um schließlich bei einer idealen Eindeutigkeit des logischen Ausdruckes und bei rein objektiven Verhältnissen und Strukturen zu landen, welche auf nichts Subjektives mehr angewiesen sind. Diese beiden Versuche sind höchst bedeutend und können nicht genug betont werden. Aber sie sind natürlich in der Sprache beheimatet und für sich unvermögend, einen Sinn des Ganzen, welcher das Einzelne, Spezielle und Bruchstückhafte übersteigt, entstehen zu lassen. Und die Philosophie, welche nichts anderes ist als ein Versuch, alle diese Mittel zusammennehmend zur überindividuellen Sinnebene, zur Wahrheit über den Standpunkten nach ihrem Durchgang zu gelangen – ist sie nicht sowohl historisch aus Dichtung und Mythos hervorgewachsen, hat sie sich nicht mit ihnen, sowie mit Wissenschaft und menschlicher Praxis auseinandergesetzt, ist sie nicht erst dadurch zu dem geworden, was sie in unserer Tradition ist? Wahrt sie nicht notwendig innere Beziehungen zur Dichtung, gibt es nicht philosophische Lagen und Gestalten, für welche Dichtertaten und -gestalten eine grundsätzliche Bedeutung haben? Gewiss gibt es Descartes und Kant, aber es gibt auch Plato und Hegel, und die stehen mit den Dichtern in einer eng verzahnten Diskussion.

So scheint mir, dass man folgende These wagen darf: Die geistige Existenz einer Gesellschaft ist mit ihrer Literatur untrennbar verbunden – ich meine mit dem literarischen Kunstwerk. Es scheint mir, dass das literarische Kunstwerk es ist, dessen erste und grundlegende Tat es war und immer wieder ist, uns zu befähigen, im Verhältnis nicht nur zum Einzelnen in Sondersituationen, sondern auch zum Ganzen des Seienden zu leben und das heißt: geistig zu leben. Das literarische Werk gibt es uns erst an die Hand, auf Grund einer geschlossenen Spracharchitektur darauf zu reflektieren, dass wir in der Sprache leben, welche an reale Ereignisse, an die begegnende Präsenz nicht gebunden ist, welche immer als Ganzes da ist und ganzheitlichen Bezug ermöglicht.

Bislang habe ich aber eigentlich nur von der künstlerischen Funktion des Sprachwerks gesprochen. Doch jetzt erst kommen wir zu unserem eigentlichen Thema: Der Sprachkünstler steht im Zentrum der Geistigkeit einer Gesellschaft als Sprachgemeinschaft. Er ist mit dieser Gemeinschaft auf mannigfaltige Art verbunden: Vor allem ist sein eigentliches Ziel, nämlich die menschliche Transzendenz, das Hinaus aus der Einseitigkeit und Bruchstückhaftigkeit der Einzelsituation, auf die gemeinschaftliche Pflege des Wortes angewiesen. Dieses Streben ist aus dem Wesen der Sache her ein Mit-Streben. Es geht beim Sinngehalt, bei der Aussage des Kunstwerkes, bei demjenigen, was es offenbart, um Intersubjektivität, um Anerkennung. Das Gelingen ist hier Ausnahmefall einer Bemühung, welche Scheitern dem inneren Sinn nach voraussetzt. Viele müssen sich am Wort abmühen, damit es dann einem gelingt, den von ihm erblickten Sinnzusammenhang bündig auszudrücken, und so sind die Vielen am Erfolg des Einen mitbeteiligt; und der Erfolg ist nichts als das Überzeugtsein derjenigen, die auf das Wort hören können, die Anerkennung eines gemeinsamen geistigen Besitzes, eine Übereinstimmung darüber, dass hier ein gegenseitiges Verständnis gelungen ist.

Dann ist aber die Pflege des künstlerischen Wortes etwas anderes als jede sonstige Arbeit. Sie ist nicht zu trennen von der Sorge um das geistige Sein des Menschen überhaupt, und das heißt: von seinem moralischen Kern. Als geistige Wesen sind die Menschen ja Personen, im Worte und seiner Pflege werden sie sich wesentlich dessen bewusst, dass Weltzusammenhang um die Person und ihre Bezüge kreist. Die Transzendenz des Menschen ist wohl der Grund des Sittlichen und das Sprachkunstwerk also dem vorhergehenden nach eine Grundmanifestation, Grundenthüllung dieses sittlichen Seins. In der gemeinsamen Pflege des Wortes bildet sich die sittliche Substanz einer Sprachgemeinschaft aus. Das Sittliche ist aber wesensmäßig kein gleichgültiger Bestand, sondern eine Forderung, ein Unerfülltes, das erfüllt werden will, kein Gegenwärtiges oder Vergangenes, sondern wesentlich Zukünftiges. So wirkt es dynamisch, und zwar gegen Kräfte, die es verengen, partikularisieren, zum bloßen Ding unter Dingen machen. Dem Schriftsteller bleibt nichts übrig, als für diese Kräfte aufmerksam zu sein, um gegen sie anzukämpfen. Er kann sich da irren, kann den Gegner falsch anvisieren und definieren, aber sofern er bleibt, was er ist, kann er vom geistigen Kampf, vom Kampf um und für das Geistige nicht ablassen. Aus diesem Grund sind die Schriftsteller, und vorzugsweise sie, dazu berufen, das Gewissen einer Gemeinschaft zu behüten und wach zu erhalten. Der Schriftsteller ist kein Handwerker, der Bücher macht, kein Spezialist eines besonderen Produktionszweiges, sondern er ist Ritter des Geistes, der zwar irren kann, aber sich immer in Gefahr begibt und den Gegner herausfordert.

Es kann da scheinen, dass seine Mühe umsonst ist und dass er verurteilt ist, im Spiel der Kräfte bloße Imponderabilien oder unselbständige Komponenten zu verkörpern, die sich auf den Schultern wirksamerer Mächte durchsetzen. Es wäre aber, glaube ich, ungerechtfertigt und schließlich unrealistisch, den Beitrag des Sprachkünstlers und Sprachgestalters zur Ausbildung, zur Bewahrung und Bearbeitung der Gesellschaft, soweit sie Sprachgemeinschaft ist, zu unterschätzen. Die Sprache, ihre Gestaltungskraft und der Wille zur Transzendenz, welcher dahintersteht, sind mächtige gesellschaftsbildende Kräfte, wie ein Blick auf die Geschichte zeigt. Ich möchte hier nur auf drei Beispiele hinweisen, welche meine Thesen gut illustrieren. Die Geschichte wird nicht bloß durch Kampf und Anwendung von Gewalt gemacht, auch nicht bloß durch eingebildete (z. B. magische) Gewalt, auch nicht bloß durch Gewalt und Arbeit, sondern auch durch die stille Macht der Geistigkeit. Man denke an die einigende Kraft Homers über die Zersplitterung der griechischen Klein- und Stadtstaaten hinaus, man denke an das Werk der Paideia, welches in Anknüpfung an dies Gemeinsame weitergeführt werden konnte. Dass es so etwas wie Hellenen gegeben hat, ist weit mehr eine Wirkung des Sprachwerkes als von geschichtlichen Gewaltaktionen. Hat aber nicht auch die mittelalterliche höfische und bürgerliche Literatur einer Volkssprache im allgemeinen und damit dem modernen Volksbewusstsein vorgearbeitet? Und was den modernen deutschen Sprachbereich betrifft, lassen Sie mich einen bekannten zeitgenössischen Schriftsteller zitieren, der da sagt: "Bevor es überhaupt eine deutsche Nation gab, gab es, seit Klopstock und Lessing, eine deutsche Literatur. (…) Als die Herrschenden in diesem Land ihren separatistischen Klein- und Großkriegen nachgingen, schrieb der schwäbische Pietist F. K. Moser 1765 seine aufklärende und bahnbrechende Schrift *Vom deutschen Nationalgeist*. Der Schwabe Schubart, die Brüder Stollberg und der Balladendichter Bürger stehen neben Klopstock, Lessing und Herder am Anfang unserer immer noch jungen literarischen Tradition. Denn Deutschland ist, hundert Jahre vor Bismarck, durch deutsche Schriftsteller und Philosophen, die den Geist der Aufklärung durch dieses Land wehen ließen, kraft der Sprache geeinigt worden."[1] Und als drittes Beispiel führe ich die Entstehung des modernen Tschechenvolkes an, welches eine so merkwürdige, in Mitteleuropa einzigartige Geschichte und in ihrem Gefolge eine so elementar demokratische Struktur besitzt. Im Laufe der unglückseligen Entwicklung seit dem 16. Jahrhundert sind ihm die oberen Gesellschaftsschichten, der Groß- und Kleinadel, das ein-

---

[1] [Günter Grass, "Des Kaisers neue Kleider" (Sept. 1965), in: Werkausgabe, Bd. 14: *Essays und Reden I*, hg. v. V. Neuhaus u. D. Hermes, Göttingen 1997, 125.] Alle Fussnoten sind von mir L.H.

gesessene große Bürgertum abhandengekommen. Was da blieb, waren Überreste einer Intellektuellenschicht, vor allem Schriftsteller.

Genug aber dafür, um mit den neuen potentiellen Staatsbürgern, den befreiten tschechisch-sprachigen Bauern und dem davon stammenden neuen städtischen Proletariat durch Zusammenschluss eine Einheit herauszubilden, die aller höheren gesellschaftlichen Funktionen, zuerst der geistigen, später auch der politischen, fähig war. Es gibt auch Gegenbeispiele: der Zerfall des römischen Raumes in sprachlich unterschiedene "romanische" Einzelgebiete in Ermangelung einer ausgedehnten populären literarischen Bildung.

Aber das literarische Werk ist nicht nur gemeinschaftsstiftend, sondern es kann diese auch behüten und bewahren dort, wo die Gemeinschaft bedroht ist von gegnerischen, vor allem politischen Mächten. Nicht nur die Deutschen, auch die slawischen Völker wissen davon. Nachdem den Tschechen wie den Polen ihr eigenes, wenn auch nicht aus Volkskräften im modernen Sinne gewachsenes Staatswesen verloren gegangen war, ist ihnen die vom Schriftstellerwort verwaltete Sprache zur eigentlichen Heimat, zum wirklichen Asyl geworden, das nur schwer erreicht, erobert und zerstört werden konnte. Um dieses Faktum herum hat sich dann auch die Herdersche Volkstheorie herausgebildet, die das Volk als Naturcharakter fasst, der sich in der Sprache und Volksliteratur und erst zweitrangig in Phänomenen wie dem Staatswesen seinen gesetzmäßigen Ausdruck schafft; das Staatswesen als Erscheinung des Volkscharakters ist nicht notwendig, da dieses immer aus dem Verborgenen nach außen auszubrechen bereit ist — eine Theorie *ad usum* der Unterdrückten und als Stütze ihrer Hoffnungen.

Aber das Wichtigste scheint mir die Möglichkeit zu sein, die einmal gestiftete und bewahrte Sprachgemeinschaft immer wieder zu stimulieren zur wirklichen Transzendenz, zum Verwirklichen der Aufgaben des Geistes. Das notwendige Engagement des Schriftstellers zeigt sich darin, dass er über seine eigenste Aufgabe, das Schaffen des sprachlichen Kunstwerkes, hinaus bereit ist, die Realbedingungen dieses Schaffens zu verteidigen, die ihm drohenden Gefahren zu enthüllen, ihnen von vornherein zu begegnen und sie abzuwehren. So sind die besten tschechischen Schriftsteller im Verlauf der letzten Jahre zugleich zu Publizisten geworden, welche auf die Gefahren einer unkontrollierten politischen Macht hinwiesen und ihre Folgen im staatlichen Leben, im Rechtsverfall, in der weitgehenden Demoralisierung bis ins Einzelne verfolgten. Sie haben da eine Arbeit geleistet, für welche Theoretiker, Soziologen, Philosophen sich nicht zu schämen bräuchten, und sie sind vor drohenden Gefahren nicht zurückgewichen. Darin liegt aber noch ein weiteres: Die Schriftsteller haben die schwierige Aufgabe, dasjenige in Worte zu setzen, was schwer zu sagen ist, weil man gerade dem am liebsten aus dem Weg geht, dasjenige zu formulieren, was die Gemeinschaft dumpf bedrückt, ohne objektiviert, ohne ausgesprochen zu sein. Das kann der Schriftsteller sowohl zum Thema seines Kunstwerkes machen als auch zum Vorwurf eines direkten Kommentars. Viele deutsche Schriftsteller der Zeit nach dem Zweiten Weltkriege sind beide Wege gegangen und man verdankt ihnen Vorbildliches. Sie haben manches zum Ausdruck gebracht, was später in der Wohlstandseuphorie einfach entschwamm, die Qual einer namenlosen Heimatlosigkeit, einer unerträglichen Welt, die trotzdem ertragen werden muss: "sich ausdrücken können in einer fast ausdruckslosen Welt, diese Tatsache erhebt ihn [den heutigen Autor] in den Stand der Bildung (...), sich ein

Bild machen können, ist ja der höchste Stand der Bildung" – so hat es ein berühmter Schriftsteller ausgedrückt, und zwar nicht nur für Deutsche.[2] "Er kann auch nicht wie Abraham sein eigenes Volk zeugen, er muss auf es zu, er muss ihm zuwachsen. Er braucht nicht nur Freunde, Leser, Publikum, er braucht Verbündete, öffentliche Verbündete, die sich nicht nur ärgern oder nicht nur triumphieren, die *erkennen* (…) *Erkannt* werden sollte, was wichtiger ist: die Suche nach einer bewohnbaren Sprache in einem bewohnbaren Land."[3] Nicht nur die deutsche, auch z. B. die östlichen Literaturen, soweit sie Literatur sind, sind diese Suche.

Dieser notwendige Einsatz des Schriftstellers bedeutet keineswegs, dass er sich einem eindeutigen politischen Programm zu verschreiben hätte. Die Frage, in welcher politischen Verfassung der Geist am besten gedeiht, ist von der Geschichte her schwer zu beantworten; es gibt da Beispiele des Zusammengehens der politischen und der geistigen Reife, wobei die politische Gesellschaftsgestaltung weit entfernt gewesen sein mag von jeder Geistesfreiheit im modern-demokratischen Sinn. Es gab Tyrannenherrschaften, die bildungsfördernd waren: die Epoche des Augustus, le siècle de Louis XIV. Aber zu keiner dieser Zeiten wurde das Geistige zu einem bloßen Instrument der gesellschaftlichen Manipulation herabgewürdigt, zu Schraube und Hebel, die keine Autonomie und Spontaneität besitzen dürfen. Diese Spontaneität ist und bleibt Voraussetzung jeder literarischen Betätigung im eigentlichen Sinn, sie ist es, welche Verbündete braucht, sie ist es, die erkannt sein will – wie Heinrich Böll es so schön, so tiefgründig sagt im obigen Zitat –, sie ist es, welcher es an einer bewohnbaren Sprache in einem bewohnbaren Land gelegen ist.

Nun liegt aber die Sache so, dass diese Spontaneität des Geistes, und vor allem die des Schriftstellers vielleicht nie so bedroht und so prekär war wie in unserer Gegenwart. Gerade die eigenartige Kombination des heutigen Kapitalismus mit seinem liberal-demokratischen Gepräge des politischen Lebens sowie der allergreifenden, keinen Widerstand duldenden industriellen Zivilisation lässt keine Stelle frei für die Ausübung einer sich auf sich stellenden Spontaneität, für geistige Freiheit; für sie gilt kein Privileg mehr, ist kein Sonderplatz ausgespart. Gesellschaftliche Mächte scheinen keine menschliche Transzendenz mehr zu dulden. Nicht nur hat der gesellschaftliche Betrieb von der Literatur weitgehend Besitz ergriffen, die Schriftstellerei ist zu einer Art Produktion geworden, die geplant, durchkalkuliert, bestellt, eingeteilt wird, sondern der Schriftsteller, bis vor kurzem der einzig wirklich freien, keine "Vorbildung" und Legitimation verlangenden Beschäftigung nachgehend, ist ebenfalls zum Objekt des Organisierens und Gruppeneifers geworden; die Massenmedien nivellieren das Wort oder lassen es zurücktreten gegenüber dem Attraktiven der stummen Sensation. In einer Zeit, wo Verbrechen sich breit machen als wären sie eine normale, gewinnbringende Tätigkeit, wo Effektivität der einzige Imperativ zu sein scheint, dem man zu gehorchen befähigt ist, wo Selbständigkeit und Unabhängigkeit, von vornherein verdächtig, unter fadenscheinigen Vorwänden liquidiert werden, scheinen die Chancen der schriftstellerischen Transzendenz verschwunden. Und noch trost-

---

[2] [Heinrich Böll, "Frankfurter Vorlesung" (1964), in: ders., *Werke. Kölner Ausgabe*, Bd. 14, Köln: Kiepenheuer & Witsch 2002, 139-201, hier: 155.]

[3] [Ibid., 159]

loser wird das Bild, wenn man bedenkt, wie es heute mit der großen Hoffnung auf eine Revolution bestellt ist, welche die entfesselten Produktionskräfte dem Chaos zu entreißen hoffte und durch Vergesellschaftung und Beherrschung den Produktionsmitteln ihre menschliche Bestimmung zurückzugeben versucht. In einer Welt der Gewalt und unbarmherzigen Gegnerschaft hat sie sich in einem selbstfabrizierten Sicherungsnetz gefangen, das nicht mehr durchsichtig ist; eine unvollendete Revolution, die steckengeblieben ist und belastet mit komplizierten Problemen eines ungeheuren Staatswesens, das sie trägt, und mit einem schwerfälligen Apparat gepaart, der nicht mehr diskutiert, sondern befiehlt. Das scheint mir die Lage zu sein, mit welcher das Gewissen heute konfrontiert ist. Nirgendwo scheinen ausreichende gesellschaftliche Kräfte vorhanden, auf welche die noch vorhandene menschliche Transzendenz sich stützen könnte – im einen Teil der Welt ist die ehemals revolutionäre Klasse um ihren Elan betrogen und ins Vorhandene eingebettet, im anderen ist sie durch einen Apparat vom Außen gegängelt, der jede Spontaneität zum Ersticken bringt. Die neuen Unzufriedenen sind zwar auch schon Masse, aber eine chaotisch agierende. Dabei hat aber die Gegenwart auch durchaus Positives und Energisches in sich. Das Planetarische, das Kosmische wirkt sich in ihr aus wie früher noch nie. Der Mensch steht an der Grenze zu Bereichen, die niemand noch ahnte. Vielleicht brauchen wir nur auf eine neue Generation zu warten, welche im Osten den Antrieben der Aufklärung gegenüber offener ist als die jetzige. Vielleicht aber müssen wir auf die gesellschaftliche Auswirkung der neuen technischen Revolution warten, in welcher Wissen selbst die entscheidende Produktionskraft darstellt. Hoffentlich erlangt dann der von Automatismus und Arbeitsversklavung befreite Mensch auf höherem Niveau den Sinn der Transzendenz wieder? Hoffentlich ist ihm dann nicht, wie ein zeitgenössischer Denker befürchtet hat, Sein mit dem Gestell, der Mobilisierung der ganz abstrakt gewordenen Kräfte und Mächte des Universums zum Unzwecke ihrer extremsten Zusammenballung identisch? Hoffentlich schöpft er dann erst aus dem Kontrast seiner Macht und Ohnmacht, aus seiner Sterblichkeit und Gebrechlichkeit mitten in seiner Machtentfaltung den Anstoß zu einer neuen Sinngebung? Wie dem auch sei, es gilt auszuharren und zu warten, nicht nachzugeben und nicht zu verraten. Es gilt, alle Kräfte der Transzendenz wach zu erhalten; es gilt jede Gelegenheit wahrzunehmen, die unvollendete Revolution wieder auf die Bahn zu bringen; nicht beklagen darf man das augenblickliche Geschick, die Diagnose darf nicht zur Resignation werden. Die Niederlage muss man versuchen zu keinem neuen Sieg umzuformen.

Ist jedoch nicht alles, was hier gesagt wurde, reiner Idealismus im schlechten Sinne von Ideen, die sich angesichts der realen Mächte blamieren? Ist die Rede von menschlicher Transzendenz, die wir bestrebt waren, an Hand des sprachlichen Kunstwerks zu entfalten, nicht bloße Phänomenologie, welche das Wesen der geschichtlichen Wirklichkeit nicht trifft, d. h. den schaffenden, sich selbst in gesellschaftlicher Produktion formierenden Menschen? Ist das Gesagte nicht der Gefahr erlegen, Erscheinung und sogar Schein für Wesen zu halten, im Interesse einer privilegierten Schicht, die sich angesichts der gesellschaftlichen Lage selbst erhalten möchte? Ist sie nicht eine typische Intellektuellenideologie?

Zur Beantwortung dieser letzten Frage gestatte ich mir, auf unsere ersten Überlegungen zu zurückverweisen. Wir haben uns da offen zur Auffassung bekannt, dass der Anfang menschlichen Weltverhältnisses und Weltbewusstseins praktisch, interessen- und situationsbedingt ist. Darin ist die sozial-wirtschaftliche Bedingtheit impliziert. Was wir bestreiten, ist bloß, dass dieses Bewusstwerden ein mechanischer, rein objektiver Prozess ist, in welchem das Subjektive die Rolle eines bloßen Begleitphänomens hätte. Wir glauben durch unsere Hinweise auf die Rolle der Sprache und des Sprachwerks gezeigt zu haben, dass hier eine Kraft der Transzendenz am Werk ist. Diese Kraft darf allerdings nicht zum Moment einer objektiven dialektischen Entwicklung uminterpretiert werden, sondern wir beanspruchen bloß, hart am Phänomen zu verharren und keine Geschichtsmetaphysik zu treiben. Nicht nach Idealistenmanier wird die menschliche Fähigkeit – die Fähigkeit, nicht in der Trieb- und Tendenzrelativität zu erstarren, sondern zur Wahrheit durchzustoßen – in einem Arsenal von a priori-Ideen gesucht. Wir haben ja gesehen, dass die Ideen, die einheitlichen Bedeutungen und Zusammenhänge erst Erzeugnisse eines vielfachen Umgangs mit der Sprache sind. Das Eindeutige, Präzise, das Rationale, die Einsichten im spezifischen Sinn sind Erzeugnisse, Resultate. Beim Menschen wird nun die Reflexionsmöglichkeit, die Fähigkeit, sich der eigenen Situation bewusst zu werden und sich damit über sie zu erheben, vorausgesetzt – alles andere ist Ergebnis eines langwierigen Ringens im Miteinander, in der Intersubjektivität, in der Auseinandersetzung zwischen Standpunkten, in der Infragestellung seiner selbst durch den anderen, im sorgfältigen Prüfen der verzerrenden und verfälschenden Motive.

    So glaube ich, dass die hier gebotenen Streiflichter aus der Phänomenologie der Sprache und des Sprachkunstwerkes grundsätzlich keine ideologische Verzerrung darzustellen brauchen. Der Idealismus erliegt einfach der Verführung, welche in unserem Bewusstseinsleben angelegt ist: Wir leben und verweilen ursprünglich immer bei den Resultaten, nicht beim Leisten des Bewusstseins, welches die Resultate erarbeitet, und so tendieren wir immer dazu, diese Arbeit zu überspringen und den Prozess von seinem Ergebnis auszulegen. Der Idealismus sucht die Sprache, als wäre sie von vornherein ein Gewebe aus eindeutigen Bedeutungen, aus Vorstellungen und Sätzen "an sich", und sieht nicht, dass das alles erst Ergebnisse, erst Idealisierungen sind. Er will von Einsichten ausgehen, als ob das Leben sich von vornherein in der Helle der Reflexion vollzöge und sich nicht im Dunkel der Praxis erst die Instrumente dieser Reflexion erarbeiten müsste. Aber an der Transzendenz als Prozess, welcher zum Überschreiten von Einzelsituationen führt, ist festzuhalten; hier liegt die Fähigkeit des Menschen, dasjenige, was er meint und denkt, zu verantworten, eine zugleich praktische und einsichtsmäßige Fähigkeit, die man seit je Vernunft genannt hat und von welcher das Wort des Heraklit gilt, dass der Seele ein *logos* einwohnt, der sich selbst vermehrt.

Übersetzung aus dem Tschechischen: Ludger Hagedorn

AN ICONIC TEXT
RETRANSLATED AND RECONSIDERED

JAN PATOČKA (Prague)
On the Matters of *The Plastic People of the Universe* and DG 307[1]

Dostoevsky once wrote a short story[2] in which a single man from our sinful world – a land of pain, anxiety, and struggle – is transported onto an analogous satellite of the star Alpha Centauri where sinless and blessed human beings live. There, he infects the entire planet and brings it to the state that ruled on Earth when he left it.

Perhaps one could also write a story with a reversed plot: a small group of people transported in a similarly utopian, futuristic, or magical way to a different planet (say, in a different galaxy) encounters the inhabitants of a large cosmic body on which a struggle currently rages for the exclusive rule over it. The society which has more or less prevailed over the others was never too healthy, let alone without sin, thus leading another one, far more malicious than the first, to rise up against it. This had given an opportunity to a third society, which had until then just suffered and hadn't had opportunities to sin, to stand up against both, to use their bad conscience, and in the name of the future happiness of all to commit so much evil among its own people, as well as among others, that this evil had long remained hidden due to its sheer incredibility. And so that it remains hidden, this society has renamed good to evil and evil to good, freedom to slavery and enslavement to freedom, and has undertaken thousands of similar changes in language so that no one may understand that which *is*, so that everyone has to imbibe deception together with the universal mother's milk that is language. People then sacrifice themselves and others to some *bonum* (*malum*?) *futurum*, whether with the best, worse, or completely bad conscience, and not just by individuals or by dozens, but by the millions, by the tens of millions. These are not always obviously bloody sacrifices; where struggle has become routine, blood may no longer flow visibly, but everything people can live for has been taken away from them as the price for the petty things that are allowed to them. So they cheat themselves and each other out of their lives without anyone knowing about it at all.

---

[1] Published in Czechs in the edition of Jan Patočka's *Collected Works (Sebrané spis,* vol. 12, Oikoymenh: Praha, 2006, 425–427).

[2] "Son smeshnogo cheloveka" ("The Dream of a Ridiculous Man"), a short story by Fyodor Dostoevsky written in 1877 and published in his diary *Dnevnik pisatelya* (2 vol., published 1877 and 1881).

In the midst of this turmoil, this chaos, this cheating of others as well as of oneself, a group of cosmonauts now lands with no clue about this situation and without instructions from any side. They have their two good hands, healthy hearts and lungs, and they conduct themselves with a good dose of what a great spirit once said is best distributed among men. (*Discours de la méthode*: "Le bon sens est la chose du monde la mieux partagée".) And maybe for this reason – but maybe also for some other, deeper reason – they are no simpletons, no Candides who can be fooled into thinking that they are the citizens of the best of all possible worlds; rather, they can hear that which speaks without words within the human being.

How will these people behave in a situation in which the entire world around them, in its confusion, will try to win them over to its side by threats, promises, by the necessity to work for one's daily bread, for one's future, and maybe also for one's loved ones and others? So far, they are guiltless human beings – except for that universally human guilt of finitude, of the necessity to take a position and vouch for it. A reversed situation to that of Dostoevsky's story – a group of innocents whom the entire world, the entire planet is trying to draw into its malevolent and often even criminal confusion. What will they do? I believe they will try not to fall into that confusion, they themselves won't attempt to play that game – the game for the planet, for the cosmic body – not even in their thoughts. They will take care of their own life, for which, for the content of which, for the "leading" of which everyone has an inalienable responsibility, a responsibility which is felt increasingly as the external pressure grows sharper. Each of them will fill their soul, discovered in this contrast, with that which gives them joy in the simplicity of their spirit without causing any harm or pain to others. That these people will be loud in doing this, in order not to hear the external confusion, is a necessary part of the thing and no boasting; "although I come from a different part of the universe", they will say, "I am a human being, even all-too-human, and I like to remind myself of this, as well as those among the others who lure us with an apparent mess of pottage cooked from the leftovers of ideals."

How will it end? Again, a plot for Dostoevsky – I myself admit that I don't know. Only this much is certain: the external world has *appearance*, slander, the making of images among its most powerful means; it can present these people as the very opposite of what they are; it will cover them with a layer of filth so that they will appear as the world wishes; they will become disseminators of moral contagions for it; they will become morbid phenomena. Such people are then to be taken away, to the court, to jail, and to the prison, and then Hades' cap of invisibility will be put on them – the world will surround them with silence, ignore their existence, and forbid even the mention of their names.

Despite all this, could the outcome be the reverse of the outcome of Dostoevsky's story? What magic could accomplish it? But the human being may be directed at such magic somewhere in his depths and still not cease to believe in it. For the only real help and care for the other comes when I step forward and do what I have to do, whether in hiding or out in the open, whether anyone knows about it or not, and perchance let my awakened conscience awaken the conscience of others.

But what else is youth, after all, if not a guest that comes from the unknown to begin life anew? The story of our cosmonauts can happen anytime and anywhere – we don't want to give the impression that they are exceptional. To begin anew means in the first place to reject, to reject partially or almost completely (to reject *completely* does not seem to be possible for anyone). What is the true approach to this grace, given to us from who knows where, namely that life always begins anew? That we, older people, mired in our already habitual and worn-out routines and perspectives, have the possibility and even the necessity to revise ourselves, test ourselves – in a word, to renew ourselves – not by slavish imitation, nor by flattery, but by coming to an understanding with something that we do not produce ourselves. And what is a greater joy than to see that there is always and again the time to struggle against relief, against comfort, leveling, dishonesty to oneself and to others, against talking oneself into untruth and confusion?

We don't want to give only praise to the young cosmonauts, we also want to warn them – not against the world and the others, but against themselves. Their strength and their weakness lie solely in themselves. They themselves will write, will finish writing, the anti-story to Dostoevsky's story. May it be worthy of the story!

Translated from Czechs by Jozef Majernik[3]

---

[3] I would like to thank Paul Cato, Mat Messerschmidt, and Daniel Watling for their helpful comments to earlier drafts of this translation – J.M.

JOZEF MAJERNIK (Chicago)

Jan Patočka's Reversal of Dostoevsky and Charter 77

Abstract

Jan Patočka became politically active for the first time as a spokesperson of the dissident movement Charter 77. In this capacity he wrote several essays, the first of which, entitled "On the Matters of The Plastic People of the Universe and DG 307", I interpret as the explanation and justification of his turn toward political engagement. The following article is a reading of Patočka's essay that pays particular attention to a peculiar formal feature of the essay – namely that it's presented as a reversal of Dostoevsky's short story "The Dream of a Ridiculous Man". In reversing this story, Patočka shows us the two basic ways of human life and explains his political engagement as an action taken on behalf of the properly human way of life, which he calls "life in truth" or "the responsible life". The purpose of his political engagement thus wasn't defending human rights, but defending life in truth, to which human rights provide suitable conditions. "On the Matters..." also presents Patočka's assessment of the Communist regime with clarity and severity not seen elsewhere in his writings, and shows a shift in his views of youth and youthful rebellion.

Keywords: Jan Patočka, Fyodor Dostoevsky, Charter 77, responsibility, political engagement, way of life

Although Jan Patočka has been drifting toward political activity in the years after 1968 – for example, by holding private seminars and lectures that were *de iure* legal but *de facto* carried significant risks for everyone involved[1] – his first and only act of overt political engagement was becoming one of the original three spokespersons of Charter 77. As is well known, the Charter was initiated as a reaction to the 1976 arrest and trial of members of the Czech underground bands *The Plastic People of the Universe* and *DG 307* on trumped-up charges of "hooliganism" (a catch-all term readily usable against anyone opposing the regime) in what seemed like a beginning of a new wave of repression. The opposition to this trial brought together dissident intellectuals and underground musicians and fused them into a common movement of resistance against the Communists. To make this alliance public, to gain any possible public support for it, and to clearly delineate what they did and did not aim for, this movement was announced by the *Manifesto of Charter 77* on

---

[1] Findlay expresses this accurately by saying these seminars were "for interested students willing to risk their careers for the sake of truth and their studies." (Findlay 2002, 131)

January 1, 1977. The *Manifesto* claimed to desire no change in the government, the Constitution, or the laws, and to be in full conformity with the Czechoslovak laws; it merely called on the government to observe the human rights of the Czechoslovak citizens to which it committed itself in the Helsinki Accords of 1975. The *Manifesto* – as was expected – was met with a furious reaction by the Communists,[2] and just a little more than two months later, on March 13, 1977, Patočka died of brain hemorrhage which he suffered as a consequence of prolonged interrogations by the authorities (Kohák 1989, 3).

It is, however, less well-known what led Patočka himself to this risky undertaking that ultimately cost him his life. The scholarly opinions show little consensus on this issue. Tucker (2000, 87) believes Patočka did it for the sake of "basic and absolute human rights – the basis of justice and the preconditions of truth". Kohák (1989, 130–1) thinks this was an act of assuming responsibility, but he sees it as merely the responsibility of one concerned citizen among many, a "modest concrete gesture" striving to improve the conditions in Communist Czechoslovakia. Findlay (2002, 151–4) explains Patočka's engagement as morally motivated and is concerned mainly with showing that Patočka didn't base it in a metaphysical conviction that would subvert his overall effort to overcome metaphysics.

I believe none of these explanations hits the nerve of Patočka's thinking about his political engagement, and in this article I want to demonstrate it on the basis of Patočka's own – widely neglected – essay on this subject. He produced six short essays and an interview during his brief tenure as the spokesperson of Charter 77, all of which have been published in Vol. 12 of his *Collected Works*. Most of these are "public" writings[3] and hence take an appropriate tone – they use a Kantian language that is accessible to anyone and does not require philosophical training to be understood, such as that "it is morality that defines what being human means" (Patočka 2006a, 429/341)[4] or that morality entails an obligation to oneself to resist injustice. However, the first of these essays, *On the Matters of The Plastic People of the Universe and DG 307*,[5] dated to December 1976 and hence written before

---

[2] Patočka himself speaks of a "furious onslaught" and "vicious attack" against Charter 77 (Patočka 2006b, 441–2/344–5).

[3] In so far as that was possible. Charter 77 and its representatives were not allowed any space in the media to present their cause and all that appeared in the media about it was Communist lies. The *Manifesto of Charter 77* and other related writings including Patočka's essays were distributed as *samizdat*, and their "public" character lies in that their intended audience was outside of Patočka's phenomenological circle. To these "public" essays belong both of the Charter 77 essays translated by Kohák (see Kohák 1989).

[4] Page numbers to *Plato and Europe*, *Heretical Essays*, and other texts that have also been translated into English refer first to the original Czech, then to the English translation.

[5] There have been two earlier translations, which I have consulted in translating *On the Matters...* anew: one in Skilling 1981, 205–207, the other is listed under Patočka 2006c. These however take certain liberties with Patočka's text and do not accurately render his terminology. Furthermore, this

Charter 77 was proclaimed, is "private":[6] it is addressed only to Patočka's friends and students. Patočka speaks here in his own voice, in words which he thought through many times over and which are properly his own; and being written not long before his death, this essay demonstrates his most mature thought.

The purpose of this paper is to explain the grounds of Patočka's engagement in Charter 77 by means of a close reading of this essay. My point of departure will be a peculiar formal feature of it – namely that it is presented as a reversal of Dostoevsky's short story *The Dream of a Ridiculous Man*. The notion of the reversal is a central structuring element of this essay, and I shall track the reversals of various elements of *The Dream...* to show that it contains a synoptic expression of Patočka's philosophic politics. *On the Matters...* explains on the space of a mere three pages, in great shorthand and with enormous artfulness, Patočka's understanding of that which is and of the attitude it calls for from the one who sees it – and thereby it explains and justifies his political engagement. Thus I agree with Kohák (but differently than Kohák means it) that Patočka never considered "the particular problems that emerge in the history of the human sojourn in this world [as] unrelated to perennial philosophical issues" (Kohák 1989, 4). I intend to show that the main subject of *On the Matters...* is the fundamental question of $πῶς βιωτέον$. This essay outlines not just Patočka's answer to this question, namely that the good life is life in truth which also means a responsible life, but also his conclusion that when this way of life itself is at stake, as it was when the Communists prosecuted the underground musicians for their attempts to live it, it is necessary for one who understands its importance – in this case, for Patočka himself – to stand up in its defense so that this substantial human good may be perpetuated. Besides this central subject, *On the Matters...* informs us about two other aspects of Patočka's thought. First, it contains his assessment of Communism with clarity and severity not seen elsewhere in his writings: namely that it is a regime of the universal lie, and that it differs in kind – not just in degree – from the Western forms of technological civilization.

---

essay was merely a timely feuilleton for the earlier translators, and no thorough interpretation of it has been written yet.

[6] Findlay (2002, 133) suggests that this may be a version of Straussian exotericism. That is a tempting idea given that Patočka knew of Strauss and even speaks of his "highly remarkable conclusions" in *Heretical Essays* (p. 86n of the Czech edition; this and all other Patočka's footnotes are absent from the English translation). However, there are two important differences in their respective approaches. First, the Straussian exoteric writing contains both the exoteric and the esoteric message within a single text, while Patočka divides his messages into separate essays. Second, the purpose of Straussian exotericism is to attract "trustworthy and intelligent readers only" by concealing the true message of the text from the eyes of the censors (Strauss 1988, 24–5), while Patočka's "exoteric" texts rather seek to attract a more varied general readership by providing them with a more accessible version of the same message, hiding nothing from the censors. Also see Findlay (2002, 179–80) for a more general comparison of Patočka's and Strauss' approach to politics.

And second, it shows a more benevolent view of the value of youthful rebellion than his earlier writings.

1. The reversed story

The first paragraph of "*On the Matters...*" gives us a brief summary of *The Dream of a Ridiculous Man*. Patočka highlights four features of the story: 1) that a sinful man, 2) a product of a sinful world, which is to say *our* world, 3) was transported to a world of "sinless and blessed human beings", 4) whom he irreversibly corrupts. At the beginning of the second paragraph Patočka speculates on how it would be possible to reverse this story, and fleshes out this idea in the second to fifth paragraphs. He immediately performs a reversal of three of the highlighted features of *The Dream...*: now, 1) innocent, sinless human beings, 2) coming from a different galaxy, 3) are transported to a planet, which clearly is our sinful Earth. Our Earth's sinfulness is demonstrated in the short summary of the previous few decades: Patočka points out the flaws of the interwar democracies and the manifest evils of Nazism which rose up against them. Both democracy and Nazism are however a matter of the past now: the present is ruled by the Communists.

A closer look at what Patočka says about Communism[7] here reveals that *On the Matters...* contains a sober and penetrating understanding of the nature of this regime and of the effects it has on the human beings living under it. Communism is for Patočka less *manifestly* evil than the Nazi regime, but not any better for it. If anything, the opposite is the case: while the manifest evils of Nazism make it manifestly intolerable to any respectable person, Communism is very adept at disguising its malice. First of all, it justifies itself by pointing toward the sins of others, playing upon their "bad conscience", and presenting itself as the solution to the evils of all previous regimes. The Communists claim that the evils of human life are essentially caused by the deficient regimes mankind has so far lived in, and that the key to "the future happiness of all" is a radical reshaping of the previous regimes to create a new, just, socialist society. The declared need for this radical reshaping and the (alleged) *bonum futurum* of a classless society to which the reshaping shall lead then serve as a smokescreen which hides the absolutely criminal means used to this end. The crimes of Communism thus remain (by and large) unbelieved by those who have not experienced them, whether because of their incompatibility with the noble ends to which they allegedly work and because those affected by these crimes were always presented by

---

[7] I use "Communism" as a shorthand for the absolute rule of the Communist party, the "leading role" of which had even been enshrined in the Czechoslovak Constitution from 1960 until 1989.

the Communists as persons inimical to those noble ends (i.e. they were branded as dangerous criminals), or, as Patočka points out, "due to [their] sheer incredibility".

But the Communists went even farther to hide their evils and preserve their noble appearance. They subjugated the language of their citizens (or rather: *subjects*) by making "thousands of [...] changes" to it with the aim that "no one may understand that which is". The Communist rule imposes mandatory indoctrination on every single individual from an early age, and thereby the only way in which one learns to think about themselves is suffused with Communist ideological clichés. The indoctrinated subjects thus would not be able to arrive at truth about that which is, especially about their own lives – and that is the work of language under ordinary circumstances[8] – but only at "deception" useful to their rulers. The end result of these strategies is the destruction of human life on multiple levels: millions have been murdered or maimed by Communism for the sake of its "*bonum futurum*", thus being bereft of their bare lives; and virtually all others have been made to live not just in untruth (which is the element of ordinary human life – see Section 2 below), but in outright, officially mandated lie, thus being bereft of the possibility of living well. What makes this lie about who they are in which they are made to live and think fundamentally different from the more common kinds of untruth is that this lie robs those who live in it of the very awareness that there *could be* a life different and better from what they live right now *at all*.

Into this world and into this regime are transported our cosmonauts, the underground musicians. Patočka stresses that they are healthy human beings, of a sound body and a sound mind. But their health lies most fundamentally in the fact that, coming from elsewhere, they have not yet succumbed to the ruling lie. Hence they see that this is decidedly not "the best of all possible worlds", that a different and better life is possible. That they are able to see this at all is intolerable for the regime: the efficacy of the universal lie depends on it being universal and unchallenged, on nobody seeing what the musicians see. The regime therefore uses all the means at its disposal, all its carrots and sticks, in an attempt to coopt the musicians into the universal lie. They are promised petty pleasures, peace, and even a small share of power if they submit, and are threatened with persecution of themselves and their loved ones if they don't. Our musicians however cannot submit to the lie. They know that they themselves are responsible for living their own lives, that no one can either deprive them of this responsibility or solve the problem of living for them (as the Communist regime pretends to, parading itself in noble words of which it understands nothing). Their wish is not to challenge the regime, but to care for their own lives. And so they

---

[8] "Die Sprache ist das Haus des Seins. In ihrer Behausung wohnt der Mensch." (Heidegger 1976, 313)

continued living in their own way and playing their music, thereby incurring the wrath of the regime anyway.

The significance of their music in this story is twofold: for them and for others who enjoy it, it is a harmless pleasure fitting for a good life.[9] For the regime, however, their loud and dissonant music,[10] as well as their unorthodox lifestyles, are a most welcome piece of ammunition. Their lives, shaped by the desire not just to live well, but also to make it visible how different they are from the "decent people" (and thereby implicitly exposing the lie in which they live, as Patočka suggests at the end of the fourth paragraph of *On the Matters...*), make them repulsive to the said "decent people". They lack good manners, they dress unusually, they present strange and subversive ideas in their lyrics; they offend the public sensibility by almost everything they do. What happened to our musicians – their arrest and imprisonment for "hooliganism", which was basically the same as offending the public sensibility – seems almost inevitable in this light. The regime could – and did – easily present them as "disseminators of moral contagions" and "morbid phenomena" (to the extent that their affairs were presented to the public at all),[11] and the "decent people" wouldn't bat an eye; they would in fact be happy that these ugly sights have disappeared from their world ("they will appear *as the world wishes*" – emphasis added). But, as Patočka knows, this is merely an appearance, a fabricated slanderous image. The "decent people" are in fact lackeys of a criminal regime, and this already gives them no right to criticize our musicians. Worse, since their lives are ruled by the universal lie, they have no idea of what does it mean to live well. Their understanding of their lives is warped by the ruling lie, and they have no way of seeing what is worthwhile about the musicians' activity, and how the musicians live a better life than the "decent people" despite their unconventional lifestyles. All they see – all they *can* see – is a bunch of lowlifes who are "immoral" *and enjoy it*. What they cannot see is that their own "morality" and "decency" is but a self-

---

[9] "It is the part of a wise man, I say, to refresh and restore himself in moderation with pleasant food and drink, with scents, with the beauty of green plants, with decoration, music, sports, the theatre, and other things of this kind, which anyone can use without injury to another." (Spinoza, *Ethics* IV, P45, Scholium 2).

[10] Patočka himself was no fan of their music either – they "played a style of music that Patočka considered unlistenable" (Findlay 2002, 131).

[11] To give an example: the hugely popular 1970s TV series *The 30 Cases of Major Zeman*, which presented the Communist view of postwar history through criminal cases solved by the titular Major Zeman from 1945 to 1973, alluded to the case of the *Plastic People* in the episode "Mimikry" (first aired in 1978). Here, the members of a fictional underground band were portrayed as aimless drug addicts and criminals with no civic spirit, no sense of responsibility, and no loyalty even to each other. The episode ends with two of them hijacking a plane to take them to West Germany; one of the pilots of the plane is shot in the process by the musician-cum-hijacker, who is at the time also high on heroin.

serving justification of their comfortable petit-bourgeois existence in the service of the regime of the universal lie.

2. The fundamental reversal

The musicians have been tried and imprisoned at the end of the fifth paragraph of *On the Matters...*, which was their actual situation at the time of the writing of this essay. Our story ends now, inconclusively for the time being. But the essay does not end yet. Patočka returns at the beginning of the sixth paragraph to the fourth feature of *The Dream...* that he highlighted in the opening paragraph and wonders if the *outcome* of our story could against all odds also be a reversal of Dostoevsky. In order to understand what would be the reversal of the universal corruption effected by the Ridiculous Man, we have to take closer look at the story as *Patočka* understood it. It is no accident or mere ornament that *On the Matters...* is framed as a reversal of Dostoevsky's story, and only by grasping the logic of Patočka's reversal will we be able to understand what he is driving at here.

Patočka did produce a reading of *The Dream...* in an essay called *Kolem Masarykovy filosofie náboženství* [*Around Masaryk's Philosophy of Religion*] (2006d, 382–90). On this reading, the Ridiculous Man is a representative of an "underground" kind of life, i.e. decadent life which is aware of its own decadence. But unlike the Underground Man, he sees in his dream that an authentic life – life in truth – is possible, and this revelation shakes and awakens him. On the other hand, the authentic life is capable of falling into inauthenticity, as it indeed happens due to the influence of the Ridiculous Man, who unintentionally but irreversibly corrupted the authentically-living humans in his dream. Patočka analyzes this story as a meditation on the two basic modalities of human life that it showcases. Truth understood as "not any [particular] reality, but the key to *all of them*" (ibid., 385) is the element of the authentic life (hence: life in truth), and conversely, (particular) lies and (general) untruth are understood as the element of the inauthentic life. Patočka's reading proceeds in terms highly consistent with *On the Matters...*, and therefore I will leave the *Masaryk* essay aside and bring these elements out from this essay in the next section.

However, *On the Matters...* is not just another interpretation of *The Dream...*, but its *reversal*. Since the two ways of life present in both Patočka's reading of Dostoevsky's story and in his reversal of it are congruent with each other, the reversal is not a matter of a change in Patočka's thinking. It rather derives from a feature of *The Dream...* which Patočka does not discuss at all in the *Masaryk* essay: namely that it is a retelling of the biblical Fall. This is well established by the Ridiculous Man, the narrator of his own story. The inhabitants of the planet to which he is transported in his dream are clearly identified as pre-lapsarian humans, "unstained by the Fall" (Dostoevsky 1955, 311), who "dwelt in a

Garden of Eden just like the one in which our ancestors [...] had once dwelt before they knew sin" (ibid.). They live in perfect harmony with each other as well as with the animals around them. And the teaching that the Ridiculous Man identifies as the source of their blessedness is "to love your neighbor as yourself" (ibid., 321).

The Fall in this story shares crucial features with its Biblical model. First, it captures the moment in which the human being has attained its present condition. This is said to be irreversible: even though the Ridiculous Man knows the truth now and is committed to spreading it, he admits that "I do not know how to establish a heaven on earth" (ibid., 321). And it doesn't seem as if he would ever find out, for, as Christians know, once man has fallen, he is fallen forever, at least in this world. Second, the present human condition is interpreted as one of inescapable misery. Third and most importantly, the Fall is related to the truth about who we as human beings are. This has been shown by Walter Bröcker, whose essay *Der Mythos vom Baum der Erkenntnis* is approvingly discussed by Patočka in *Plato and Europe* (Patočka 1999, 189–190; 2002, 47–48). Bröcker notes that the first consequence of the eating of the fruit of the tree of knowledge was *shame*, shame at one's nakedness (Gen. 3:7), and that "eben dadurch [...] sind [die Menschen] nach Gottes eigenem Urteil geworden wie Gott" (Bröcker 1950, 39–40). Adam and Eve have ceased to be like animals and have become like God in that for them, "das beim Tier ineinander gebundene Auffassen und Deuten auseinander tritt; es wird voneinander frei" (ibid., 41). In other words, the eating of the forbidden fruit dramatizes the way in which the human being has become *Geist*, a free being. A free being is one for whom – unlike for an animal – the meanings of things it encounters in the world are not fixed beforehand, but who is free to interpret the meanings of things, and hence is free to act. However, he is not *completely* free; in particular is he not free from the rule of the sexual drive. And, says Bröcker "das Bewusstsein, nicht mehr Tier zu sein und doch dem tierischen Triebe noch gehorchen zu müssen, ist die Scham" (ibid.). Before becoming *Geist*, Adam and Eve's sexual drive acted itself out like that of other animals: "nicht in kindlicher, sondern in tierischer Unbefangenheit lebten die Menschen" (ibid., 37). But now the sexual drive becomes a source of shame for humans; its rule cannot be overcome, it can only be covered up, literally (by clothes) as well as figuratively (ibid., 42). Finally, God's punishments of Adam – the necessity of work, the awareness of death – are indistinguishable from the direct consequences of eating from the tree of knowledge, of having become *Geist* (ibid., 43). In this manner the myth explains the present situation of mankind as a consequence of our awareness of being the kind of being that we are (ibid., 48).

Bearing this in mind, let's take a closer look at Ridiculous Man's account of the corruption he effected on the pre-lapsarian humans:

> [...] so did I infect with myself all that happy earth that knew no sin before me. They learnt to lie, and they grew to appreciate the beauty of a lie. Oh, perhaps, it all began *innocently*, with a jest, with a desire to show off, with amorous play, and perhaps indeed only with a germ, but this germ made its way into their hearts and they liked it. The voluptuousness was soon born, voluptuousness begot jealousy, and jealousy – cruelty... (Dostoevsky 1955, 316)

Their corruption then progressed until they have become like humans on our Earth. The Ridiculous Man presents this as the necessary consequence of lie, the supposed original corruption. However, it is worth noticing how he introduced them to lies: "with a desire to show off, with amorous play". The amorous play, or seduction, was done by one who had shame to one who was yet shameless, i.e. in an animal-like, unaware state. Being seduced is something altogether different from an animal's yielding to its sexual drive. Seduction addresses our sexual drive under the guise of addressing another of our interests. But our response to this advance is not purely "rational" (i.e. it isn't simply a response to the overt question, such as "Would you like to come up and see my etchings?"); we rather respond to it on the basis of our passions, of the attraction (or repulsion) we feel toward the seducer. In seduction, the seduced person's "reason", their capacity to think freely, is used as a means to provide a palatable pretext for yielding to the sexual drive. Thus being seduced shows us how deeply we are ruled by our animal drives despite our freedom, and how easy it is for our freedom to be enslaved by our drives. It shows us our "nakedness" and brings about the shame that the awareness of being naked means. It reveals to the seduced that they are *Geist*, a self-aware subject – and that they are ruled by their sexual drive even though they are not determined by it. Being seduced is for the pre-lapsarian humans in *The Dream...* tantamount to gaining the (self-)knowledge about the human way of being that constitutes the Fall. Hence, not the lie itself, but the "amorous play" which provided the occasion for the first lie is the true cause of the Fall.

The Fall is then understood in Dostoevsky's story, just as in its biblical model, ultimately as a matter of our self-knowledge – once we learn the truth about ourselves, about the kind of beings that we are, this truth hangs above us like a curse forever. What is once known cannot be un-known; fallen humanity has to remain fallen. The truth about man is deadly to man. Patočka is familiar with this kind of "deadly truth": it constitutes the core of what he calls "the mythical framework" in *Plato and Europe*. Myth, Patočka tells us, is a truthful articulation of the fundamental human predicament, of the fact that "man is a creature of the truth – which means of the phenomenon – and that this is his *damnation*" (Patočka 1999, 179; 2002, 35). Patočka sees this framework at work in the most influential myths of the past, such as the myth of Oedipus, the myth of Gilgamesh, or – indeed – the biblical myth of the tree of knowledge of good and evil. All these myths show human beings as open – or rather *exposed* – to the truth which is overwhelmingly powerful in relation to them and which can at any moment overturn even the greatest apparent happiness into the greatest misery.

Truth holds this destructive power over human life because ordinary human access to it is accidental, haphazard, partial, and/or contradictory, and because our actions are based on this access. We act without truly knowing what it is that we do. In Patočka's words, "we are left to blind wandering" (Patočka 1999, 188; 2002, 45), our life originally *is* blind wandering over the course of which we have no real control.[12] Blind wandering means living in untruth while being exposed to the truth. As long as we blindly wander, it is always possible that our wrongdoings – which may be unwitting, but no less terrible because of that – will be revealed to us, and there is nothing we as blindly wandering beings can do to protect ourselves from this ever-present danger of unwittingly ruining our lives.

This is the lesson of the mythical world, in which there moreover is no way out of this predicament – myth understands human beings *as* blindly wandering beings. The solution offered by the mythical framework is a sharp division of the world into two separate realms, that of the "Day", in which human beings work and try to protect the transitory goods of their lives, and that of the "Night", the realm of the terrifying and destructive phenomena which always lurk just beyond the limits of the cultivated world (Patočka 1999, 187 and 196; 2002, 44 and 54).[13] But even though our worlds are in many ways very different from the mythical world, the mythical framework is not a thing of a distant past, but very much alive: we, here and now, are still in a way within the mythical framework and live exposed to the terrible power of the truth (Patočka 1999, 186; 2002, 43). Truth is the supreme human predicament as long as we blindly wander.

But how is it possible *not* to blindly wander? That question, according to Patočka, was a central concern of Greek philosophy. The mythical framework, being an expression of the supreme human predicament, was something the Greek philosophers were acutely aware of – and something they found the way out of. Patočka summarizes this foundational element of Greek thought as follows:

---

[12] "Blind wandering" translates *bloudění*, the Czech equivalent of the German *Irren*, which Heidegger names as one of the primary forms of untruth in *Vom Wesen der Wahrheit* (Heidegger 1976, 196–198).

[13] It is interesting to trace the parallels between the "Day" of the mythical framework and the "Day" as discussed in the sixth of the *Heretical Essays*. The Force readily coopts the mythical framework of Day and Night; Day becomes the rational calculation of everything as resources to be efficiently deployed. The blind wandering characteristic of mythically living humans is thereby deepened. And Night, the shaking of all the meanings that Day arrogates to itself, becomes the way out of this domination and false determination of the human being by the metaphysics of the Force, as we read in the sixth of the *Heretical Essays*. No wonder that *this* Day should be terrified of its Night.

> The greatness – that which made Greek philosophy what it is and that which made it the foundation of all of European life – is that from [this predicament] Greek philosophy developed *a plan for life*, that it understood [this predicament] not as a curse, but as *human greatness*! Of course, only under certain circumstances: only if we make this clarity, the phenomenon as such, the phenomenalization of the world, the placing into clarity – the program of the entire human life. (Patočka 1999, 180; 2002, 35; translation amended)

And the finitude of human life is not a problem for this "plan for life", since it does not bear on our ability to understand the truth of the phenomenon:

> [Since] the phenomenon and its lawful ordering is at the very roots of the entire universe, man does not fare any worse than a being which would have the entire universe in its power – so long as he systematically pursues the phenomenon as such. Human life differs from the life of the gods only in its quantitative dimension, but not in its essence: *that is the solution of Greek philosophy*. (Patočka 1999, 180; 2002, 36; emphasis added)

The great achievement of Greek philosophy was the working out of a new way of life that constitutes the overcoming of life as blind wandering. Here too the human being is understood as a being essentially open to the truth, but this openness may become the greatest blessing if one undertakes to live according to it. This way of life, which Patočka calls by the Platonic word "care for the soul" (τῆς ψυχῆς ἐπιμελεῖσθαι), consists in a ceaseless conscious effort at working out the human essence and leading one's life according to it. It is the life of the thinker led in the explicit awareness of human openness to the truth and in a constant effort to live in accordance with the truth by examining one's opinions and thus arriving at the coherent, simply true speech (Patočka 1999, 230; 2002, 92). It is an effort to understand things as what they are rather than according to the practical use we can make of them, to understand the whole in which we encounter all things, and so – most importantly – to understand what the human being is and what its place in the whole is.

Care for the soul was the first version of the life in truth. Patočka stresses two features of the care for the soul: first, it is the *attitude* of the knower rather than the state of having attained the desired knowledge (ibid.). Hence, philosophy is *love of wisdom* rather than attained wisdom. Second, it is a "philosophical ideal that *does not depend* on a particular philosophic view" (Patočka 1999, 230; 2002, 93); it is not the Platonic way of life, but rather the philosophic way of life as such. The rightness of this way of life lies in the fact that from this perspective alone is it possible to live without fear of the truth and protected, not from the unpleasant accidents of life, but from the risk that one lives fundamentally in the wrong. It is a kind of awakening from the unreflected, ordinary human condition of which myth is a truthful expression, into (the possibility of) the condition of true happiness which consists in reflection and which effects the unity of one's soul and the awareness of one's place within the whole. For one who is able to live in this way, the human essence comes to be understood as a blessing rather than as a curse; the world ceases being divided into day and night, and becomes a single whole; and one comes to understand their place within this whole and so no longer blindly wanders. Only for one who practices life in truth (whether as care for the soul, or in a different form) can truth be a "friend", as Aristotle is said to have put it, rather than something to be afraid of or an instrument in the struggle for power. The Greek discovery of life in truth is the most fundamental reversal of the human condition that has ever been enacted.

I believe that by presenting the musicians' story as a reversal of *The Dream...*, Patočka hints that the musicians are enacting precisely this kind of reversal. In our world, there are originally no unfallen humans; we are born as, and live with, fallen humans. The musicians too have begun as "fallen", blindly wandering humans, but they have managed to raise themselves up to a life truer than that of succumbing to the ruling lie. And their example has the effect of raising others up as well. Hence, Patočka's story reverses also the outcome of Dostoevsky's story, and this is the most fundamental way of reversing it. While in *The Dream...* a fallen man irreversibly drags others down to his fallen state, in our story the musicians who strive to live in truth are able to raise others up to their level, or at least to show them the way there. They make the truth a blessing instead of a curse. But how do the musicians do this? Why does Patočka see *them*, of all people, as enacting this fundamental reversal? After all, they were not known for having produced any great works of thought. What did their way of living in truth consist of? What did they *know*? More radically, what did they know that a man like Patočka did *not* know?

3. The two ways of life

We have in fact already read, in the fourth paragraph of *On the Matters...*, what the saving knowledge brought to Patočka and us by the musicians is: it is the knowledge that each of us has an "inalienable responsibility" for the leading of our own life. This suggests that responsibility is in an important way *the* alternative to the Communist lie, as well as to life in untruth in general. To understand how this is the case, and what does responsibility entail, I will now take a closer look at the fifth of the *Heretical Essays*, where life in truth is discussed through the phenomenon of responsibility.

Responsibility is introduced here as the criterion for judging whether a life is decadent or not, inauthentic or authentic (Patočka 2002a, 99; 1996, 97). Patočka begins from our perception of life as a burden, as something difficult to carry – both in the sense of the difficult labor we have to carry out in order to provide the material necessities of survival,[14] and in the sense of the difficult choices life forces upon us. In other words, human beings cannot simply be, but have to *lead* their lives (Patočka 2002a, 100; 1996, 98); in Heidegger's phrase, they have to take care of their own being. A responsible life is one that *responds* to this character that human life possesses: it is taking care of our own life "in the sense that we truly bear it, that we identify with its burden." (ibid.) It is a life led in awareness of and in accordance with the truth about its own essence, *life in truth*. On the other hand, an untrue, inauthentic life is characterized by an avoidance of the problematic character of human life, most clearly visible in various modern attempts (such as Communism) to resolve the problematic by external means: it is "avoidance, escape, deviation into inauthenticity and relief." (ibid.)

Patočka then brings out three basic features of the responsible life. It entails first of all leading *my own* life in its particularity and in its irreplaceability: it means doing "what no one else can do in my place" (Derrida 1995, 44). In *On the Matters...* Patočka also tells us that responsibility means "doing what *I* have to do" (emphasis added), I as the particular individual that I am in my particular situation. Second, it is "*doing* what I have to do"; it is the *activity* of leading one's own life, "involvement in action, doing, a *praxis*" (Derrida 1995, 25). If we are to live responsibly, we have to consciously face the difficulties life brings with itself and take them upon ourselves rather than try to avoid them in one way or another. Third, if I am to do what I have to do, I have to *know* what it is that I have to do. The responsible life hence requires "explicit clarity about the mode of being of the responsible beings that humans are" (Patočka 2002a, 103; 1996, 101). This clarity consists in knowing that the specifically human mode of being is relation to our own being (*Heretical Essays* 114/116), the fact that our life isn't something simply given to us but has to be led: in other words, it is the understanding of ourselves as responsible for the way we live, and the understanding of the possible ways of human life. The element of clarity points back to the Platonic "care for the soul" and shows us why it is the original form of responsible life. The responsible life is then essentially the same as life in truth; they are two sides of the same coin. The truth about the human way of being is no mere abstract proposition, but entails the injunction to strive living according to it, i.e. to live responsibly. And conversely, the awareness of responsibility for our life issues from an understanding of this characteristic of human life. As we have seen, for Patočka there are two fundamental ways of life: the life of blind wandering, of inauthenticity and escaping the call to care for our own life by attempting to relegate our responsibility to someone or something else; and the life that cares for itself, that responds to the essential need to lead our lives and strives to attain

---

[14] "Work is always forced labor" (Patočka 2002a, 101; 1996, 99).

clarity about it as much as possible, life oriented on the truth about human life. To summarize: living responsibly means leading one's life in the full awareness of what this leading demands from us, both as human beings and from us in our particularity.

In the history of Europe, responsibility has taken on two main forms so far: the Platonic and the Christian, which for all their differences are best understood as two renewals of the same fundamental idea rather than as something essentially different.[15] Such periodic renewals of the thought of responsibility are necessary for it to perpetuate itself. In fact *every single person* that comes to understand themselves as responsible for leading their own life makes a kind of renewal for themselves, for responsibility has to be won for oneself by one's own effort rather than learned from others (as discursive knowledge is).[16] What the musicians did in refusing to succumb to the Communist lie and in taking up the responsibility for leading their lives despite the consequences they had to face for it is then no "ineffectual posturing", as Kohák (1989, 130) dismissively describes the underground. It is rather something deserving of the highest praise. If we understand the story of our musicians as another renewal of the thought of responsibility in the midst of a regime dedicated to stamping it out, we can see it (as a whole) as a final reversal of *The Dream…*: the story of our musicians as told to us by Patočka is no "fantastic story" (the subtitle of *The Dream…*), but a truthful account of the typical interaction between the two basic modalities of the human life.

Patočka's remark in *On the Matters…* that the musicians discovered their souls "in this contrast [between the life in truth and the life in the Communist lie]" is an expression of the transformative character that the thought of responsibility has on those who accept it. Once we assume the responsibility for our life and strive to live in truth, we come to see 1) that this is a fundamentally different way of life from the life of inauthenticity and blind wandering, 2) that these are the two basic alternatives that stand before human beings, and 3) that the difference between them lies in understanding the nature of our existence.

---

[15] Derrida's reading of the fifth *Heretical Essay* in *The Gift of Death* is very rich and insightful, although I believe his arguments as to why responsibility is not fully attainable miss the nerve of Patočka's understanding of it. Taking up responsibility for one's own life has a profoundly transformative effect even if it's not fully realized. In this it is analogous with the Platonic care for the soul, whose ostensible goal – the coherent speech about the whole – is strictly speaking unattainable. As I argued above, it nevertheless has a real, attainable effect: the attitude of openness to the truth and of ceaseless questioning of one's opinions. Patočka understands philosophic activity precisely as this attitude which has to be periodically renewed: "*We have to say that which is, again, over and over, and always in a different way, but it always has to be the same thing!*" (Patočka 1999, 229; 2002, 90; emphasis original, translation amended). In fairness to Derrida, I agree with Findlay (2002, 197) that "Derrida is […] not searching for Patočka's or Kierkegaard's concept of responsibility as much as for his own."

[16] "Whatever one generation learns from another, no generation learns the essentially human from a previous one" (Kierkegaard 1983, 121).

Patočka speaks of the "soul" here because he understood our existence in terms of three fundamental movements and because he took up the Greek notion of the soul as the principle of motion.[17] Tucker suggests that "soul" is for Patočka a similar kind of determination of the human being as *Dasein* is for Heidegger, for both of them have to be discovered by rising up to the task of taking care of our own being. Insofar as the discovery of the two ways of life is tied up with clarity about the specifically human mode of being, it does entail the discovery of one's soul in Patočka's meaning of the word (see Tucker 2000, 118).

But even though our musicians may have been leading their lives responsibly, it seems hardly possible that they, a small group without any access to media, would be able to spread the thought of responsibility against the will of the Communist regime with all the resources it had available to suppress them. After all, we know that the musicians have been imprisoned and we have seen what image was assigned to them by the Communists. Patočka acknowledges that this seems highly improbable in saying that it would take "magic" to accomplish it; but he nevertheless thinks it to be possible. In one sense, the "magic" is precisely the immense power of attraction which the thought of responsibility has and which allows it to propagate itself despite the huge resistance on part of the powers that be. From the Communists' perspective, this power is simply incomprehensible, coming from nowhere, and thus "magical" or, as it were, supernatural (or they understand it as the work of their enemies from the other side of the Iron Curtain). However, for those who have taken up responsibility for their own lives, the "magic" is something altogether different, namely a way of expressing the wonder that the understanding of oneself as responsible for leading one's own life naturally arouses. This "magic" being inherent in the essential human possibility of life in truth, it is indeed something on which the human being is "directed" and in which it "[doesn't] cease to believe."

In the seventh paragraph of *On the Matters...* we finally learn why Patočka chose to speak of the musicians as if they were beings from another galaxy. The reason for this is twofold and has nothing to do with a wish to accommodate himself to the structure of *The Dream...*, which he has reversed so thoroughly. First, it has to do with their nature as young people. Being young, they are thrown into life and "begin life anew", literally as well as figuratively – by their great sensitivity to what is wrong with the established forms of life, with the compromises and routines in which we tend to get "mired" as we grow older, and by being prone to reject them on grounds of their inauthenticity or wrongness.[18] For them,

---

[17] See e.g. *The "Natural" World and Phenomenology* in Kohák 1989, or *Plato and Europe* 320/187.
[18] Patočka agrees on the subject of youth with Nietzsche, according to whom "Der Mensch, welcher nicht zur Masse gehören will, braucht nur aufzuhören, gegen sich bequem zu sein; er folge seinem Gewissen, welches ihm zuruft: "sei du selbst! Das bist du alles nicht, was du jetzt tust, meinst, begehrst." Jede junge Seele hört diesen Zuruf bei Tag und bei Nacht und erzittert dabei" (Nietzsche

thrown here, the conventions of our way of life are strange and clearly wrong in countless ways, as they would be for enlightened aliens from a science fiction story. This capacity of youth, its specific gift, is universally and inalienably human, no matter how hard the Communists or anyone else may try to suppress it, as Patočka points out by saying that "the story of our cosmonauts can happen anytime and anywhere". Patočka's second reason goes even further than this: the musicians are not just guests thrown into the life we older humans have prepared for them – they are *cosmonauts*. A "cosmonaut" is here not simply the Communist equivalent of "astronaut": it is another way of expressing the essential character of human life. We all, whether we know it or not, whether we act like it or fail to do so, sail through the *kosmos* and seek a way of navigating it, a clarity about what our life is and what it asks from us. And as we have seen, our musicians have been performing this essentially – but by no means *universally* – human activity of seeking clarity and living in truth with remarkable success.

Patočka calls this beginning-life-anew a "grace" and says that although our musicians' approach to the responsible life has been mostly negative – pointing out what is wrong with the current practices rather than offering better practices in their stead – they are not to be blamed for it, for such is the nature of youth. Their way of living responsibly is as of now insufficient, but therefore not yet without value; it is a first step in the right direction; it already partakes in the attitude of living in truth. The "true approach" to this grace is to embrace it, to listen to their criticisms and use them to revise and improve our own practices. Their struggle is Patočka's own struggle, the struggle for life in truth and against relief, and to take part in this struggle alongside others who see the importance of this struggle too is for him the greatest joy, as his rhetorical question at the end of the seventh paragraph of *On the Matters*... makes clear. After all, this story could happen "anytime and anywhere": what our musicians did in Communist Czechoslovakia – namely, demonstrated by deed what leading a responsible life means here and now – was and will be done by others at other times and places. Their example led Patočka himself to reconsider his own practice of responsibility and "to do what I have to do", which he came to understand as publicly stepping up in their defense not merely because they were persecuted but because they were persecuted for attempting to live the life which alone is fitting for a human being. They have taught him to step up in the defense of life in truth when its very possibility is under attack. The example of their fearless resistance to the ruling lie in the face of the

---

1999, 1.338). Both Nietzsche's and Patočka's understanding of youth emphasizes their capacity to recognize the wrong or the untrue even without knowing the good or the true, and identifies the former in being comfortable, in unwarranted relief of one's responsibility for one's life.

Patočka also appears to echo Hannah Arendt's famous sentence: "With each new birth, a new beginning is born into the world, a new world has potentially come into being." (Arendt 1953, 311)

powers that be has awakened Patočka's conscience, just as he was trying to awaken the consciences of his compatriots by relating them the story of our musicians as he understood it (that is, by writing *On the Matters*...), and by his engagement as the Charter 77 spokesperson in general.

In the final paragraph of *On the Matters*... Patočka once again stresses the irreplaceably and inalienably personal dimension of the responsible life. No one can take away from our musicians their way of life – only they themselves can give up on it, and this risk is ever-present to us as human beings (as it happened in *The Dream*...). Only on them depends which of the two ways of life they will choose – whether the life in truth, responsibility, and care for their souls, or the life of blind wandering (or lie), relief, and care for dominating the world.[19] In so far as these are the two fundamental alternatives of human life, we all, as human beings, are faced with the same choice. As Patočka says, "they themselves will write, will finish writing the anti-story to Dostoevsky's story" – and the same is true of *our own* stories.

* * *

I hope to have brought out the great richness hidden in this unassuming little essay. Its principal subject is life in truth, the properly human way of life as Patočka understands it. Life in truth is the leading of one's life in the awareness of the nature of human life as something which we have to actively take care of, something we have to take care of *well* – i.e. with the effort to attain the greatest possible clarity both about human life as such and its good, and about the particular situation of my own life and its requirements. It is a life which one strives to lead on the basis of truth, which takes truth as the highest and only criterion of action. In short, it is "*doing* what *I* have to do," with the silent addendum that no effort is to be spared at *knowing* what I have to do. And that is no pastime of an ivory-tower intellectual, for, as Patočka said (and as he *did*), it is rather "the only real help and care for the other".

In this light it becomes clear why, in contrast with the "public" Charter 77 essays, the core of Patočka's argument here is decidedly not morality or human rights, the *raison d'être* of Charter 77. This essay is rather an articulation of that for the sake of which it is

---

[19] That is the name which Patočka gives in *Plato and Europe* (228/89) to the ultimate outcome of the tendency of the inauthentic life to bend things and other human beings according to its desires, the opposite of which is the tendency of life in truth to "let all that is be as and how it is, not distorting it, not denying its own being and its own nature to it" (Patočka 2002, 100; 1996, 98). This distinctly echoes Heidegger's definition of love (see Heidegger 1976, 316), and Patočka elaborates on this understanding of love in the *Masaryk* essay (Patočka 2006d, 388).

important that human rights be observed. There is a strong continuity in Patočka's view of the human good as life in truth that persists throughout the different articulations of *Plato and Europe*, the *Heretical Essays*, and of his other mature writings, and *On the Matters...* shows how his commitment to life in truth is the foundation of his defense of human rights by engaging in Charter 77. Thus, I also disagree with Rorty's judgment that "Patočka's conscience led him to do the right thing, but he did not supply good philosophical reasons for doing what he did" (1991, 37). Patočka indeed did not provide a "firm philosophical foundation" (ibid.) to democracy and human rights. That is because his defense of them is instrumental rather than substantial. They are only historically contingent juridical constructs rather than substantial goods, but they offer the space and opportunity for those who seek to live in truth to do so. Life in truth has to be attained by overcoming blind wandering – it has to be aware of its counterpart, of the falsity below it that it may fall into. And the blind wandering of a democratic society can be overcome without one's life being destroyed in the process, which was not possible under the rule of the Communist lie. In short, the goodness of democracy and human rights lies for Patočka in their being (at least in comparison with the relevant alternatives) good conditions for the substantial human good that life in truth is.[20]

We can now answer the question of what made Patočka become a spokesperson for Charter 77. His reasons for this step were twofold. First of them is his assessment of the nature of the Communist regime, so "heretical" that it could not be stated directly even in a private text; even here it needs to remain hidden behind allegory and reversal. Communism is understood by Patočka as the regime of the universal lie that uses all its power to make life in truth unthinkable; it is a truly *inhuman* regime because it denies that which is essential to being human. This assessment of the evils of Communism, founded upon substantial philosophical (rather than merely political or economic) grounds, has no parallel that I know of. The second reason ties in directly to the first one. Living in such a regime, the best

---

[20] It is true that Patočka argues that not just Communism, but modern technological civilization as such is decadent, since it has made the possibility of living the responsible life even more difficult than it was before, and since it has led to the rule of the Force over human life (Patočka 2002a, 115; 1996, 117). However, he does not follow Heidegger (1983, 40–41) in seeing a metaphysical equivalence between Communism and Americanism or modern technological civilization in general. Patočka would reply to Heidegger that although modern technological civilization fosters life in untruth, untruth has always been the element of ordinary human life, and life in untruth is essentially different from life in the lie in that life in mere untruth contains the possibility of rising above the untruth and does not deny and violently suppress it. Unlike Communism, technological civilization has not declared itself to be the truly human life, it did not strive to make other ways of life literally unthinkable, and it did not mete out furious and draconic punishments to those who refused its way of life. The difference between Americanism and Communism is for Patočka the difference between life in untruth and life in the lie.

Patočka could do was to step up publicly and do his utmost to counteract this pernicious tendency of Communism. Contrary to Tucker's view (2000, 87), Patočka's political engagement was not for the sake of "absolute" human rights, nor was it *merely* an act of "assuming the responsibility of free citizens", as Kohák (1989, 131) thinks. It was rather the final fruit of his lifelong striving to live in the best possible, truthful and *clear* way – to live the properly human life, which is the only true good and the only true happiness. The young underground musicians, with their capacity to recognize the evils of Communism and with their passionate opposition against them, showed Patočka by their example what does it mean to *lead* life in truth there and then, under the rule of the Communist lie. They have improved his understanding of what *he* had to do – which for him meant to stand up publicly in defense of the musicians and of life in truth itself when the very possibility of this substantial human good was endangered by the powers that be.

For us Patočka is an example to rise up to, but not one to imitate – *we* have to lead our lives ourselves and find out what life in truth means and asks from us here and now (as Patočka stresses throughout *On the Matters…*). Patočka himself, by reconsidering his own way of living in truth and by defending its possibility even at the cost of his own life decisively proved his adherence to it in its strongest form (in its *true* form), expressed by the Socratic dictum that "the most important thing is not life, but the good life" (Plato, *Crito* 48b).

Jozef Majernik, Ph.D. Cand., The John U. Nef Committee on Social Thought, University of Chicago, jmajernik[at]uchicago.edu

References

Arendt, Hannah. "Ideology and Terror: A Novel Form of Government." *The Review of Politics*, Vol. 15, Nr. 3 (1953): 303–327.
Bröcker, Walter. "Der Mythos vom Baum der Erkenntnis" in s.a. *Anteile: Martin Heidegger zum 60. Geburtstag*. Frankfurt am Main: Vittorio Klostermann, 1950. 29–50.
Derrida, Jacques. *The Gift of Death*. Translated by David Wills. Chicago: The University of Chicago Press, 1995.
Dostoevsky, Fyodor. "The Dream of a Ridiculous Man. A Fantastic Story," in David Magarshack (trans.). *The Best Short Stories of Dostoevsky*. New York: Modern Library, 1955. 297–322.
Findlay, Edward F. *Caring for the Soul in a Postmodern Age: Politics and Phenomenology in the Thought of Jan Patočka*. New York: SUNY Press, 2002.
Heidegger, Martin. *Gesamtausgabe Bd. 9: Wegmarken*. Frankfurt am Main: Vittorio Klostermann, 1976.

Heidegger, Martin. *Gesamtausgabe Bd. 40: Einführung in die Metaphysik.* Frankfurt am Main: Vittorio Klostermann, 1983.
Kierkegaard, Søren. "Fear and Trembling," in Howard V. Hong and Edna H. Hong (ed. and trans.). *Fear and Trembling, Repetition.* Princeton: Princeton University Press, 1983. 1–123.
Kohák, Erazím. *Jan Patočka: Philosophy and Selected Writings.* Chicago: The University of Chicago Press, 1989.
Nietzsche, Friedrich. *Unzeitgemäße Betrachtungen* (*Kritische Studienausgabe*, Bd. 1). Berlin: De Gruyter, 1999.
Plato. *Complete Works.* Edited by John M. Cooper. Indianapolis: Hackett, 1997.
Patočka, Jan. "Platón a Evropa," in *Sebrané spisy [Collected Works] vol. 2.* Praha: Oikoymenh, 1999. 149–355. Translated by Petr Lom as *Plato and Europe.* Stanford: Stanford University Press, 2002.
Patočka, Jan. "Kacířské eseje o filosofii dějin," in *Sebrané spisy [Collected Works] vol. 3.* Praha: Oikoymenh, 2002a. 13–131. Translated by Erazím Kohák as *Heretical Essays in the Philosophy of History.* Chicago: Open Court, 1996.
Patočka, Jan. "Čím je a čím není Charta 77," in *Sebrané spisy [Collected Works] vol. 12.* Praha: Oikoymenh, 2006a. 428–30. Translated by Erazím Kohák as "The Obligation to Resist Injustice," in Kohák 1989, pp. 340–343.
Patočka, Jan. "Co můžeme očekávat od Charty 77?" in *Sebrané spisy [Collected Works] vol. 12.* Praha: Oikoymenh, 2006b. 440–4. Translated by Erazím Kohák as "What We Can and Cannot Expect from Charta 77," in Erazím Kohák. *Jan Patočka: Philosophy and Selected Writings.* Chicago: The University of Chicago Press, 1989. 343–347.
Patočka, Jan. "K záležitostem Plastic People of the Universe a DG 307" ["On the Matters of The Plastic People of the Universe and DG 307"]. In *Sebrané spisy [Collected Works] vol. 12.* Praha: Oikoymenh, 2006c. 425–427. Translated by Paul Wilson as "The Planetary Game," *Ethos*, Vol. 2, Nr. 1 (1986): 15.
Patočka, Jan. "Kolem Masarykovy filosofie náboženství" [Around Masaryk's Philosophy of Religion]. In *Sebrané spisy [Collected Works] vol. 12.* Praha: Oikoymenh, 2006d. 366–422. Translated by Jiří Rothbauer et al. as "On Masaryk's Philosophy of Religion", in Ludger Hagedorn and James Dodd (ed.). *Religion, War and the Crisis of Modernity* (*The New Yearbook for Phenomenology and Phenomenological Philosophy*, vol. XIV). London & New York: Routledge 2015. 95-135.
Plato. "Crito," in idem. Five Dialogues: Euthyphro, Apology, Crito, Meno, Phaedo. Transl. by George Maximilian Antony Grube, revised by John M. Cooper, 2 ed. Hacket Publishing Company: Indianapolis/Cambridge, 2002. 45-57.
Rorty, Richard. "The Seer of Prague." *The New Republic*, 1 July 1991, 35–40.
Skilling, H. Gordon. *Charter 77 and Human Rights in Czechoslovakia.* London: Allen & Unwin, 1981.
Spinoza, Benedict. *A Spinoza Reader: The Ethics and Other Works.* Edited and translated by Edwin Curley. Princeton: Princeton University Press, 1994.
Strauss, Leo. Persecution and the Art of Writing. Chicago: The University of Chicago Press, 1988.
Tucker, Aviezer. *The Philosophy and Politics of Czech Dissidence from Patočka to Havel.* Pittsburgh: The University of Pittsburgh Press, 2000.

THE HERETICAL PERSPECTIVES OF JAN PATOČKA

LUDGER HAGEDORN (Wien)

Die "unermessliche Leichtigkeit und Zerbrechlichkeit des menschlichen Faktums." Jan Patočka und die Krise des Humanismus

---

"The Immeasurable Lightness and Fragility of the Human Fact".
Jan Patočka and die Crisis of Humanism

Abstract

The article addresses Jan Patočka's writings in the immediate aftermath of the Second World War. The paper's title – "The Immense Lightness and Fragility of the Human Fact" – is taken from a short, yet immensely crucial 1946 text of his that formulates a severe criticism of ideology/ideologies and eventually offers a profound questioning of humanist ideals. Accentuating his critique against the backdrop of Sartre's and Heidegger's contemporaneous challenges to humanism, the paper argues that Patočka debunks a misconceived "cult of the human being" and ideologies of progress while insisting on the integrity of a human life in confrontation with its inherent weakness and fragility.

Keywords: Patočka, Sartre, Heidegger, Humanism, Metaphysics, Post-War Philosophy, Ideology

---

Es wird nicht verwundern, dass ein Philosoph unmittelbar nach dem Ende des Zweiten Weltkriegs zu einer Reflexion über die jüngsten zeitgeschichtlichen Ereignisse ansetzt, nicht verwundern auch, dass sich diese Reflexion – nach den Schrecken und politischen Katastrophen der vorhergehenden Jahre – auswächst zu einer grundsätzlichen Erwägung über die Rolle und das scheinbare Scheitern des Humanismus. "Ideologie und Leben in der Idee", so der Titel eines kleinen Essays, mit dem Jan Patočka im Jahre 1946 gleich nach der Okkupationszeit und dem weitgehenden Erliegen der Publikationstätigkeit den Schritt in die neue Zeit wagt (vgl. Patočka 1988, 379-388). Es ist eine kostbare Reflexion, die die "Leichtigkeit und Zerbrechlichkeit des menschlichen Faktums" (ibid., 387) nicht nur thematisiert, sondern diese in einzelnen Sätzen gleichsam zu inkorporieren scheint, eine Reflexion auch, die bei aller

Fragilität festhalten möchte an der menschlichen Freiheit, ja deren Möglichkeit gerade im "Bewusstsein der eigenen Schwäche, Verwirrung und Beschämung" (ibid., 388) konstituiert sehen möchte. Es ist aber auch die gleichermaßen konzise wie anspruchsvolle Skizze eines politisch-gesellschaftlichen Programms, das aus der gerade erfahrenen existentiellen Erschütterung eine grundlegende Kritik der Ideologie formuliert. Bedeutungsvoll und markant ist der kurze Text in vielerlei Hinsicht; einige maßgebliche Ansätze sollen im Folgenden umrissen werden, stets jedoch mit Blick auf die drängende Frage, die hier nur andeutungsweise verhandelt wird, aber aus vielen anderen Überlegungen dieser Jahre spricht: *Was* bleibt vom Humanismus bzw. *wie* bleibt ein Humanismus überhaupt möglich?

1. Zeitgeschichtlicher Kontext:
Nachdenken über den Humanismus im Jahre 1946

Trotz des knappen Umfangs, trotz seiner allzu gedrängten Gedankenführung und einer nicht zu bestreitenden begrifflichen Unschärfe, gehört der Aufsatz zu den Preziosen von Patočkas politischer Philosophie. Kaum eine Auslegung seines politischen und geschichtsphilosophischen Denkens, die dieses kleine Juwel außer Acht gelassen hätte; allerdings auch kaum eine ernsthafte Auseinandersetzung, die nicht bemerkt hätte, dass es ein ungeschliffenes Juwel ist – vorläufig, skizzenhaft, eher eine verheißungsvolle Ankündigung als die Exposition eines Gedankens. Kaum ein Rezipient aber auch, bei dem die Lektüre dieser philosophisch-literarischen Skizze nicht irgendwie verfangen, *nolens volens* ihre kleinen Widerhaken zurückgelassen hätte – es mag sein, dass man sich genarrt fühlt von der scheinbar allzu eingängigen Argumentation und der plötzlichen Überwältigung durch diesen kleinen Entwurf von großer Tragweite, doch auch das innere Widerstreben ist einmal mehr Bestätigung für die rhetorische Kraft des Essays.

Der Aufsatz erschien gleich in der ersten 1946er-Ausgabe (Nr. 1/2) von *Kritický Měsíčnik* (Kritische Monatsschrift), einem anspruchsvollen Journal, das sich vor allem der Literatur- und Kunstkritik widmete. Die Veröffentlichung liegt also ganz am Anfang der Aufbruchszeit nach dem Ende des Krieges, in der es überhaupt wieder möglich war zu publizieren. Entstanden ist die Reflexion vielleicht schon im Jahre 1945, d.h. während der Koalitionsregierung unter Edvard Beneš, die auf Geheiß Moskaus gebildet worden war, jedenfalls aber vor den ersten Wahlen im Jahre 1946 (die mit einem Ergebnis von 40% für die Kommunistische Partei endeten). Den Umständen seiner Entstehungszeit geschuldet, ist der Artikel dementsprechend voll von Hinweisen auf die Unsicherheit und das politische Lavieren dieser Zeit: von einer "Vertrauenskrise" (Patočka 1988, 380) ist die Rede, von Zweifeln an den "Idealen der politischen Freiheit, der Demokratie und der nationalen Selbstbestimmung" (ibid.), von Zweifeln, die schon in der Zwischenkriegszeit offenkundig gewesen seien – um wieviel mehr aber nun, nach einer Zeit, deren Schrecken alles Vorherige in den Schatten stellen. Trotz seiner Kürze, trotz der schwierigen Umstände seiner Entstehung – was der kleine Artikel versucht, ist nicht weniger als eine Neubestimmung der politischen Ideologie(-n) und ihrer philosophischen Begründungen. Hellsichtig benennt er die Symptome einer Krise des Humanismus sowie die begründeten Zweifel an der zukünftigen Geltendmachung humanistischer Ideale, verbleibt aber auch in einer Perspektive, die den Humanismus gerade nicht verabschieden will, sondern umso vehementer, fast verzweifelt, an der Notwendigkeit des Humanismus festhält.

2. Editorischer Kontext: Die "Kritische Monatsschrift"

Wie erwähnt, wurde Patočkas wegweisender Artikel zu Ideologie und Humanismus publiziert in *Kritický Měsíčník* (Kritische Monatsschrift). Das Journal propagierte eine ideologisch unvoreingenommene Betrachtung von Literatur und Kunst; dabei orientierte es sich eher an moralischen und ästhetischen als an politischen Kriterien. Es erschien von 1938-42 und dann, nach der Okkupationszeit, wieder von 1945-48. Die Publikation des Artikels fällt also in die Zeit eines optimistischen Neuanfangs und der Wiederbelebung nach dem Zweiten Weltkrieg, welcher allerdings nicht lang anhielt, da die Zeitschrift schon im Oktober 1948 aus politischen Gründen wieder eingestellt wurde. Jan Patočka publizierte hier einige seiner bedeutendsten Studien aus dieser Zeit, und zwar in beiden Erscheinungsperioden: so vor dem Krieg u.a. den grundlegenden Artikel über "Die Idee der Bildung und ihre heutige Aktualität" (1938, dt. in: Patočka 1992), sowie die Essays "Leben im Gleichgewicht, Leben in der Amplitude" (1939, dt. in: Patočka 1999) und "Über die Philosophie der Geschichte" (1940, dt. in: Patočka 2006). Beide Essays sind markante, wegweisend Stellungnahmen des jungen Philosophen: Mit "Leben im Gleichgewicht, Leben in der Amplitude" positioniert sich Patočka als existentialistischer Denker, der – natürlich – dem *Leben in der Amplitude* den Vorzug vor dem *Gleichgewicht* gibt. Ebenso kann die 1940-er Studie zur Geschichtsphilosophie als eine Art Einführung oder fundamentale Exposition seines philosophischen Zugangs zur Geschichte gelten, die erstmals das lebenslange Forschungsfeld des Autors umreißt. Sie entwirft die Grundzüge eines großangelegten geschichtsphilosophischen Projekts, an dem er während der Zeit des Zweiten Weltkriegs arbeitete (erhalten als sog. Strahov-Nachlass; vgl. hierzu die ausführlichen Erläuterungen in: Karfík 2006), nämlich eine Ideengeschichte des neuzeitlichen Europas, die sich – wie man formulieren könnte – an der geistigen Dimension der Moderne orientiert bzw., so Patočka selbst, der Frage nachgeht, wie aus dem christlichen Europa das "nach-christliche" wurde. Die geistige Geschichte Europas vom Mittelalter bis ins 19. Jahrhundert wird dort als die Ausfaltung zweier divergierender Radikalismen gesehen: eines religiösen Eskapismus einerseits, z.B. in den eschatologischen Motiven der frühen Neuzeit, und einer forcierten Implementierung des objektivierten und rationalisierten Weltbezugs andererseits, der immer stärker zu einem techno-wissenschaftlichen Reduktionismus wird. Was, so die Analyse des jungen Autors, in dieser doppelten Radikalisierung verloren gehe, sei die *Spannung* konfligierender Anschauungen (etwa der Religion und der Wissenschaft), die den unerlässlichen Grundtonus für das eigentlich philosophische Denken bildet.

Nach dem Krieg folgten neben "Ideologie und Leben in der Idee" noch die beiden politisch bedeutsamen Artikel "Der tschechische Humanismus und sein letztes Wort in Emanuel Rádl" (frz. in: Patočka 2006b) sowie "Der Humanismus des Edvard Beneš" (tschech. in: Patočka 20011), beide erschienen im Jahr 1948. Beide Artikel sind wenig bekannt und spielen in der Patočka-Forschung kaum eine Rolle. Dennoch sind sie gerade in politisch-historischer Hinsicht alles andere als unbedeutend. Emanuel Rádl, die philosophisch herausragende Persönlichkeit der tschechoslowakischen Geschichte der Zwischenkriegszeit, und Edvard Beneš, der Nachfolger und Erbe Masaryks, der in zwei historisch äußerst bedeutsamen Perioden (1935-38 sowie 1945-48) als Staatspräsident die Geschicke seines Landes mitbestimmte, sind zentrale Referenzen einer philosophischen Auseinandersetzung mit den auch in europäischer Dimension folgenschweren Wendepunkten der tschechoslowakischen Geschichte dieser Jahre. Beide Artikel markieren schon im Titel gerade die Frage nach der Geltung des Humanismus als ausschlaggebendes Kriterium der Auseinandersetzung.

Es ist vielleicht keine Übertreibung, wenn man in den Studien für die *Kritische Monatsschrift* so etwas wie das Grundgerüst von Patočkas Philosophieren aufgespannt sieht: eine existentialphilosophisch inspirierte Kritik am Humanismus und eine daraus hervorgehende Neubestimmung von Politik und Geschichte, die – wie es später in den Ketzerischen Essays heißen wird – nicht mehr den "Faktologen und Routiniers", den Ideologen und ihren "Parolen des Tages" (Patočka 2010, 158f.) folgt, sondern den Durchbruch zur Wahrheit des Politischen einer grundlegenden Erschütterung überantwortet.

Auch einige weitere Umstände von Patočkas Liaison mit *Kritický Měsíčnik* sind von besonderer Bedeutung und sollten nicht unerwähnt bleiben: Unter der Leitung ihres Herausgebers Vacláv Černý war die politische Orientierung der *Kritischen Monatsschrift* dezidiert demokratisch und progressiv. Das Adjektiv "kritisch" in ihrem Titel war erklärtermaßen nicht nur schmückendes Beiwort, sondern politisches und künstlerisches Programm. Černý engagierte sich während der Okkupationszeit im Widerstand und wurde 1945 inhaftiert. Sein Journal stand dem Sozialismus keineswegs feindlich oder ablehnend gegenüber. Den Versuch einer progressiven politischen Neuorientierung nach 1945 gestaltete es aktiv mit, dennoch wurde die Zeitschrift 1948 indiziert (Černý selbst wurde ab 1950 mit Lehrverbot belegt, ein Jahr später als Patočka – auch in den folgenden Jahrzehnten weisen beider Biographien große Parallelen auf – Černý gehörte später ebenfalls, wie Patočka, zu den Erstunterzeichnern der *Charta 77*). Das Hauptkriterium für das Verbot der Zeitschrift im Jahr 1948 war ihre eindeutige *demokratische Positionierung* und ihr striktes Eintreten für *künstlerische Freiheit*. Dass Patočka gerade hier seine bedeutendsten Artikel dieser frühen Jahre publizierte, ist mehr als eine Koinzidenz und widerlegt all diejenigen, die sein spätes Eintreten für die *Charta 77* als eher zögerliches oder gar den Umständen geschuldetes, beinahe zufälliges Engagement sehen möchten.

Die Artikel in der *Kritischen Monatsschrift* sind somit auch ein Hinweis darauf, wie stark Patočkas Denken, gerade das Denken dieser frühen Jahre, sich politisch-kritischen Prinzipien verpflichtet weiß. Stärker als es zunächst den Anschein haben könnte, scheint das "Kritische" im Titel der Zeitschrift für Patočka auch ein Vorbote seiner späteren Entwicklung zu sein. Das Verbot der Zeitschrift aus "politischen Gründen" (vulgo: aus Angst vor ihrem liberal-kritischen Geist) ist Manifestation des Wirkens einer (jeder!) Ideologie, die Patočka fortan nur noch als denkfeindlich begreifen kann. Seine Ablehnung *aller* Programme ist in gewisser Weise eine deutliche radikalisierte Fortsetzung eben dieses frühen Kritizismus. Wenn die Umstände Kritik nicht mehr zulassen, dann wird sie verstummen – oder sie wird verfemt als *Ketzerei*.

3. Historische Entwicklungslinien hin zur Krise des Humanismus

Eine ersichtliche Leitlinie von Patočkas Artikel aus dem Aufbruchsjahr 1946 ist der Versuch, die soeben zurückliegende Katastrophe des zweiten Weltkriegs nicht kurzsichtig oder im Sinne einer zeitweiligen Verirrung zu betrachten, sondern an die Wurzeln einer Entwicklung zu gelangen, deren Anfänge in der europäischen Geistesgeschichte der frühen Neuzeit zu verorten sind. Es wäre – so die stillschweigende Annahme – nicht möglich, die jüngsten Ereignisse zu verstehen, wenn man nicht bereit ist, ihre langfristigen Ursachen zu sehen und sich auf eine kritische Reflexion des grundlegenden zivilisatorischen Projekts der europäischen Neuzeit einzulassen. Auch in diesem Punkt findet sich eine deutliche Parallele zu den rund 30 Jahre später entstandenen *Ketzerischen Essays*. Dort heißt es im 4. Essay unter dem Titel "Europa und das Europäische Erbe bis zum Ende des 19. Jahrhunderts" markant:

Das 16. Jahrhundert scheint den großen Bruch im westeuropäischen Leben zu bezeichnen. Von dieser Zeit an tritt statt der Sorge um die Seele ein anderes Thema in den Vordergrund, das einen Bereich nach dem anderen – Politik, Wirtschaft, Glauben und Wissen – erobert und dem neuen Stil entsprechend umformt. Nicht die Sorge um die Seele, die Sorge zu sein, sondern die Sorge zu *haben*, die Sorge um die äußere Welt und ihre Beherrschung, wird dominierend. (Patočka 2010, 103)

Ausgehend von dieser ebenso einschneidenden wie historisch ausgreifenden Diagnose erscheint dann im letzten der sechs Essays das 20. Jahrhundert gleichsam als die radikalisierte Zuspitzung und die nihilistische Konsequenz dieser lang grassierenden Vergessenheit der "Sorge für die Seele". Als Kulminationspunkt der Geschichte der europäischen Neuzeit ist es nicht nur ein Jahrhundert, das die historisch sich ereignenden Kriege und humanitären Katastrophen zugelassen hat, sondern erscheint als deren wesentlicher Ausdruck: "das 20. Jahrhundert *als* Krieg", wie es im Titel des Essays heißt.

Im Vergleich dazu wirken die historischen Anspielungen in seiner Kritik an der Ideologie im 1946er Artikel geradezu bescheiden, fast schon kryptisch. Und doch sind die Parallelen unverkennbar: Gleich zu Beginn diagnostiziert der Autor eine "Krise jener Idee des Menschen, die als die spezifisch moderne bezeichnet werden kann" (Patočka 1988, 379). Ohne einen Hinweis, was denn diese "spezifisch moderne" Idee des Menschen eigentlich meint, wie sie zu bestimmen wäre oder worin sie sich artikuliert, geht Patočka unmittelbar zu den historischen Quellen über. Die moderne Idee des Menschen habe "ihre Wurzeln (…) in der Aufklärung", um dann mit frappierender Datierung fortzufahren: "von 1715 bis in die Gegenwart sind dieser Idee immer wieder neue Programme entsprungen" (ibid.). Es sind diese spärlichen Andeutungen, die den gesamten historischen Horizont des Artikels umreißen, nämlich dass die "großen sozialen Bewegungen" der Gegenwart allesamt im "Aufklärungsbegriff des Natürlichen verwurzelt" (ibid., 380) seien. Allerdings, so sparsam die Hinweise auch sein mögen, die Richtung ist mehr als klar: Die Jahreszahl 1715 bezieht sich ersichtlich auf den Tod Ludwigs XIV., des sogenannten "Sonnenkönigs". Als Jahr markiert es symbolisch den Beginn der Aufklärung bzw. des aufgeklärten Absolutismus, der auf den "monarchischen Absolutismus" Ludwigs XIV. folgte. Kennzeichen dieser Periode sind eine Stärkung der Rolle der Parlamente, Religionsfreiheit und – was vor dem Hintergrund einer Debatte um den "Humanismus" nicht unwesentlich ist – eine Auffassung des Menschen, die individuelle Würde und Freiheit des Einzelnen betont und den Glauben an die Vernunft postuliert.

Inhaltlich beschränkt sich Patočka auf den (ebenfalls deutungsbedürftigen) Hinweis, dass die Wurzeln für die Krise der modernen Idee des Menschen in der Aufklärung zu finden seien, "und zwar im Gedanken der Natur und der Natürlichkeit" (ibid., 379; im Original: "osvícenská myšlenka přírody a přirozenosti"). Es steht zu vermuten, dass der Autor hier insbesondere das von der Aufklärung betonte Naturrecht (bzw. Vernunftrecht) im Blick hat, d.h. die natürlich gegebenen Rechte eines jeden Individuums, unabhängig von Geburt und sozialer Schicht (Abschaffung der Leibeigenschaft als Errungenschaft der Aufklärung). Diese universellen und natürlichen Rechte erscheinen hier abgelöst von ihren religiös-theologischen Fundierungen, die göttliche Vorsehung wird aber dennoch oft gleichsam durch die Hintertür wieder eingeführt mit der Behauptung, dass das Naturrecht und die göttliche Offenbarung konvergierten und letztlich dieselbe Quelle in Gott hätten.

In Bezug auf die Geschichte wird dieser Gedanke paradigmatisch formuliert von Johann Gottfried Herder, der die Geschichte der Menschheit als Weiterung und Fortsetzung der Naturgeschichte konzipiert, wobei die Vernunft die Ausführung des göttlichen Plans übernimmt (Herder 2002). Bei ihm als zweiter wichtiger Aspekt auch hinzu, dass er in seinen umfangreichen Schriften zur Philosophie der Geschichte nicht nur die Vielfalt und Gleichheit der einzelnen Menschen und Charaktere betont, sondern diese Haltung auch auf Völker und Nationen überträgt. Dieser Teil seiner Geschichtsphilosophie fand gerade unter den slawischen Völkern im Laufe der nationalen Erweckungen des 19. Jahrhunderts ein enormes und nachhaltiges Echo. Wenn man nun hinzusetzt, dass Patočka eben während der Zeit des Zweiten Weltkriegs intensiv an der Übersetzung Herders arbeitete und 1941/42 zwei größere Studien zu ihm veröffentlichte ("J.G. Herder und seine Philosophie der Humanität", bzw. "Zweierlei Vernunft und Natur in der deutschen Aufklärung", dt. Übers. beide in: Patočka 2006a), dann erhellt sich der ansonsten kryptische Hinweis auf die Rolle von "Natur und Natürlichkeit" in der Aufklärung. Ganz wichtig ist in diesem Zusammenhang, dass die aufklärerischen Ideale nicht nur als Individualrechte gefasst werden, sondern von Beginn an in den politischen Kontext von Emanzipation und nationaler Selbstbestimmung eintreten. Dies ist besonders vor dem Hintergrund der tschechischen Geschichte von Bedeutung, gewinnt aber für Patočka eine grundsätzliche Dimension: Was einerseits nationale Unabhängigkeit und Freiheit bedeutet, schlägt andererseits leicht in nationalen Partikularismus und Nationalismus um – und ist in dieser Form einer der Gründe für das, was Patočka später als das Ende Europas und das Ende einer universellen Idee Europas beschreiben wird.

Die unmittelbar nach dem Ende des Krieges geschriebene Reflexion beschränkt sich also keinesfalls auf die politischen Verirrungen der unmittelbaren Gegenwart, sondern sieht diese eingebettet in eine lange Entwicklung, die bis zu ihren Anfängen in der Aufklärung verfolgt wird. Gleichwohl artikuliert die Studie (anders als später die *Ketzerischen Essays* mit ihrer Kritik am "Primat des *Habens* vor dem *Sein*" [Patočka 1988, 110]) keine pauschale Abgrenzung von der neuzeitlichen Entwicklung. Der Grundton ist mehr fragend als urteilend – eher Ausdruck einer Sorge darum, ob die Ideale der Aufklärung wirklich noch die intellektuelle Überzeugungskraft besitzen, um der politischen Krise antworten zu können. Somit artikuliert der Artikel eine vorsichtige Anfrage, die nicht abschließend beantwortet wird. In der folgenden kurzen Passage wird dieser Zweifel ("Unsicherheiten") deutlich:

Von Krieg zu Krieg können wir beobachten, wie sich die Krise des menschlichen Nachdenkens über den Menschen, ja mehr noch, wie sich die Krise des Verhältnisses des Menschen zu sich selbst immer weiter vertieft. Die großen sozialen Bewegungen, die in dem Aufklärungsbegriff des Natürlichen verwurzelt sind, behalten zwar immer noch die Führung, aber zugleich tauchen Unsicherheiten auf – Unsicherheiten, die nicht nur theoretischen, sondern auch politischen und moralischen Charakters sind. Der Enttäuschung durch den Weltkrieg und später durch den Frieden folgt eine gewaltige Krise des sozialen Humanismus. (Patočka 1988, 380)

Zwar wird den "großen sozialen Bewegungen", die auf den emanzipatorisch-humanistischen Idealen der Aufklärung gründen, noch immer die maßgebliche Bedeutung für die Lösung der gegenwärtigen Probleme zugeschrieben, zugleich haben sie aber sowohl theoretisch als auch politisch-moralisch an Überzeugungskraft verloren. Besonders bemerkenswert ist in diesem Zusammenhang die Behauptung einer "gewaltigen Krise des sozialen Humanismus" – eine Formulierung, die auf Sozialismus und Marxismus zielt. Es ist dies – geschrieben im Jahr 1946 – nicht nur eine treffende Antizipation zukünftiger Zweifel an der politischen Ideologie des "sozialen Humanismus", sondern eine grundsätzliche Anfrage an die wirkmächtigste Strömung des Humanismus und somit auch an den Humanismus überhaupt.

4. Krise des Humanismus – Konjunktur der philosophischen Humanismen

Der philosophische Kern von Patočkas Schriften dieser Zeit wird augenfällig, sobald man sie als einen ausgedehnten Kommentar zur tiefen Krise des Humanismus liest. Patočka steht damit in diesen Jahren keineswegs allein. Die mit Händen zu greifende Infragestellung humanistischer Grundwerte, die mit dem Erlebnis von Krieg und Vernichtung einherging, fordert geradezu die philosophische Reflexion heraus. Deshalb ist die vielfach beschworene Krise des Humanismus auch eine Zeit der Konjunktur philosophischer Humanismen: 1946 publiziert Jean-Paul Sartre seinen Essay *L'existentialisme est un humanisme* (den Patočka später eingehend in seiner Studie *Ewigkeit und Geschichtlichkeit* [frz. Übers. in: Patočka 2011] kommentieren wird); im selben Jahr verfasst auch Heidegger seinen *Brief über den "Humanismus"* als Antwort auf ein Schreiben Jean Beaufrets (der aber bei seiner Publikation im Jahr 1947 auch zu einer Antwort auf Sartre wurde), und schließlich könnte man noch György Lukács mit seinem Buch *Existentialismus oder Marxismus* hinzunehmen, das ebenfalls um die gleiche Zeit herum geschrieben wurde (die frz. Übersetzung erschien 1948, die deutsche Ausgabe 1951).

Vor diesem Hintergrund trägt es nicht unmaßgeblich zur Faszination für die Lektüre Patočkas bei, dass er seine Kritik am Humanismus exakt zur selben Zeit wie die genannten Autoren entwickelt, dabei aber zunächst ganz unabhängig formuliert, schlicht weil die anderen Studien zu dieser Zeit noch nicht erschienen bzw. ihm nicht bekannt waren. Umso erstaunlicher ist es, welch deutliche Parallelen und welche Ähnlichkeit der philosophischen

Motive sich bei einer Zusammenschau offenbaren. Erst einige Jahre später erfolgte dann bei Patočka eine ausdrückliche Auseinandersetzung mit diesen parallel entstandenen Kritiken am Humanismus, deren eindrücklichste Zeugnisse (wie die lange Studie über *Ewigkeit und Geschichtlichkeit*, vgl. Patočka 1996) jedoch unpubliziert blieben und somit nie Teil der Diskussion wurden, in die sie unzweifelhaft gehören.

4.1. Sartres "Negativismus"

Während György Lukács' Analyse der Unvereinbarkeit von Existentialismus und Marxismus bei Patočka gänzlich unbeachtet bleibt, obwohl gerade die Engführung auf den Marxismus reichlich Anknüpfungspunkte für eine Diskussion böte,[1] ist es bemerkenswert zu sehen, wie Patočka seine Sorge um den Humanismus zunächst ganz unabhängig von den anderen Autoren formuliert, ehe es später zu direkten Referenzen kommt. Für Sartre ist zunächst kennzeichnend, dass er grundsätzlich zwei Arten des Humanismus unterscheidet: 1) Eine Lesart des Humanismus, die den Menschen als höchsten Zweck stilisiert und letztlich eine *Selbstermächtigung des Menschen* postuliert, inklusive aller Exzesse, die einen "Kult des Menschen" begründen – dieses Verständnis des Humanismus lehnt Sartre als überkommen ab. 2) Ein Verständnis des Humanismus, das den Menschen als ein Wesen sieht, das nicht fertig ist, sondern ein stets noch zu schaffendes bleibt und sich insofern der *Suche nach der Menschlichkeit des Menschen* verpflichtet weiß – diese Auslegung hält Sartre bei aller Kritik am traditionellen Humanismus für weiterhin relevant. Es resultiert daraus eine Philosophie, die den Menschen in der Notwendigkeit zur Entscheidung sieht, er ist, wie es in Sartres berühmter Formulierung heißt, "zur Freiheit verurteilt" ("l'homme est condamné à être libre"; Sartre 1970, 38).

Die Kritik an der ersten Lesart des Humanismus teilt – so darf man wohl behaupten – Patočka voll und ganz. Unter seinen vielen Nachlass-Manuskripten findet sich eines mit dem bezeichnenden Titel *Der "Kult des Menschen" und sein Umsturz in heutiger Zeit*. Wenn auch ein kurzes Manuskript, bietet es doch eine profunde Kritik am "Kult des Menschen", der mit seiner Vorstellung von einer Selbsterlösung des Menschen als Idee des 19. Jahrhunderts präsentiert wird, die jede Glaubwürdigkeit verloren hat. Denn "was ist seit dieser Zeit geschehen? Die Mittel, mit denen der Mensch sich selbst zu erlösen meinte, die Mittel eines sinnlich-materiellen und praktischen Wirkens, haben sich zwar bewährt, aber keineswegs als Mittel der Erlösung und Selbstverwirklichung, sondern als (…) eine eigene Wesenhaftigkeit, die in keiner Weise Rücksicht nimmt auf die menschliche Erlösung, son-

---

[1] Wie überhaupt Lukács in seinem Werk kaum einmal Erwähnung findet, was angesichts der geschichtsphilosophischen Interessen oder der ausgeprägten Hegel-Rezeption beider Philosophen eine durchaus bemerkenswerte Auffälligkeit darstellt.

dern im Gegenteil den Menschen in ihre Dienste einzubeziehen weiß" (Patočka 2002a, 707; Übers. LH).

Hegel und Comte sind es, die nach Patočka als die größten Vordenker einer solchen Selbsterlösung des Menschen zu gelten haben ("Marx ist bloß eine Folge"; ibid. 706). Diese Philosophie glorifiziert die menschliche *Arbeit*, die *Mühe*, sie steigt hinab in die endlichen Tiefen des Menschseins, um gerade dort die Unendlichkeit zu finden und von dort aus die Erlösung des Menschen zu erwarten. Es gibt jedoch eine Bedingung dieser Anschauung: Sie ist gerichtet auf ein letztes Ziel, die Selbsterlösung des Menschen, und sie muss insofern getragen sein von einer "*totalen* Sinnerfülltheit". Nichts kann hier außerhalb der sinnerfüllten Verständlichkeit bleiben, und mit einer großartigen Charakterisierung dieser menschlichen Selbstbefreiung a la Hegel setzt Patočka hinzu: " In die Totalität des Sinnes sind wir geradezu *eingekerkert*." (Patočka 2002a, 708; Übers. LH). Die totale Sinnerfülltheit beruht auf der Überzeugung eines letztlichen Glaubens an die Harmonie, die sich – wie in einem weiteren Nachlass-Manuskript zu finden – so formulieren ließe: "Die Welt muss in dem Maße menschlich werden, wie der Mensch weltlich…" (Patočka 2002c, 715; Übers. LH). Es ist dieser Glaube an die "Menschlichkeit" der Welt – philosophisch spätestens seit Nietzsche in Frage gestellt –, der in den Kriegen und Katastrophen des 20. Jahrhunderts grundlegend erschüttert wurde. Für Sartre wie für Patočka ist damit der Humanismus als "Kult des Menschen" seiner Grundlagen beraubt.

Weit schwieriger fällt es dagegen, beider Positionen zu bestimmen, wenn es um die für Sartre angedeutete zweite, "positive" Haltung zum Humanismus geht, d.h. um die Frage, inwiefern der Humanismus auch weiterhin relevant bleibt. Sartre beantwortet dies mit der Verantwortung des Menschen für sein Leben: es ist nicht alles gleichgültig und alles erlaubt, sondern der Mensch muss sich selbst entwerfen, ja er *ist* nichts anderes als dieser Entwurf. Zwar ist dieser grundsätzlich offene, suchende Weg der Philosophie einer, den auch Patočka mit seiner unablässig wiederkehrenden Betonung des sokratischen Fragens hervorhebt – so hält etwa der letzte, markante Satz seiner langen Studie *Was ist Phänomenologie?* fest: "Das Bestreben … der Moderne einen *suchenden* Weg entgegenzustellen, das ist Phänomenologie."(Patočka 1991, 452). Jedoch lässt sich kaum verkennen, dass dieses suchende Element eines ist, das einer existentialen Erschütterung entspringt und in einer grundsätzlichen Offenhaltung der Möglichkeit einer solchen existentialen Erschütterung besteht. Es ist mehr ein Moment des Frei-Machens nicht des Entscheidens und Sich-Selbst-Wählens, wie es bei Sartre gedacht wird. Vor allem aber ist es die vermeintliche grundsätzliche Freiheit, die nach Sartre in dieser Entscheidung liegen soll, die Patočka anzweifelt. In seinem kleinen Artikel *Zweifel am Existentialismus* von 1947, also ebenfalls aus der philosophisch hochintensiven Phase der unmittelbaren Nachkriegszeit stammend, referiert er Sartres Position, wonach der Mensch so sei, wie er sich selbst wähle (bzw. zu wählen in der Lage sei), um dann die Frage anzuschließen:

Ist aber der Umstand, dass sich der Mensch selbst wählt, sich für sich selbst entscheidet, nicht wieder nur etwas Essentiales? Und ist es nicht so, dass jede Wahl nicht nur das Gegebene voraussetzt, welches wir zu beurteilen haben, wenn wir über es entscheiden sollen, sondern auch die Werte, in deren Namen wir uns entscheiden, und die folglich bereits gegeben sein müssen? (...) Prinzipiell lässt sich sagen, dass es einen ausschließlich individuellen Wert, der Wert nur für eine bestimmte Person in einem bestimmten Lebensmoment wäre, gar nicht geben kann." (Patočka 1991, 512)

Damit ist in der Tat ein grundlegender Zweifel angemeldet ("Zweifel am Existentialismus"), der den Kern von Sartres vielleicht bekanntestem Leitmotiv in Frage stellt, wonach beim Menschen die Existenz der Essenz vorausgeht. Patočka hält aber in der Umkehrung der Verhältnisse von Essenz und Existenz die philosophische Frage nach den Grundlagen eines (wie auch immer gearteten) "Humanismus" keineswegs für überwunden oder gelöst, sondern sieht diese im Gegenteil verschärft zurückkehren. Er formuliert damit exakt dieselbe Kritik wie Heidegger in seinem zeitgleich entstandenen *Brief über den "Humanismus"*. Dort heißt es:

> Sartre spricht (...) den Grundsatz des Existentialismus so aus: die Existenz geht der Essenz voran. Er nimmt dabei *existentia* und *essentia* im Sinne der Metaphysik, die seit Plato sagt; die *essentia* geht der *existentia* voraus. Sartre kehrt diesen Satz um. Aber die Umkehrung eines metaphysischen Satzes bleibt ein metaphysischer Satz. Als dieser Satz verharrt er mit der Metaphysik in der Vergessenheit der Wahrheit des Seins. (Heidegger 1991, 19)

> Auch in dem langen Essay zu *Ewigkeit und Geschichtlichkeit* findet sich eine ganz ähnlich formulierte Kritik, die zwar nicht direkt auf die Heidegger'sche Wahrheit des Seins als Unverborgenheit Bezug nimmt, aber doch deutlich erkennen lässt, dass Sartres "Sein" (wie auch das "Nichts"!) zu sehr im ontischen Sinne eines vorhandenen, verfügbaren Seins gedacht sind, weshalb seine Philosophie dahin zurückkehrt, wogegen sie sich ursprünglich wenden wollte: Sie kehrt zurück zu dem Ausgangspunkt, gegen den eigentlich die existentielle Bewegung und vor allem die existentiale Metaphysik, die existentiale Ontologie ausgezogen war: während diese Philosophie die Frage nach dem Sinn des Seins neu stellen, sie im Status einer Frage, im Status einer offenen und vertieften Problematik belassen sollte, sind hier im Gegenteil alle Fragen auf einen Schlag (wenn auch scheinbar) gelöst und das alte eleatische Sein, das verfügbare, dingliche, gegenständliche Sein feiert seinen größten Triumph (...) (Patočka 1996, 217; Übers. LH)

Entsprechend gilt auch für das prominent in seiner Philosophie figurierende "Nichts", dass es zu einer eigenen Entität wird, die fungiert wie in der alten Metaphysik. Es stimmt, dass das "Nichts" für Sartre zwar nicht "existiert", aber dennoch soll es etwas sein, das uns fortwährend "bedrängt", auf dessen Grundlage wir erst die Dinge begreifen und auseinanderhalten können. Wenn es aber dergestalt "wirkt", so muss das "Nichts" auch eine ganz eigene Wertigkeit, ein "Sein" haben: "Es ist klar, dass dieses 'Nichts' (…) allen Protesten Sartres zum Trotz als Hypostase zu betrachten ist" (Patočka 1991, 513). Zu dieser Hypostasierung des "Nichts" gehört dann auch, dass der Mensch bei Sartre – wie in der obigen Kritik angedeutet – angeblich die Werte, die seinen Entwurf und sein Sich-Selbst-Wählen leiten, ganz unvoreingenommen, "weltlos" bestimmen kann. Der Irrtum liegt aber – für Patočka – darin, dass diese Werte ganz entschieden zur Welt dazugehören, dass sie von Anfang an in die Welt der menschlichen Möglichkeiten hineingestellt sind. Zurückgewendet auf die leitende Frage nach dem Humanismus und dem Bild des Menschen, das ihm zugrundliegt, ließe sich die Kritik demnach so zusammenfassen, dass auch Sartres Philosophie entschieden ein bestimmtes Wesen des Menschen voraussetzt, dieses allerdings aus einem hypostasierten "Negativismus" entwirft, so dass er allein "die negierende Bestimmung (…) für ausschließlich, wesentlich, definitiv hält" (Patočka 1996, 217; Übers. LH).

4.2 Heidegger und die Zurückweisung der Metaphysik

Obwohl sich die direkten (kritischen) Referenzen beim Patočka dieser Jahre stärker auf Sartre beziehen, ist es kaum möglich, seine Positionierung zum Humanismus unabhängig von Heideggers zeitgleich entstandener Abhandlung zu sehen. Einige Parallelen zu Heidegger, gerade in der Kritik an Sartre, wurden schon benannt, wobei wichtig ist zu betonen, dass ein großer Teil dieser Studien noch ohne Kenntnis von Heideggers *Humanismusbrief* verfasst wurde. Auch nach 1947, als Patočka diesen irgendwann zur Kenntnis genommen haben muss, bleiben die *direkten* Bezüge darauf in seinem Werk seltsamerweise dünn (bzw. sind so gut wie gar nicht vorhanden). Es gibt aber deutliche Indizien, dass er den *Humanismusbrief* bereits sehr bald nach dem Erscheinen gelesen haben muss. [2]

---

[2] So notiert er am 2.5. 1948 in seinen philosophischen *Heften*: "Das Sein hat also zwei Seiten, wie sich Heid. ausdrückt, *das Heile und das Nichthafte*." Und am 25.12.1948 heißt es u.a.: "*Geschick – Geschichte, Geschichtlichkeit – Hut, Obhut*, Mensch: *Hirt des Seins* (gen. subj. & obiectivus)." (Kursivierte Worte im Original deutsch. – Die *Hefte* sind noch nicht erschienen. Die tschechische Ausgabe ist in Vorbereitung, ebenso wie eine französische Übersetzung.) Beide Passagen enthalten deutliche Hinweise auf den *Brief über den "Humanismus"*, die Patočka nur diesem entnehmen konnte [vgl. bei Heidegger die entsprechenden Passagen: Heidegger 1991, 22 ("Hirt des Seins") bzw. 49 (das Heile und das Nichthafte) bzw. 51 ("Hut")].
Der Verweis auf den Menschen als "Hirt des Seins" findet sich sogar schon in einem französischsprachigen Brief Patočkas an Robert Campbell, der vom 3.5.1947 datiert – was somit eine noch frühere Lektüre des Humanismusbriefs bezeugen würde. Dort schreibt er: "Heidegger veut maintenir la distinction entre le *Seiendes* (…) et l'être lui-même, l'être qui *se dit* de toutes ces choses-là. C'est pour-

Heideggers grundlegende Distanzierung vom Humanismus erfolgt schon im Titel, in dem er dieses Wort in Anführungszeichen setzt. Damit will er keine Wendung gegen den Menschen oder eine endgültige Aufgabe des Humanismus andeuten, wohl aber eine gegen alle bestehenden Humanismen – sei es der christliche Humanismus, sei es Marxismus oder die neueste Formulierung des Humanismus bei Sartre. Alle bestehenden Humanismen kommen nach Heidegger darin überein, dass sie das Wesen des Menschen immer schon voraussetzen, also metaphysisch sind. Heidegger begegnet dem mit einem Denken der "Ek-sistenz", d.h. im wörtlichen Sinne eines "Hinausstehens" des Menschen "in die Wahrheit des Seins" (Heidegger 1991, 18). Gleich zu Anfang seines Briefes bestimmt Heidegger dies auch als ein "Denken des Seins", wobei die Doppeldeutigkeit des Genitivs als *genitivus obiectivus* und *genitivus subiectivus* anzeigt, dass nicht nur das Sein gedacht und bedacht werden soll, sondern auch das Sein selbst ins Denken fällt, "insofern das Denken, dem Sein gehörend, auf das Sein hört" (Heidegger 1991, 8). Die bisherigen Humanismen sind also nicht nur metaphysisch, weil sie das Wesen des Menschen immer schon voraussetzen, sondern setzen sich auch dem Vorwurf eines Anthropozentrismus aus, weil sie den Menschen stets in die "Mitte des Seienden" rücken. Auch hierauf antwortet das "Hinausstehen" des Menschen: "So kommt es denn bei der Bestimmung der Menschlichkeit des Menschen als der Ek-sistenz darauf an, dass nicht der Mensch das Wesentliche ist, sondern das Sein als die Dimension des Ekstatischen der Ek-sistenz." (Heidegger 1991, 24).

Neben den bereits erwähnten Parallelen gibt es viele Ansätze, wo sich Entsprechungen zwischen beiden Denkern finden. An erster Stelle wäre das "Thema" oder der "Gegenstand" der Reflexion selbst zu nennen: die Infragestellung bzw. die philosophische Vergewisserung über den "Humanismus". Daher kann es nicht nur darum gehen, über diese oder jene Ideologie, über diese oder jene gesellschaftliche Veränderung nachzudenken, sondern die Krise als eine Herausforderung der Philosophie und eine grundlegende Anfrage an den "Humanismus" zu nehmen. Am Ende seines *Humanismusbriefes* formuliert Heidegger markant, es sei an der Zeit, dass "man sich dessen entwöhnt, die Philosophie zu überschätzen und sie deshalb zu überfordern." Was Not tue "in der jetzigen Weltnot", so weiter, sei "weniger Philosophie, aber mehr Achtsamkeit des Denkens; weniger Literatur, aber mehr Pflege des Buchstabens." (Heidegger 1991, 54) Gemeint ist hier vor allem die Zurückweisung einer *bestimmten* Philosophie, einer *bestimmten* Tradition der Philosophie, die in ihrer

---

quoi il dit aussi que l'homme est le voisin de l'être (ou son « pâtre », celui dont la fonction est de veiller sur l'être et dont toute l'existence est conditionnée par cette fonction : dont l'être est la condition)." In einem Brief vom 25.1.1948 an denselben Empfänger heißt es dann unmissverständlich: "Dans le numéro 63 de *Fontaine* il y a un article remarquable de Beaufret sur Heidegger, d'une justesse absolue quant au dernier Heidegger. (…) La lettre de Heidegger aussi est remarquable" (zitiert nach: Patočka 1992b, 35 bzw. 57). Für diese Hinweise danke ich Erika Abrams.

bisherigen Ausprägung für Heidegger gleichbedeutend mit der Metaphysik war, wie er explizit festhält: "Das künftige Denken ist nicht mehr Philosophie, weil es ursprünglicher denkt als die Metaphysik, welcher Name das gleiche sagt" (ibid.). Das künftige Denken wird/soll also zugleich ein "ursprünglicheres" Denken sein, was gleichbedeutend ist mit Heideggers proklamiertem Bruch mit der abendländischen Philosophietradition und einer Neubesinnung auf das vorsokratische Denken.

Eine ähnliche Forderung findet sich bei Patočka nicht – oder besonders bei ihm nicht, denn sein "ursprünglicheres" Denken ist eines, das gerade die Anfänge der abendländischen Philosophie wiederbeleben will und das *sokratische* Fragen zu seinem Leitprinzip erhebt. Es verbindet sich damit jedoch ein ganz ähnliches Anliegen: die Zurückweisung einer bestimmten Art von Philosophie, nämlich der Philosophie als Metaphysik. So heißt es in dem oben ausführlich vorgestellten Artikel "Ideologie und Leben in der Idee" (1946) signifikant:

> Ideologien, Programme, Gedanken, Einfälle und Auffassungen kommen und gehen – die Idee des Menschen aber bleibt. Diese Idee ist weder ein gelehrtes Produkt der konstruierenden Vernunft, noch ein Märchen aus einer nebensächlichen Welt. Sie ist das, was dem Menschen immer dann verbleibt, wenn ihm die Situation, in die er gestellt ist, als eine fundamentale Bedrohung seines ganzen inneren Seins erscheint. (Patočka 1988, 388).

Die Unterscheidung zwischen "Idee" und "Ideologie" ist die zentrale Leitlinie dieses Artikels – Ideologie als das, was den Menschen "von außen her" ergreift, die Idee hingegen als etwas, das "unser eigenstes Inneres" berührt, etwas, dem gegenüber wir "nie gleichgültig sein" können (ibid., 379). Wichtiger ist im Zusammenhang des Vorherigen jedoch, wie die Idee hier eingeführt und charakterisiert wird: Sie ist gerade nicht ein "gelehrtes Produkt der konstruierenden Vernunft" – soll heißen: sie entspringt nicht der Metaphysik, ist nicht "hergestellt" –, sie ist aber auch nicht "Märchen aus einer anderen Welt" – soll heißen: kein Ausfluss der Religion oder Mythologie.[3] Diese Distanzierung von jeder Metaphysik – die sich nicht nur in der Abgrenzung gegen die abstrakte Philosophie findet, sondern auch den zweiten Bereich der Religion einschließt – ist ein durchgängiges Leitmotiv von Patočkas Philosophieren. Charakteristisch ist auch die positive Bestimmung der Idee im letzten zitierten Satz: Gerade das ist die Idee, was in der Situation einer "fundamentalen Bedrohung" bleibt, anders gesagt, was gerade in dieser Situation "erscheint", "sich zeigt". Damit ist das Grundmotiv eines "Durchbruchs zur Wahrheit" (verstanden als fundamentale existentiale Wahrheit) benannt, das seine Philosophie durchzieht und später in den *Ketzerischen Essais*

---

[3] Es scheint angebracht, hier mit "Märchen aus einer anderen Welt" zu übersetzen. Das Original spricht von "postranní svět", was in der Tat auch die Bedeutung von "Nebenwelt" hat, aber gemeint sein dürfte vielleicht die Welt, die "neben" unserer die ganz "andere" ist.

als "Erschütterung" seinen prominenten Platz hat. Immer dringt hier der Versuch einer "armen Philosophie" durch, d.h. die Geste eines existentialisierenden, "kenotischen" Denkens (vgl. Hagedorn 2014), das den Versuch wagt, den Ausgangspunkt (wie auch in gewisser Weise den Kulminationspunkt) zu sehen in einer inneren Reflexion, die sich freimacht von Ideologien, Konzepten, Programmen und allen metaphysischen Vorgaben. Bei Patočka gehört in diesen Gedankengang auch mit hinein, dass die so verstandene "Idee" tatsächlich und ganz konkret auch die "Umgestaltung der Gesellschaftsverhältnisse" erhellen soll, was in dieser klaren politischen Abzweckung bei Heidegger gänzlich fehlt. Entscheidend ist aber auch, dass die Wendung gegen *die* Metaphysik (und *die* Theologie) bei Patočka – wie auch bei Heidegger – nicht nur die traditionelle Metaphysik und Theologie meint, sondern ganz entschieden auch die modernen (vermeintlichen) Überwindungen miteinschließt. In einem seiner Nachlassmanuskripte findet sich eine Sentenz, die dies schön zusammenfasst und auf das leitende Thema des Humanismus zurückbezieht: "Die humanistische Ära – sie richtet sich gegen die Theologie und Metaphysik, welche in ihr enthalten ist. Doch sie ist selbst metaphysisch, nur dass es eine Metaphysik der modernen Naturwissenschaft und Geschichte ist, eine "positive" Metaphysik." (Patočka 2002c, 715; Übs. LH).

Sogar in sprachlichen Dingen stehen sich Patočkas und Heideggers Entwürfe dieser Zeit nah, doch ein gewichtiger Unterschied wird nicht zu übersehen sein. Heidegger schließt seinen *Humanismusbrief* mit den Sätzen: "Das Denken ist auf dem Abstieg in die Armut seines vorläufigen Wesens. Das Denken sammelt die Sprache in das einfache Sagen. Die Sprache ist so die Sprache des Seins, wie die Wolken die Wolken des Himmels sind" (Heidegger 1991, 54). Das ist die poetisierende, besondere, oft belächelte Sprache Heideggers – Heidegger-Poesie, eine Rede, die Sammlung, Lauschen, Aufmerksamkeit, Gabe, Empfang in der Sprache selbst zu artikulieren sucht. Nimmt man Sätze Patočkas zum Vergleich, so fällt seine Vorliebe für eine gewisse existentielle Dramatisierung und Wendung der Sprache nach innen auf – in Anspielung auf einen seiner Titel könnte man auch sagen: sie zeigt eine Präferenz für Extreme und das "Leben in der Amplitude" (vgl. Patočka 1999). Fast ganz am Ende seines 1946er Artikels (an ähnlich prominenter Stelle also wie bei Heidegger) heißt es etwa:

> Die Zerbrechlichkeit ist kein äußerlicher Zufall, es ist vielmehr eine Grenze, hinter der der Mensch nicht mehr gestellt und daher auch nicht verfolgt oder belangt werden kann, eine Grenze, an der wir innehalten müssen. Wer dort ungebrochen, von seinem letzten Sinn ungetrennt verharrt, wird sich selbst im höchsten den Menschen möglichen Maße erfüllen – er wird frei bleiben. Die innere Einheit erleben wir dann im Bewusstsein der eigenen Schwäche, Verwirrung und Beschämung. (Patočka 1988, 387f.).

Eingeleitet wird diese Passage von einer noch bemerkenswerteren Formulierung. Es ist eine Formulierung, die – so möchte ich vermuten – vielleicht den Kern seines philosophischen Menschenbildes überhaupt ausmacht – und die deshalb diesem Artikel titelgebend voransteht. Patočka spricht nämlich von der "besonderen Leichtgewichtigkeit und Zerbrechlichkeit des Faktums ‚Mensch'" (Patočka 1988, 387). Im tschechischen Original hat diese Formulierung einen speziellen Klang dadurch, dass sich die beiden ersten Substantive reimen: "nesmírná lehkost a křehkost lidského fakta", wörtlich (und vielleicht treffender) übersetzt hieße es: die "unermessliche Leichtigkeit und Zerbrechlichkeit des menschlichen Faktums".[4] Es ist eine existentiell dramatisierende Beschreibung, die aber doch eine besondere Innigkeit und Nähe zum "Faktum Mensch" ausdrückt – trotz oder gerade wegen der immensen Gefährdung und Leichtigkeit, die sie beschwört. Das Menschenbild, das sie evoziert, könnte an die Anfänge des abendländischen Denkens erinnern, an Pindar, der über die Menschen als *ephemeroi*, "Eintagswesen", spricht (8. Pythische Ode, Vers 95).

Bei aller Kritik am Humanismus, die Patočkas Philosophie der Nachkriegszeit kennzeichnet, bei aller "Krise des Humanismus", die sie beschwört, scheint doch eines unverkennbar: Mit einer fast verzweifelten Geste hält er energisch am Menschen und an der Hoffnung auf den Humanismus fest. Ganz zum Schluss seines Artikels von 1946 setzt er im Lichte dieser "Idee des Menschen" zu einem Appell an, der den "Kampf um einen neuen Menschen und um die Umgestaltung der Gesellschaftsverhältnisse" (Patočka 1988, 388) als wichtiges politisches und soziales Ziel dieser Zeit benennt. Es ist eine Schlussfolgerung, die in dieser Form bei Heidegger sicher nicht vorstellbar wäre. Aber mehr noch: Wenn es bei Heidegger heißt, dass nicht der Mensch das Wesentliche ist, so gilt für Patočka, dass bei ihm in den Essays dieser Zeit (wie vielleicht in seinem Denken überhaupt) sehr wohl der Mensch das Wesentliche bleibt. Während für Heidegger ein neues "Denken des Seins" gefordert ist, weil der Humanismus einhergeht mit "Seinsvergessenheit", ist es analog bei Patočka gerade die Vergessenheit der "Sorge für die Seele", die sein Denken umtreibt. Die Krise des Humanismus ist, dass er die Sorge um die Seele vergessen und die Idee des Menschen der Ideologie überantwortet hat.

Dr. Ludger Hagedorn, Institute of Human Sciences, Vienna
hagedorn[at]iwm.at

---

[4] Im Tschechischen erlangte das Wort "lehkost" nachmals eine fast ikonische Bedeutung durch Milan Kunderas 1984 erschienenen Roman *Die unerträgliche Leichtigkeit des Seins*. Patočka verwendet es in seinem Artikel zweimal. Beide Male wird es begleitet von dem Adjektiv "nesmírná" = "unermesslich". Durch die Verwendung dieses Adjektivs verliert die "Leichtigkeit" eben die menschliche Dimension und wird zu der brutalen Diagnose, die sie ist.

Literaturangaben

Hagedorn, Ludger. "Kenosis. Die philosophische Anverwandlung eines christlichen Motivs bei Jan Patočka", in: Michael Staudigl and Christian Sternad (eds.), *Figuren der Transzendenz. Transformationen eines phänomenologischen Grundbegriffs*, Würzburg: Königshausen & Neumann 2014. 349-366.

Heidegger, Martin. *Über den "Humanismus"* (EA 1947), Frankfurt: V. Klostermann ^{9}1991.

Herder, Johann Gottfried. *Ideen zur Philosophie der Geschichte der Menschheit* (1784-91), München/ Wien: Carl Hanser Verlag 2002.

Karfík, Filip. "Jan Patočkas Strahov-Nachlass und sein unvollendetes opus grande", in: Patočka 2006a, 31-63.

Karfík, Filip. *Unendlichwerden durch die Endlichkeit*, Würzburg: Königshausen & Neumann 2008.

Lukács, György: *Existentialismus oder Marxismus*, Berlin: Aufbau 1951.

Patočka, Jan. "Ideologie und Leben in der Idee", in: *Ketzerische Essais zur Philosophie der Geschichte*, Stuttgart: Klett-Cotta 1988, 379-388.

Patočka, Jan. *Die Natürliche Welt als philosophisches Problem. Phänomenologische Schriften I*, Stuttgart: Klett-Cotta 1990.

Patočka, Jan. *Die Bewegung der menschlichen Existenz. Phänomenologische Schriften II*, Stuttgart: Klett-Cotta 1991.

Patočka, Jan. *Schriften zur tschechischen Kultur und Geschichte*, hg. v. K. Nellen, P. Pithart u. M. Pojar, Stuttgart: Klett-Cotta 1992.

Patočka, Jan. *Lettres à Robert Campbell (1946-50)*, in : Les Temps Modernes 48, Paris 1992, Nr. 554, 2–77. (=1992b)

Patočka, Jan. "Věčnost a Dějinnost" (Ewigkeit und Geschichtlichkeit), in: *Péče o duši I* (= Sebrané Spisy 1), Praha 1996, 139-242.

Patočka, Jan. *Body, Community, Language, World*, Chicago-La Salle: Open Court, 1998 (=1998)

Patočka, Jan. "Leben im Gleichgewicht, Leben in der Amplitude", in: Ludger Hagedorn u. Hans Rainer Sepp (Hg.), *Jan Patočka. Texte – Dokumente – Bibliographie*, Praha: OIKOYMENH / Freiburg: Alber Verlag, 1999. 91-102

Patočka, Jan. "'Kult člověka' a jeho převrat v dnešní době" (Der „Kult des Menschen' und sein Umsturz in heutiger Zeit), in: *Péče o duši III* (= Sebrané Spisy 3), Praha 2002, 706-709. (=2002 a)

Patočka, Jan. "Humanismus" (Humanismus), in: *Péče o duši III* (= Sebrané Spisy 3), Praha 2002, 710-713. (=2002 b)

Patočka, Jan. "Humanismus, pozitivismus, nihilismus a jejích překonání" (Humanismus, Positivismus, Nihilismus und deren Überwindung), in: *Péče o duši III* (= Sebrané Spisy 3), Praha 2002, 714-731. (=2002 c)

Patočka, Jan. *Andere Wege in die Moderne. Studien zur europäischen Ideengeschichte von der Renaissance bis zur Romantik*, hg. v. L. Hagedorn, Würzburg: Königshausen & Neumann 2006 (=2006a).

Patočka, Jan. "Humanismus Edvarda Beneše" (Der Humanismus des Edvard Beneš), in: *Češi I* (= Sebrané Spisy 12), Praha 2006, 122–126. (=2006b)

Patočka, Jan. *Ketzerische Essays zur Philosophie der Geschichte*, Berlin: Suhrkamp, 2010.

Patočka, Jan. *Éternité et historicité*, Übers. E. Abrams, Lagrasse: Verdier 2011.

Sartre, Jean-Paul. *L'être et le néant*, Paris 1943.

Sartre, Jean-Paul. *L'existentialisme est un humanisme* (1946), Paris : Éditions Nagel 1970.

OVIDIU STANCIU (Paris)

Subjectivité et projet. La critique patočkienne du concept heideggérien de "projet de possibilités"

Abstract

Subjectivity and Project.
Patočka's critique of Heidegger's concept "project of possibilities"

The purpose of this article is to lay out the main aspects of Patočka's critical reading of Heidegger's fundamental ontology. More precisely, I intend to restate the central arguments Patočka raised against Heidegger's characterization of "understanding" (Verstehen) as a "project". In the first part, I will single out Patočka's project of an "asubjective phenomenology" by distinguishing it from another asubjective project (that of Aristotle) and from the subjective phenomenology. In the second part, I will examine some central theses Heidegger puts forth in §31 of Being and Time *in order to show the inescapable difficulties they bring about. In the final part, I will describe the tenets around which Patočka's critical reading of Heidegger revolves. I will explore the two directions of this critique that correspond to the double orientation of asubjective phenomenology: a) on the one hand, the priority of the phenomenal field with regard to any subjective sense-bestowal; b) the importance of the phenomenon of corporeity for an accurate apprehension of subjectivity.*

Keywords: Patočka, phenomenology, asubjectivity, project, possibility, body

---

La voie singulière que Jan Patočka a tracée au sein du mouvement phénoménologique est habituellement ressaisie à l'aide du terme d'"asubjectif", que le philosophe tchèque emploie lui-même, à partir de la seconde moitié des années 1960, pour caractériser sa propre démarche. C'est ainsi que, dans deux textes programmatiques du début des années 1970, il place le renouvellement de la phénoménologie qu'il propose sous l'égide de ce concept, en faisant apparaître, de manière successive, la "possibilité" et "l'exigence" d'une phénoménologie asubjective. Ce programme de recherche est développé et détaillé dans d'autres textes importants qui datent du milieu des années 1970 – notamment "*Epoché* et réduction" et "Qu'est-ce que la phénoménologie ?" – ainsi que dans de nombreux manuscrits de travail de la même période.

Il est indéniable que cette tentative de situer la phénoménologie dans un horizon asubjectif est animée par une intention polémique. Patočka cherche à mettre en évidence la radicale originalité de l'espace théorique propre à la phénoménologie et, partant, son excès à l'égard de toute démarche philosophique tributaire du subjectivisme postcartésien. Ce travail de délimitation à l'égard de l'héritage cartésien dévoile toute son importance dès lors que l'on reconnaît que les décisions philosophiques qui constituent le soubassement de cette pensée qui a inauguré la modernité continuent de déterminer les engagements théoriques des fondateurs de la phénoménologie. En formulant le projet d'une phénoménologie asubjective, Patočka cherche donc simultanément à affranchir la phénoménologie des formulations que lui ont donné ses initiateurs et à recueillir l'inspiration première de sa percée (*Durchbruch*), qu'il situe dans "la découverte du champ du se-montrer, champ qui, afin que la chose même puisse se présenter et apparaître, doit dépasser la chose et sa structure matérielle, et qui recèle en soi une légalité *sui generis*, inconvertible tant à celle de l'objet dans son être propre qu'à celle de l'être mental dans son caractère purement égologique". (Patočka 1998a, 200). Mais si Husserl mettait en avant, dans son œuvre de 1900-1901, le champ phénoménal neutre à l'égard de la distinction du subjectif et l'objectif, ses développements ultérieurs l'ont conduit à donner un poids illégitime, aux yeux de Patočka, au "pôle subjectif", qui, du moment indispensable pour la structuration de l'apparaître, en devient le centre constitutif. Le geste premier de la phénoménologie asubjective est de contester ce privilège constitutif et de montrer que "la subjectivité n'en est pas le corrélat, elle *y* apparaît de même que tout le reste de l'étant" (Patočka 1995, 129). Saisir la place véritable que le subjectif occupe dans le dispositif de l'apparaître exige que l'on passe – pour employer une formule très saisissante de Steven Crowell – du "nominatif de la constitution" au "datif de la manifestation" (Crowell 2011, 16).

Si dans la plupart des textes publiés le terrain propre de la phénoménologie asubjective est gagné à travers une confrontation avec la phénoménologie husserlienne, on peut également trouver, dans des notes de travail de même que dans des notes préparatoires pour les cours prononcés à l'Université "Charles" de Prague, une opération similaire effectuée à l'égard de l'ontologie phénoménologique de Heidegger. Le texte le plus explicite et le plus radical à cet égard nous semble être le manuscrit de travail publié sous le titre "Corps, possibilités, monde, champ d'apparition" (Patočka 1995, 118-129) auquel il faudra sans doute rajouter les notes préparatoires pour le cours de 1968-69 "Corps, communauté, langage, monde"[1]. Patočka tente de ressaisir le geste philosophique fondamental d'*Etre et temps* à travers le concept de "projet des possibilités" (*Entwurf von Möglichkeiten*) que Heidegger introduit, au §31 d'*Etre et temps*, pour caractériser la compréhension et voit dans l'importance attribuée à ce concept le signe du maintien chez Heidegger d'une perspective subjectiviste. Nous nous proposons dans ce qui suit de restituer les linéaments de cette critique et

---

[1] Les notes de Patočka sont publiées en traduction française sous le titre "Leçons sur la corporéité" (cf. Patočka 1995, 53-116). Une traduction anglaise basée sur les notes prises par des étudiants a été publiée dans le recueil *Body, community, language, world* (Patočka 1998b).

de faire apparaître, par-delà cette dimension polémique, les pivots sur lesquels s'édifie la compréhension positive de la phénoménologie propre à Patočka.

1. Le sens de l'asubjectif

Avant d'entamer cette lecture, il est nécessaire de faire deux précisions qui nous permettent de circonscrire avec davantage de précision le lieu théorique à partir duquel Patočka déploie son interprétation critique de Heidegger et qui sont à même d'écarter un certain nombre de contre-sens que son projet peut susciter. Le premier point est de nature historique. Il faut ainsi rappeler que, empêché durant de longues années à poursuivre ses recherches phénoménologiques, brillamment entamées dans les années 30, Patočka se tourne à la fin des années 50 vers la pensée aristotélicienne à laquelle il consacre un ouvrage majeur : *Aristote, ses devanciers, ses successeurs*. L'angle sous lequel l'œuvre du Stagirite est envisagée n'est pas d'ordre historique ou "antiquaire". Patočka cherche à mettre au jour l'affinité structurale qui unit l'œuvre d'Aristote au projet phénoménologique, allant jusqu'à parler de cette "phénoménologie du monde naturel qu'est la *Physique*" (Patočka 2011, 427) aristotélicienne. Mais davantage qu'un précurseur de la phénoménologie, Aristote apparaît comme un guide théorique à même de procurer les biais nécessaires pour remettre en cause tout un ensemble de décisions théoriques propres à la pensée moderne. Plus précisément, le recours à Aristote permet de dépasser le dualisme caractéristique des philosophies post-cartésiennes, de retrouver l'unité qui sous-tend la fracture moderne du monde en un pôle subjectif et un pôle objectif, et ainsi de "réunir le plus bas et le plus haut, à fournir une explication unitaire de tout étant, de la pierre qui tombe jusqu'à la pensée philosophique et aux faits et gestes historiques de la communauté" (Patočka 2011, 213). C'est précisément dans ce contexte, celui d'une appropriation critique de la philosophie aristotélicienne[2] mise au service d'une reconfiguration du champ de la philosophie contemporaine, que Patočka introduit le terme d'"'asubjectif". Ainsi, il note qu'"Aristote cherche à découvrir des structures *asubjectives* propres à inclure et à expliquer, à partir des principes les plus universels, même les phénomènes humains, la compréhension et le comportement humains, des choses aussi spécifiques à l'homme que la vie dans la vérité, la volonté et le choix" (Patočka 2011, 251). Il s'agit donc, à travers la réactivation d'une position aristotélicienne, de contester le privilège octroyé à la conscience et de surmonter les dualismes qui vont de pair avec cette préséance, afin de retrouver un horizon de sens unitaire à partir duquel on

---

[2] Une lecture extrêmement précise et rigoureuse des implications de la pensée d'Aristote pour la constitution de la philosophie patočkienne est proposée par Dragos Duicu (cf. Duicu 2014).

peut rendre compte à la fois de l'effectuation subjective et de la manifestation chosique. L'"asubjectif" est le terme qui permet de mettre en résonance la philosophie aristotélicienne et la percée vers l'apparaître comme tel, de faire apparaître que ces deux orientations sont mues – au moins sur leurs versants négatifs – par des exigences convergentes.

Pourtant, si Aristote permet d'ouvrir un accès vers une pensée de l'asubjectif, il reste à savoir si la phénoménologie peut assumer intégralement et de manière positive l'engagement de fond de l'aristotélisme. En effet, il faut savoir gré au Stagirite d'avoir fait ressortir que "ce qui fait apparaître, ce qui amène la chose à sa forme essentielle, ce n'est ni la *psyché* ni, moins encore, la 'conscience', mais bien le mouvement" (Patočka 2011, 429). Pourtant, l'accord indéniable de la phénoménologie avec l'aristotélisme sur leurs versants négatifs – à savoir la lutte contre les dualismes, et plus particulièrement celui de la chose et de la conscience – n'implique nullement que l'aspiration positive qui traverse chacune de ces deux entreprises soit identique. Afin de saisir le lieu où leur divergence éclate, il faut interroger la direction vers laquelle les dualismes évoqués sont dépassés. Si, pour Aristote, le site vers lequel ce dépassement s'opère est un champ unitaire qui est de l'ordre de la réalité – ou plus précisément du réel –, pour Patočka ce dépassement vise à atteindre le champ de l'apparaître. Qui plus est, la promotion du champ phénoménal comme domaine où tout ce qui apparaît prend sa source est compatible avec l'introduction d'une nouvelle dualité, celle de l'apparaître et de l'apparaissant. Or c'est précisément cette distinction – qu'on pourrait qualifier de *différence phénoménologique* – qui constitue le noyau essentiel de la phénoménologie comme telle et qui la sépare radicalement de la pensée aristotélicienne. Dans la formulation que le philosophe tchèque en donne au cours d'un séminaire privé de 1973, cette distinction revient à affirmer que "la légalité ou la structure de l'apparaître est entièrement indépendante de la structure des choses étantes ; on ne peut déduire la manifestation en tant que telle ni des structures objectives ni des structures psychiques" (Patočka 1983, 39). Le plan unitaire vers lequel la phénoménologie s'avance, le domaine au sein duquel l'écart entre la chose et l'effectuation subjective est annulé, est le plan phénoménal. Or, à la différence d'Aristote qui a mis en évidence des structures asubjectives *réelles*, "le plan de l'apparition n'est pas un étant au sens de l'effectivement réel" (Patočka 1995, 129) : on y accède précisément par la "mise entre parenthèse", grâce à l'inhibition de toute thèse concernant le réel. Par conséquent, la phénoménologie peut circonscrire avec précision son domaine et peut faire apparaître sa nouveauté seulement si elle admet que ce domaine n'est pas total. Cette enquête doit nécessairement s'abstenir de toute considération relative au réel : la cartographie du réel au sens strict ne rentre pas dans la sphère de compétences de la phénoménologie.

La deuxième précision que nous souhaitons formuler a trait à la manière précise dont Patočka délimite le champ de la phénoménologie en le rapportant cette fois non pas à un autre projet philosophique asubjectif, mais en le distinguant de la phénoménologie classique, qu'il qualifie de "subjective". Ainsi, dans un manuscrit de travail de 1972 Patočka formule l'écart entre son projet phénoménologique asubjectif et la compréhension usuelle de l'enquête phénoménologique dans les termes suivants :

> Quelle est la différence entre la phénoménologie subjective et la phénoménologie asubjective ? Le plan d'explication de la phénoménologie subjective se situe dans le sujet. L'apparaître (de l'étant) est reconduit au subjectif (le moi, le vécu, la représentation, la pensée) comme ultime base d'éclaircissement. Dans la phénoménologie asubjective, le sujet dans son apparaître est un "résultat" au même titre que tout le reste. Il doit y avoir des règles a priori tant de ma propre entrée dans l'apparition que de l'apparaître de ce que je ne suis pas. Et cette entrée dans l'apparition fait apparaître quelque chose qui en est indépendant. Cela ne signifie pas, dans le cas du moi, [qu'il est] indépendant de tout apparaître, car il ne peut y avoir du moi que pour autant que quelque chose lui apparaît, pour autant qu'il se rapporte à lui-même à travers l'apparition d'un autre ; mais ce se-rapporter-à-soi-à-travers-l'apparition, c'est-à-dire cet apparaître à soi, est une structure d'être tout aussi indépendante de la conscience que celles qui n'apparaissent pas à elles-mêmes. (Patočka 1995, 127)

On le voit, la conséquence majeure de la réforme patočkienne de la phénoménologie réside dans la contestation de l'ancrage de l'apparaître dans la subjectivité, ce qui conduit à un décentrement de la position de l'homme dans le dispositif de l'apparaître. Il s'agit ainsi de reconnaître a) l'autonomie du champ phénoménal, le fait qu'il constitue un domaine articulé par un ensemble de légalités spécifiques, impossible à déduire à partir de la sphère de l'étant ; b) la priorité de la manifestation, de l'apparaître, à l'égard de tout étant qui se manifeste, à l'égard de tout apparaissant. Or, recueillir l'apparaître pour lui-même sans le référer à un étant apparaissant implique avant tout de contester que la subjectivité soit une instance "donatrice de sens", qui porte la charge de l'apparaître. Loin d'être le sol sur lequel l'apparaître repose, la subjectivité n'est qu'un résultat ou – selon la formulation d'un texte contemporain – "quelque chose de manifeste" et non pas "le fondement et la base de la manifestation" : "*Aber sowohl die Dinge als auch Ich sind etwas Manifestiertes, nicht selbst der Grund und Ursprung der Manifestation*" (Patočka 2000, 282). La phénoménologie asubjective conduit donc à une reconfiguration des relations entre apparaître et subjectivité : si la légalité de l'apparaître s'avère être autonome à l'égard de toute légalité issue de la sphère de l'étant – y compris de la subjectivité –, en revanche, la subjectivité doit être saisie dans son dépendance à l'égard de l'apparaître. Comme le note Patočka dans la suite du texte : "croire que l'apparition *soit quelque chose* qui aurait besoin des sujets comme porteurs et fondements, c'est un préjugé ; peut-être en va-t-il inversement – le sujets ne sont possibles que s'il y a le plan de l'apparition qui rend possible quelque chose comme le rapport à soi" (Patočka 1995, 129). La subjectivité n'existe comme telle que pour autant qu'elle s'apparaît à elle-même et, partant, qu'elle est engagée dans l'apparaître.

Or, la phénoménologie subjective n'a pas ignoré l'apparaître-à-soi de la subjectivité et en a même fait la pierre de touche de son édifice conceptuel. Pourtant, la manière dont cette thèse est orchestrée dans l'économie d'ensemble de cette démarche est de nature à défigurer le sens même de la subjectivité. En effet, dans la mesure où la subjectivité assume le rôle de fondement de l'apparaître, il faut que sa donation soit absolue, qu'elle ne comporte aucune faille ou écart. La saisie de la subjectivité dans cette optique conduit à l'assomption de deux préjugés d'origine cartésienne dépourvus de toute support phénoménal : a) la donation absolue des *cogitationes* ; b) la réflexion comme mode d'accès à soi-même, comme modèle de l'auto-compréhension. Au moment même où il tente de penser le sujet à partir de l'intériorité accessible à travers la réflexion – en distinguant donc son mode de donation de celui de la chose –, la phénoménologie subjective homogénéise le sens d'être de l'*ego* avec celui de la chose intra-mondaine. Or, afin de penser la subjectivité "indépendamment de toute immanence et de toute clôture", il est nécessaire de la saisir "de manière essentiellement *dynamique*, plutôt que chosique et par conséquent statique, comme ouverture effective et donc active plutôt que comme clôture, que l'on aura le plus de chances d'en préserver la spécificité" (Barbaras 2011, 74). Le tort du subjectivisme est donc double : incapable de saisir l'apparaître sans le rabattre sur un étant apparaissant, il méconnaît également le sens véritable du subjectif en le comprenant à partir du modèle directeur de la *res*. En effet, les contraintes architectoniques qui pèsent sur la subjectivité au sein de la perspective subjectiviste conduisent à une détermination défigurée et appauvrie de celle-ci : le prix qu'elle paie pour sa position centrale est sa saisie sous la figure abstraite du fondement. Pour résumer, nous pouvons affirmer que la lutte contre le subjectivisme est menée sous une double bannière. En premier lieu, il s'agit de restituer à la phénoménologie son thème propre et, partant, d'éviter que le champ phénoménal soit assimilé à un domaine subjectif. Deuxièmement, la polémique contre le subjectivisme vise à retrouver une figure plus concrète et plus riche de la subjectivité[3].

2. Le possible et le projet

La nouvelle impulsion que Patočka cherche à imprimer à la phénoménologie est solidaire d'un double remaniement : du statut de la phénoménalité et du celui de la subjectivité. Il

---

[3] Pour une exposition plus détaillée des engagements théoriques fondamentaux de la phénoménologie asubjective, nous nous permettons de renvoyer à notre dernière étude (cf. Stanciu 2017).

reste maintenant à mesurer si le traitement que Heidegger réserve à cet ensemble problématique dans *Etre et temps* peut satisfaire à ces réquisits ou bien s'il réédite, d'une manière plus subtile, les impasses du subjectivisme. De manière anticipée, nous pouvons affirmer – mais cette thèse doit être confirmée par des analyses ultérieures – que le subjectivisme de *Sein und Zeit* réside dans la soumission du plan phénoménologique au projet existential.

Le concept de "projet de possibilités" constitue le point d'application de la critique patočkienne, pour autant qu'il semble concentrer les principales difficultés que l'ontologie fondamentale recèle. Nous pourrions organiser les réserves critiques que Patočka émet à l'égard de ce concept selon les axes suivants. En premier lieu, Patočka conteste que le champ du possible – qu'il assimile au champ phénoménal et, plus encore, au monde – ait sa source dans la subjectivité, dans le *Dasein*. Il s'ensuit, deuxièmement, que si le *Dasein* entretient une relation essentielle avec le possible, cette relation est de l'ordre d'une saisie et d'une réalisation, et non pas de l'ordre du projet. Troisièmement, le refus de voir dans le *Dasein* l'origine du projet conduit à contester que le sens du possible *überhaupt* est réductible – ou déductible – du possible existential. Il faudra alors faire la place pour un sens du possible que ne découle de la prise en charge par le *Dasein* de sa propre existence, sens pour lequel le possible corporel constitue une attestation de premier ordre.

Pourtant, le reproche de "subjectivisme" formulé à l'encontre de la position de Heidegger ne va nullement de soi. En effet, *Etre et temps* propose une critique du concept cartésien de sujet, regard théorique a-situé et source de tout sens, qui apparaît à la fois comme dérivé et comme incapable de rendre compte de la phénoménalité dans son ensemble. Plus particulièrement, on pourrait se demander si le sens que Patočka confère au concept heideggérien de projet est véritablement conforme à l'usage que *Sein und Zeit* en fait. En effet, l'on a pu reprocher au traitement patočkien de ce concept le rapprochement illégitime qu'il opère entre projet et création, entre *Entwurf* et *Schaffen*, assimilation qui facilite sans doute la caractérisation de l'approche heideggérienne comme subjectiviste (Karfik 2008, 55). Nous essayerons de questionner la légitimité de ces propos à travers une lecture du §31 de *Sein und Zeit*.

Heidegger entame son analyse du §31 en indiquant la solidarité fondamentale qui rattache le comprendre à l'existential antérieurement mis en lumière, celui de l'affection : si "l'affection (*Befindlichkeit*) a à chaque fois sa compréhension, (…) le comprendre est toujours in-toné (*Vestehen ist immer gestimmtes*)" (Heidegger 1986, 126), de sorte qu'ils déterminent conjointement l'être du Là. Pourtant, le lien profond qui unit ces deux existentiaux ne doit pas obscurcir les fonctions différentes qui leur sont assignées. Si dans l'affection l'être-au-monde est découvert comme étant déjà là – car, comme l'affirme Heidegger au §29, c'est à la ""simple tonalité" qu'on doit confier fondamentalement la découverte primaire du monde" (Heidegger 1986, 123) – en revanche, le comprendre ouvre le monde dans sa significativé. Dans la mesure où il perce jusqu'au à la significativité du monde et la prend en charge, le comprendre s'avère être un pouvoir, ce que l'équivalence ontique entre "comprendre quelque chose", "s'entendre à quelque chose" et "pouvoir faire quelque chose" le laisse déjà voir. Mais comme la compréhension co-constitue l'être du là, le *Da* du *Dasein*, celui-ci peut à son tour être caractérisé comme un pouvoir-être. La saisie du *Dasein* comme pouvoir-être vise à arracher le concept de possible à sa détermination traditionnelle et plus particulièrement à l'extraire de la triade logique du nécessaire, de l'existent et du possible, car ces catégories sont applicables uniquement à l'étant qui n'est pas de l'ordre du *Dasein*. Ainsi, comme on a pu le remarquer, "par la délimitation du possible existential par rapport à sa figure purement logique, il s'agit de restructurer les rapports classiques de la possibilité avec l'effectivité et la nécessité, en transformant son infériorité traditionnelle en primauté. C'est là un geste éminemment anti-aristotélicien, car il revient à destituer l'antériorité et la supériorité ontologique de l'acte sur la puissance" (Serban 2016, 118-119).

La prééminence octroyée au possible dans le dispositif conceptuel heideggérien tient au fait qu'il caractérise avant tout – et on pourrait dire même exclusivement – le *Dasein*. Sans le *Dasein*, c'est-à-dire sans un être qui a à être l'être qu'il est, qui est constamment "devant" lui-même et "davantage" que lui-même, il n'y a tout simplement pas de possible. C'est le *Dasein* qui porte la charge du possible, c'est grâce à lui que la loi de l'effectivité qui règne sur le domaine de la présence-subsistante se trouve contestée. Or, la préséance du *Dasein* dans la détermination du possible a son strict corolaire dans la priorité du possible dans la caractérisation du *Dasein* : "La possibilité comme existential est la déterminité ontologique positive la plus originaire et ultime du *Dasein*" (Heidegger 1986, 127), de sorte que "le *Dasein* est primairement possibilité" (Heidegger 1986, 127).

En effet, le possible n'est pas confiné à un des existentiaux du *Dasein* – le comprendre – mais transit son mode d'être tout entier. Certes, Heidegger est amené à insister sur le fait que le possible que le *Dasein* incarne n'est pas une dimension abstraite, pure de toute facticité, car "le *Dasein* est un être-possible remis à lui-même, *une possibilité de part en part jetée*" (Heidegger 1986, 127). Pourtant, l'être-jeté ne signifie pas la dépendance du *Dasein* à l'égard de quelque chose qui lui soit extérieur et, partant, l'être-jeté ne saurait être assimilé à une factualité brute, à un socle indifférent sur lequel viendrait se greffer le "pouvoir-être" du *Dasein*. En marquant une distinction entre la factualité propre à l'étant intramondain et la facticité qui est un existential du *Dasein*, Heidegger peut affirmer que "le *Dasein* est constamment "plus" qu'il n'est factuellement, à supposer que l'on veuille et que l'on puisse l'enregistrer en sa réalité en tant qu'étant sous-la-main. En revanche, il n'est jamais plus qu'il n'est facticement, parce que le pouvoir-être appartient essentiellement à sa facticité" (Heidegger 1986, 128). Ainsi, la facticité excède toute figure de la pure présence, parce qu'elle contient déjà un rapport au possible. Le caractère jeté du pouvoir-être qu'est le *Dasein* est manifeste dans le fait qu'il n'existe comme pouvoir être qu'en tant qu'"il s'est à chaque fois déjà engagé dans des possibilités déterminées" (Heidegger 1986, 127). Le comprendre est enraciné dans une situation qu'il doit éclairer : il doit reprendre, faire siennes des possibilités déjà instituées et déposées dans la situation. Si le *Dasein* se découvre comme étant toujours déjà inscrit dans un champ préalable, ce champ n'est pas assimilable à une assise opaque, mais elle est à chaque fois de l'ordre du possible.

Poursuivant son analyse, Heidegger introduit la notion de projet afin de saisir de façon plus précise la relation qui se noue entre le comprendre et le possible. Le caractère projectif de la compréhension est explicité dans les termes suivants:

> Pourquoi le comprendre, selon toutes les dimensions essentielles de ce qui peut être ouvert en lui, perce-t-il toujours jusqu'aux possibilités ? Parce que le comprendre a en lui-même la structure existentiale que nous appelons le projet. Il projette l'être du Dasein vers son en-vue-de-quoi tout aussi originairement que vers la significativité en tant que mondanéité de ce qui lui est à chaque fois monde. Le caractère de projet du comprendre constitue l'être-au-monde du point de vue de l'ouverture de son Là comme Là d'un pouvoir-être. (Heidegger 1986, 128)

Ainsi, le projet désigne une structure existentiale à travers laquelle s'accomplit une double ouverture : vers le soi et vers le monde. Dans le projet, le monde est ouvert dans sa significativité et, grâce à cette ouverture, l'étant intra-mondain est à même de paraître – mais chaque fois selon un régime déterminé du sens. De même, le *Dasein* est ouvert dans son être, pour autant qu'il est amené devant son "en vue de quoi". A la faveur de cette double ouverture, il est légitime de soutenir que dans le projet du comprendre "se jouent non seulement les possibilités de l'existence, mais aussi les possibilités de l'étant (intramondain)" (Serban 2016, 120).

Pourtant, dans la suite du texte Heidegger n'explore pas les difficultés que cette double orientation soulève et qui ont leur source dans le fait que "l'ouverture du *Dasein* (…) est à la fois ouverture soumise à l'être ou au monde, et ouverture à soi constituante du soi" (Haar 1990, 13), mais se concentre sur une ligne de faille qui traverse l'ouverture à soi du *Dasein*. Ainsi, il note que "Le comprendre *peut* se placer primairement dans l'ouverture du monde, c'est-à-dire que le *Dasein* peut de prime abord et le plus souvent se comprendre à partir de son monde. À moins que le comprendre ne se jette primairement dans l'en-vue-de-quoi, autrement dit que le *Dasein* n'existe en tant que lui-même. Le comprendre est soit authentique – jaillissant du Soi-même propre comme tel – soit inauthentique" (Heidegger 1986, 128). Le partage entre le comprendre authentique et le comprendre inauthentique introduit au sein du domaine du possible une nouvelle structuration: le spectre du possible est organisé par la possibilité insigne du *Dasein*, la possibilité de se comprendre soi-même à partir de soi-même. Toute possibilité doit être mesurée à l'aune de la possibilité radicale pour le *Dasein* de gagner une transparence sur lui-même et, partant, d'exister sur le mode du *soi*, de l'*ipse*. Dans cette optique la quotidienneté apparaît comme un obscurcissement, car elle est "aveugle au possible (*möglichkeitsblind*) et se satisfait auprès de ce qui est 'réel'" (Heidegger 1986, 161).

Exister équivaut à avoir rapport à des possibles et vivre c'est viser et traverser des horizons de possibilités. Une telle caractérisation permet de distinguer le mode d'être du *Dasein* du celui de la présence subsistance ou de l'être-à-portée-de-main. Que le *Dasein* porte la charge du possible, que toute possibilité est relative au *Dasein*, n'implique nullement que toute possibilité est possibilité de lui-même. En établissant le monopole du sens existential du possible sur le sens du possible comme tel, Heidegger affirme implicitement qu'il n'y a du possible qu'existential ou comme dérivé du possible existential. Au sein d'une démarche dont l'orientation d'ensemble nous semble être convergente avec le projet patočkien, Claude Romano explicite de manière limpide les impasses de cette conception univoque du possible :

> Heidegger ne distingue pas clairement les différents sens de "possibilités" (…). Il fait comme si tous les possibles que recèle le monde, ou plutôt, en lequel consiste, étaient des possibles au sens existential du terme, c'est-à-dire des possibles tels que le Dasein les rend possibles ou les "possibilise" en s'y projetant. Comme il l'écrit, "le possible ne se déploie en sa possibilité que si nous nous lions à lui dans sa possibilisation" (Heidegger 1992, 522). En vertu de cette conception hypertrophique des pouvoirs du Dasein tout se passe comme si l'étant exemplaire possibilisait tous les possibles – dans un seul et unique sens du verbe "possibiliser" – et, de ce fait, se rendait possible le monde lui-même. Si le monde, en effet, est la totalité des possibilités intrinsèques du Dasein (…) et si tout possible est rendu possible par le projet fini d'un pouvoir-être – par ce que Heidegger appelle la résolution – il en découle que le Dasein configure le monde en existant". (Romano 2010, 715-716)

Si c'est seulement l'existence qui peut avoir affaire à du possible, est-ce que cela implique nécessairement que toute possibilité est une possibilité de l'existence ? Une telle équivalence peut être affirmée uniquement si le plan phénoménal – l'apparaître et ses horizons de possibilités – est soumis au "projet de soi" de l'existence, c'est-à-dire au "projet d'auto-appropriation, d'auto-possession, de maîtrise absolue de soi qu'est le projet de l'authenticité" (Haar 1990, 14). C'est dans ce passage indu – d'un possible *relatif à* l'existence à un possible *de* l'existence – que réside le subjectivisme de Heidegger.

3. Champ phénoménal, pouvoir du corps, possibilités de l'existence

Dans sa discussion critique des thèses de Heidegger, Patočka insiste sur l'indétermination de l'expression "possibilités dont je fais le projet" – comprendre ou projeter des possibilités, ce n'est pas la même chose" (Patočka 1995, 125). En effet, cette expression se laisse entendre d'une double manière : a) comme un projeter (actif), comme une formation de sens, à travers laquelle la possibilité est constituée comme possibilité ; b) comme un être-projeté vers un champ déjà articulé, c'est-à-dire, selon un mouvement centrifuge, comme un être-aspiré vers …, être-amené devant une tâche qu'il s'agit d'assumer. La stratégie patočkienne consiste à faire apparaître le caractère intenable de la première option – de même que sa dominance dans les écrits du premier Heidegger – et la compatibilité de la seconde interprétation avec les engagements théoriques de la phénoménologie asubjective.

En premier lieu, Patočka s'emploie à dénoncer l'illusion consistant à voir dans la compréhension une imposition de sens – voire même une création de sens –, illusion facilitée par l'emploi heideggérien du vocabulaire du projet : "Heidegger dit : la compréhension (des possibilités) a en elle-même le caractère du projet (Heidegger 1986, 145); par là il annule le caractère du *Verstehen* – la compréhension, c'est la saisie de quelque chose que je n'ai pas créé, du moins pas de manière phénoménale, de manière que cette "création" se montre à moi" (Patočka 1995, 118). En effet, s'il est certain que la compréhension représente une dimension inéludable du rapport au possible, il n'en demeure pas moins que ce n'est pas la compréhension qui institue ce rapport et que c'est encore moins elle qui ouvre l'espace du possible : "Ce n'est pas la compréhension qui porte les renvois, mais au contraire la totalité des renvois qui rend la compréhension possible" (Patočka 1995, 123). L'écart qui sépare la position de Patočka de celle défendue par Heidegger peut être résumé de manière suivante : le rapport de l'existence au possible doit être pensé selon le modèle de l'interpellation et de la réalisation, alors que l'ouverture de l'espace du possible doit être référée au champ phénoménal lui-même, c'est-à-dire au monde.

Dans le rapport au possible l'existence est portée dans un domaine qui ne doit pas sa configuration interne à ses propres accomplissements de sens, car "ce n'est pas moi qui projette le monde des possibilités ; mais, comme je suis un être "du" possible, je suis interpellé par la possibilité, par le champ de possibilités du monde" (Patočka 1995, p. 123-124). Dans la caractérisation de l'existence, l'évocation de son rapport au possible est indispensable : la saisie heideggérienne du *Dasein* comme "pouvoir-être" est ainsi reprise par Patočka lorsqu'il affirme que le moi est un être "du" possible. Pourtant, le fait que le *Dasein* soit situé nécessairement dans l'horizon du possible n'implique nullement qu'il en soit la source. Le possible ne se dévoile pas comme le corolaire d'un projet lancé par l'existence, mais apparaît plutôt comme le lieu d'émergence d'un appel adressé à l'existence.

Patočka est donc conduit à opérer un remaniement du rapport entre l'existence et le possible, qui conduit à un renversement dans l'ordre de la possibilisation : "Contre Heidegger : il n'y a aucune *projection* primaire de possibilités – le monde n'est pas un produit de la liberté, mais simplement ce qui rend possible ma liberté finie" (Patočka 1995, 122), de sorte que "le plan phénoménal *m'*ouvre en même temps que ce que je ne suis pas" (Patočka 1995, 122). Ainsi, si l'ouverture du monde doit nécessairement octroyer une place à l'homme – car "l'homme est requis dans l'apparition : il est le *destinataire* de l'apparition, celui qui utilise les possibilités en les faisant *siennes, situées*" (Patočka 1995, 122) – la configuration de cette ouverture n'est pas l'œuvre de l'homme. Le monde s'ouvre de lui-même, de telle manière qu'il ouvre en même temps l'être au monde de l'homme : "les possibilités originaires (le monde) ne sont rien d'autre que le champ dans lequel le vivant existe et qui en est co-originaire" (Patočka 1995, 124). Ainsi, le monde se dévoile comme la dimension ultime et pré-subjective où toute apparition s'enracine, le lieu d'émergence de tout sens, la ressource dernière de toute élucidation phénoménologique.

Les réserves que Patočka formule à l'encontre de la saisie heideggérienne du rapport au possible peuvent être saisies selon un autre versant. Cette fois, il ne s'agit pas de faire apparaître que Heidegger a méconnu la priorité constitutive du champ phénoménal eu égard à tout accomplissement du *Dasein*, mais il s'agit de montrer que la restitution des possibilités du *Dasein* doit nécessairement intégrer une réflexion sur la dimension corporelle de l'existence, car sans la prise en compte du corps, tout éclaircissement de l'existence demeure abstrait. Si dans le premier cas il était essentiel de montrer que l'existence tire son sens d'un domaine qui la précède, il s'agit maintenant d'approfondir sa constitution interne.

A cet effet, il est essentiel pour Patočka de dévoiler une couche plus profonde de la subjectivité, située en-deçà du seuil de partage entre l'existence authentique et l'existence inauthentique. Ce projet de remonter vers une strate de l'existence ontologiquement antérieure et indépendante de la prise en charge radicale de soi-même s'effectue à travers l'exploration de deux phénomènes : celui du sentir pur – qui se laisse exposer de manière privilégié à travers les cas de l'animal et l'enfant – et celui de la corporéité. A chaque fois, il s'agit de faire apparaître un régime du possible qui est propre à l'existence – qui est une possibilité *de* l'existence – mais qui n'a pas été rendu possible *par* l'existence elle-même.

En prenant pour guide le rapport au monde propre à l'animal et à l'enfant, Patočka remarque qu'il s'agit d'un rapport de "sentir pur. (…) Mais ce n'est pas dire pour autant que l'animal et l'enfant soient des mécanismes, des processus en troisième personne. L'animal et l'enfant sont immergés dans un rapport sympathétique, co-sentant, au monde. Cette relation sympathétique, de sentir avec, présuppose une intériorité, une "âme". En revanche, elle ne présuppose pas la compréhension du soi, l'ouverture à l'être propre dans ses possibilités, car l'être ici n'est pas confié au vivant lui-même comme une tâche" (Patočka 1995, 101). La mise en évidence de ce rapport de "sentir pur" ne représente pas une concession faite à l'objectivisme : en rétrocédant vers ce niveau, Patočka ne cherche pas à faire ressortir une strate grise sur lequel viendraient se dessiner la couleur du rapport au monde. En effet, Patočka accorde bien que le comprendre est d'abord et toujours un comprendre de soi, mais il conteste que toute compréhension de soi doit nécessairement prendre le soi comme tâche à réaliser, comme un poids qu'il faut porter. En faisant apparaître ces niveaux souterrains de la constitution du soi, pour lesquels l'animal ou l'enfant représentent des exemples privilégiés, le philosophe tchèque soutient que si cette compréhension de soi est bien présente, elle ne prend pas la forme d'une décision, d'une assomption ou d'un refus de la tâche que représente l'existence. Il s'agit ainsi pour Patočka de faire droit à une couche perceptive, affective-impressionnelle qui précède et soutient le rapport proprement "pragmatique" que le projet de l'authenticité met en scène, à une "vie sensible" qui n'est pas encore transie par les impératifs de la conquête de soi. Or, il ne faut pourtant pas croire que ce type de rapport est quelque chose que nous avons laissé derrière nous :

> Ce mode de vie, cette consonance avec le monde est, d'une certaine manière, intégralement conservée dans notre sensibilité. (…) L'homme aussi est constamment en mouvement, d'un mouvement qui lui aussi se déroule dans un champ d'attraction et de répulsion : le monde s'impose à nous d'une part par les tonalités affectives, mais aussi par sa physionomie qui a toujours, dans sa diversité bigarrée, un cachet d'ensemble, une expression unitaire. (Patočka 1995, 102)

Il émerge ainsi un régime de possibilités qui n'est pas scindé selon le partage du propre et de l'impropre, de l'authentique et de l'inauthentique, où l'alternative entre "être lui-même ou ne pas être lui-même" n'a pas encore de sens – une strate de possibilisation où appropriation de soi n'est pas encore présente comme tâche.

L'éviction de cette dimension de l'existence dans le dispositif heideggérien transparaît dans le fait que Heidegger n'accorde pas à la corporéité la dignité d'un existential[4]. A cet égard, Patočka note que

> Heidegger ne prend jamais en considération le fait que la *praxis* originelle doit être par principe l'activité d'un sujet *corporel*, que la corporéité doit donc avoir un statut ontologique qui ne peut être identique à l'occurrence du corps comme présent ici et

---

[4] Nous avons proposé ailleurs un développement plus détaillé de la problématique de la corporéité chez Patočka (cf. Stanciu 2014).

maintenant. L'éclaircissement qui caractérise l'existence est éclaircissement d'un étant corporel. (Patočka 1988, 93).

Le refus d'accorder au corps un statut existential découle de sa compréhension comme une présence-subsistante et de la saisie de sa localisation dans le monde comme une simple insertion dans un continuum spatio-temporel. Afin de rectifier ce contre-sens, il est nécessaire de mettre en évidence la charge de possible que le corps possède en propre et qui le rend à tout jamais inassimilable à de la pure actualité. C'est ce chemin théorique que Patočka emprunte lorsqu'il note que

> Le corps relève du domaine des possibilités propres (…). Le corps est existentialement l'ensemble des possibilités que nous ne choisissons pas, mais dans lesquelles nous nous insérons, des possibilités pour lesquelles nous ne sommes pas libres, mais que nous devons être. Cela ne signifie pas qu'elles n'aient pas le caractère de l'existence, c'est-à-dire de ce qui m'est imposé dans son unicité et que je dois assumer et réaliser. Mais c'est seulement sur leur fondement que sont ouvertes les possibilités "libres" (Patočka 1988, 94).

Si le corps peut être compris comme un pouvoir sur les choses, il faut admettre qu'il ne découle pas d'une prise en charge radicale par le *Dasein* de son pouvoir-être. C'est ce pouvoir non-libre – "l'ensemble des possibilités que nous ne choisissons pas" – qui constitue le préalable à toute mise en œuvre des possibilités libres. En effet, les possibilités doivent "prendre [leur] source dans un organisme qui toujours déjà sait faire, qui toujours déjà obéit d'une certaine manière, qui est à même de réaliser un élan vers les choses" (Patočka 1995, 71). L'existence s'établit sur un socle corporel et vital : pourtant celui-ci ne relève pas de l'ordre de la factualité brute, mais représente à son tour une possibilité – une possibilité non-choisie, qui traverse et excède le *Dasein*. Le corps représente un témoignage pour un rapport au possible qui n'est pas encore déterminé par les impératifs de la conquête de soi, par le projet de rendre le soi transparent à lui-même.

Le concept de possible que l'ontologie fondamentale met en scène s'avère donc insuffisant pour autant qu'il n'offre pas les moyens conceptuels permettant d'intégrer les "possibilités que nous ne choisissons pas". Or, cette omission – qui s'appuie sur une équivalence implicite entre possibilité et liberté – n'a pas une signification seulement régionale, mais affecte l'économie de l'ensemble de la démarche. Ce qui est ainsi obnubilé, c'est la racine même de la possibilité existentiale. En effet, comme le note Renaud Barbaras commentant Patočka, "la corporéité est la *possibilité de la possibilité*, le pouvoir du pouvoir être ou encore l'existential de l'effectivité du comprendre. Non pas ce qui serait ajouté empiriquement et facultativement à l'existence mais, au contraire, son noyau même, ce qui en possibilise la possibilité" (Barbaras 2011, 102).

La tentative patočkienne de proposer un réaménagement du cadre théorique de la phénoménologie s'avère donc orientée par une double tâche. En premier lieu, il s'agit de faire apparaître que le thème propre de la phénoménologie n'est nullement la subjectivité, mais le champ phénoménal, dans sa neutralité à l'égard de toute coloration objectiviste ou subjectiviste. Pourtant, cette torsion ne signifie nullement un abandon de la subjectivité, qui doit précisément être restituée dans sa figure véritable. En s'affranchissant des préjugés cartésiens solidement enracinés, la phénoménologie asubjective est à même de dévoiler toute la richesse de sens propre à la subjectivité et à reconnaître le corps comme une dimension inéludable de celle-ci.

Dr. Ovidiu Stanciu, Institut d'Etudes Politiques (Sciences Po), Paris,
ovidstanciu[at]gmail.com

Références

Barbaras, Renaud. *L'ouverture du monde. Lecture de Jan Patočka.* Chatou: La Transparence, 2011.
Crowell, Steven Galt. "'Idealities of Nature': Jan Patočka on Reflection and the Three Movements of Human Life," in Chvatík, Ivan and Erika Abrams (eds.). *Jan Patočka and the heritage of phenomenology.* Berlin: Springer, 2011. 7-22.
Duicu, Dragos. *Phénoménologie du mouvement. Patočka et l'héritage de la physique aristotélicienne.* Paris: Hermann, 2014.
Haar, Michel. *Le chant de la Terre. Heidegger et les assises de l'histoire de l'être.* Paris: L'Herne, 1987.
Haar, Michel. *Heidegger et l'essence de l'homme.* Grenoble: Millon, 1990.
Heidegger, Martin. *Etre et temps*, trad. Emmanuel Martineau. Paris: Authentica, 1986.
Heidegger, Martin. *Les concepts fondamentaux de la métaphysique. Monde – finitude – solitude*, trad. par Daniel Panis. Paris: Gallimard, 1992.
Karfik, Filip. *Unendlichwerden durch die Endlichkeit. Eine Lektüre der Philosophie Jan Patočkas.* Würzburg: Königshausen & Neumann, 2008.
Patočka, Jan. *Le monde naturel comme problème philosophique*, trad Jaromir Danek et Henri Declève. La Haye: Martinus Nihhoff, 1976.
Patočka, Jan. *Platon et l'Europe*, trad. Erika Abrams. Paris: Verdier, 1983.
Patočka, Jan. *Le monde naturel et le mouvement de l'existence humaine*, trad. Erika Abrams. Dordrecht: Kluwer, 1988.
Patočka, Jan. *Papiers phénoménologiques*, trad. Erika Abrams. Grenoble: Millon, 1995.
Patočka, Jan. *Qu'est-ce que la phénoménologie*, trad. Erika Abrams. Grenoble: Millon, 1998a.
Patočka, Jan. *Body, community, language, world*, trad. Erazim Kohak. Chicago: Open Court, 1998b.
Patočka, Jan. *Vom Erscheinen als solchem. Texte aus dem Nachlass*, éd. par Helga Blaschek-Hahn et Karel Novotný. Freiburg/München: Karl Alber, 2000.
Patočka, Jan. *Aristote, ses devanciers, ses successeurs*, trad. Erika Abrams. Paris: Vrin, 2011.

Romano, Claude. *Au cœur de la raison, la phénoménologie*. Paris : Gallimard, 2010.
Serban, Claudia. *Phénoménologie de la possibilité. Husserl et Heidegger*. Paris: PUF, 2016.
Stanciu, Ovidiu. "Le pouvoir du corps et le phénomène de l'orientation. Lecture des "Leçons sur la corporéité" de Jan Patočka", in *Revue Transversales*, no. 2, 2014 (online: http://tristan.u-bourgogne.fr/CGC/publications/transversales/Que_peut_le_corps/O_Stanciu.html).
Stanciu, Ovidiu. "De la manifestation au réel. La phénoménologie asubjective et son autodépassement", in *Revue de métaphysique et de morale*, 2017/3 (N° 95): 303-316.

JAN FREI (Prag)

Zerstreuung, Verschließung, Hingabe.
Zur Figur des Transzendierens bei Jan Patočka

To get distracted, to enclose and to give oneself.
The Gesture of Transcendence in Jan Patočka

Abstract

The problem of transcendence can be traced throughout the whole work of Jan Patočka. The appeal to transcend our bonds to mere objectivity is a constant issue of his thought. It finds a new substantiation in the 1960s in his studies focusing on the meaning of the other as human being. The relation to the other person offers a special "occasion" or "place" of transcendence and poses the challenge to transcend one's own particular setting.

While in the mid-1960s Patočka maintains his earlier dramatic vocabulary to describe the process of transcendence, in the late 1960s his idiom becomes less vehement. Yet, it is precisely within this more "sober" framework that he symbolizes the process of transcendence with an emphatic turn to a "myth of the divine man" and its key metaphor of resurrection.

To transcend means, for Patočka, always to liberate oneself from a state of self-distraction between things. However, in his late lectures, he briefly refers to a deeper layer, suggesting that this self-distraction has its "roots" in a self-enclosure or self-isolation, in the exclusive concentration on our own interests and in the illusion of our self-sufficiency. Transcendence, then, means to overcome this self-enclosure by means of a self-forgetting love. Are these rarely mentioned "roots" perhaps implicitly present in all Patočka's accounts of transcendence?

Keywords: Patočka, transcendence, person, objectivity, otherness, Christianity

Einleitung: Die Strukturen des Transzendierens

Ein Blick auf das Thema "Transzendenz" in der gegenwärtigen philosophischen Debatte zeigt zweierlei: Erstens beweisen Titel wie *Transcendence and Beyond* (Caputo und Scanlon 2007) oder *Figuren der Transzendenz* (Staudigl u. Sternad 2014), dass das Thema unbestreitbar präsent ist. Zweitens aber erweist die Lektüre, dass sich die Fragestellung dabei unverkennbar auf Transzendenz im Sinne "des Transzendenten" konzentriert – wie immer dies auch näher bestimmt wird –, während *das Transzendieren*, Transzendenz als *Erfahrung* oder *Akt des Überschreitens*, eher im Hintergrund bleibt.

Eben diese Erfahrung ist jedoch von eminenter Bedeutung – selbst zur Transzendenz im erstgenannten Sinne haben wir ja keinen anderen Zugang. Für Patočka ist die Transzendenz ein eminentes philosophisches Motiv: wann immer sich sein Denken den großen Themen des Weltganzen, des Erscheinens als solchen oder der unableitbaren Freiheit zuwendet, bewegt es sich *transzendierend* hin auf die letzten Gründe und Kontexte.

Eine methodische Vorentscheidung ist jedoch notwendig: Das Transzendieren wird bei Patočka zumeist nicht eigens thematisiert, es verbirgt sich vielmehr hinter dem jeweiligen Thema der Erörterungen. Daher wählen wir – um den Texten keine fremden, unangemessenen Definitionen aufzuzwingen – folgenden Zugang: Wir werden von einer rein formalen Bestimmung des Transzendierens ausgehen und die Texte nur daraufhin befragen, was *in ihnen selbst* dieser Bestimmung entspricht. Unter Transzendieren verstehen wir – ungefähr wie Heidegger (Heidegger 1976, 137) – ein Überschreiten, für das folgende Momente konstitutiv sind: (a) ein Transzendiertes, d.h. etwas, von dem man ausgeht und das überschritten wird, (b) etwas, worauf das Transzendieren zielt, und (c) der Akt selbst, d. h. die Art und Weise, auf welche das Transzendieren durchgeführt wird. Auf eine kurze Formel gebracht, fragen wir also bei Patočka nach dem Akt des Transzendierens in seinem Woher, seinem Woraufhin und seinem Wie.

Bei diesen Vorgaben sehen wir zunächst, dass das Transzendieren in seinem Denken sozusagen zwei Stufen hat. Einerseits ist der Mensch "je schon" transzendierend; das Transzendieren ist ein immer präsentes Merkmal des Denkens, des Wahrnehmens, der Affektivität und des Handelns (darin sind die Einzeldinge je schon auf breitere Zusammenhänge überschritten). Andererseits können wir uns dieses "apriorischen" und "notwendigen" Transzendierens bewusst werden; wir können es aktiv übernehmen und bis zum Erkennen des letzten Woraufhin weiterführen. Es ist besonders diese zweite Form, das Transzendieren als bewusstes Handeln, das wir in diesem Beitrag zum Thema machen wollen.

Im Rahmen eines Artikels müssen wir uns natürlich auf ein Beispiel beschränken. Für dieses Vorhaben eignet sich am besten eine relativ kohärente Gruppe von Texten, die in zeitlicher Nähe entstanden sind, die das Thema unter ähnlichen Perspektiven behandeln – und die doch ihren je eigenen Zugang haben. Es handelt sich um Texte aus der zweiten Hälfte der 60er Jahre, aus einer Zeit, in der Patočka nach einer langen Unterbrechung – die er der interpretatorischen Auseinandersetzung mit Aristoteles und Hegel sowie dem Denken der frühen Neuzeit widmete – das Thema wieder "systematisch" aufgreift.

Bevor wir uns diesen Texten zuwenden, fassen wir kurz die früheren Beschreibungen des Transzendierens zusammen, die man in Patočkas Werk zwischen von den 1930er bis in die 1950er Jahre findet:

- In seinem *Wie* besteht das Transzendieren zumeist in einer Verschiebung oder Erweiterung der Aufmerksamkeit;
- das Überschrittene (das *Woher*) sind einerseits die Einzeldinge in ihrer objektiven Struktur, andererseits die von hedonischen und utilitären Motiven beherrschte Umwelt, der Bereich des Planmäßigen, Ausgewogenen, Fließenden;
- das *Woraufhin* des Transzendierens sind weitere Kontexte der gegebenen Dinge und bislang nicht bewusstgewordene Sphären der Welt (*in* der Welt können besonders die Elemente, die Fernen und Extreme als "Auslöser" des Transzendierens dienen), und schließlich die Welt als der letzte, universelle Zusammenhang bzw. unsere Stellung in ihr;
- explizite Benennungen des *Woraufhin* sind "Projektionen" und "verbale Mimesen" von etwas, wozu nur die Erfahrung des Transzendierens selbst einen direkten Zugang bietet;
- der Akt des Transzendierens umfasst einen Aspekt der Aktivität, der freien Leistung, sowie einen der Passivität, der "Ergriffenheit" und Faszination durch das Weltganze;
- diesem Akt ist eine Dynamik eigen, die sich von einer anfänglichen, unbestimmten Beunruhigung hin zu einem zunehmend klareren Bewusstsein des Ganzen entwickelt (siehe besonders Patočka 1990a; 1999; 2007a; 2014).

Wie erscheint nun Patočkas Auffassung des Transzendierens in den Texten der 1960er Jahre?

1. *Natürliche Welt und Phänomenologie* (1967)[1]

1.1. Der Gegenstand und der Andere

"Der Kontakt mit den Anderen ist die primäre und wichtigste Komponente des Zentrums der natürlichen Welt, deren Boden die Erde und deren Peripherie der Himmel bildet" (Patočka 1991b, 210). Mit diesem Satz sind in lapidarer Kürze die Koordinaten benannt, in denen die Bewegung des Transzendierens sich abspielt. Von der Beschreibung der Welt, wie wir sie aus früheren Texten kennen, vor allem aus den unvollendeten *Studien zum Weltbegriff* (Patočka 2014), wird die *Peripherie* beibehalten, jene anziehende und weiter-

---

[1] Siehe Patočka 1991b; Weiterführung von Überlegungen, die schon zwei Jahre früher begonnen wurden (vgl. Patočka 1991a).

weisende "Ferne". Der Himmel, der hier diese Peripherie verkörpert, ist weiterhin, zusammen mit der Erde, ein *Element*, so dass also das Woraufhin des Transzendierens nicht als Gegenstand erscheint, sondern eher als *Macht*.[2] Zwischen diesen Grenzen der Welt zeigt sich nun als die "wichtigste Komponente" der Kontakt mit den Anderen.

Es ist wahr, dass auch die Welt der früheren Texte nicht menschenleer war. Besonders das Zentrum der Lebenswelt, das Zuhause, wurde auch dadurch zu einem Zentrum, dass es eine Stätte unserer Annahme, unseres Aufgenommenwerdens in die zwischenmenschlichen Beziehungen war. Nach einem anderen Text aus den 60er Jahren bilden die Ich-Du-Beziehungen bzw. die Ich-Es-Beziehungen geradezu "ursprüngliche Formen" von Nähe und Ferne; dem Gegensatz Nähe-Ferne liegt also der Gegensatz zwischen der wechselseitigen personalen Beziehung und derer Absenz zugrunde. Es kann aber auch beides, Nähe und Ferne, durch wechselseitige personale Beziehungen charakterisiert werden: der Unterschied zwischen ihnen entspricht dann dem Unterschied zwischen Wir und Ihr (Patočka 1991c, 96-99). Das Neue des nun besprochenen Textes liegt darin, dass die Anderen dort inmitten der Beschreibung des Transzedierens selbst auftreten. Wie?

Die früheren Texte beschrieben die anfängliche Befindlichkeit entweder als einen unklar wahrgenommenen Appell (dem wir nachgeben können), oder als eine Beunruhigung über ein ebenso unklar empfundenes Ausbleiben des Transzendierens (die zu einer transzendierenden Aktivität führen kann). Um den zweiten Aspekt ging es in *Endlichkeit und Geschichtlichkeit*, wo konstatiert wurde, dass die bloßen unlebendigen Gegenständlichkeiten in uns Langeweile, Widerwillen oder Abscheu hervorrufen (Patočka 2011, 136). Dieses Grundmotiv bleibt auch in den späteren Auseinandersetzungen erhalten; während jedoch zuvor die Unzulänglichkeit der bloßen Gegenständlichkeiten darauf gegründet wurde, dass sie nicht lebendig sind, kein eigenes Inneres und keine eigene Beziehung zum Leben haben, ist nun die wahre Wirklichkeit, welcher gegenüber die bloßen Gegenstände als defizient erscheinen, *der andere Mensch*:

> Der gegenwärtige Gegenstand ... muss nicht ein anderes 'Ich', ein anderer Mensch sein. Ist er es nicht, so ist ihm freilich ein Mangel, etwas Unerfülltes eigen; der eigentliche Gegenstand, dem wir beiwohnen, ist nie ein 'Es', sondern ein 'Du'. (Patočka 1991b, 211)

Somit ist es der andere Mensch, der eminenter Anlass des Transzendierens ist. Gerade ihm gegenüber empfinden wir die Unzulänglichkeit des Seienden, das weniger ist als

---

[2] Besonders die Erde erscheint hier explizit "als Kraft und Gewalt" (Patočka 1991b, 206). In dem früheren Text wird stärker die Fähigkeit des Himmels und der Erde betont, weiter über sich selbst zu weisen, "zum Hinweis auf das Unermessliche" zu werden (Patočka 1991a, 138).

das menschliche; und wir empfinden sie auch dort, wo *der andere Mensch selbst* vor uns nur in einer instrumentalen Rolle dasteht, d.h. nicht in seiner vollen personalen Wirklichkeit. Es gehört zu unserer Zerstreuung in die Dinge, dass wir auch uns selbst und die Anderen mit Rollen und Funktionen identifizieren, die sich aus der Behandlung der Dinge ergeben (*dies* verdeckt uns unseren "eigenen menschlichen Charakter"); aber "da, wo ich lediglich meine Rolle lebe und in den Anderen auch nur die ihrige ansehe, (…) stellt sich ein *Mangel an Befriedigung* (…) ein" (Patočka 1991b, 217). Dieser Mangel ergibt sich aus unserem Bewusstsein, dass der Andere eigentlich mit keiner definierbaren Rolle und keinem konkreten Zustand identisch ist; dieser Mangel führt also zur "Ablehnung jeder gegenständlichen endlichen Gestalt", zur Ablehnung, den Anderen mit den angeführten Objektivitäten zu identifizieren, zur "Suche nach einer tieferen Beziehung" (Patočka 1991b, 217).

Diese Suche ist allerdings nur als eine gegenseitige denkbar: die Verdinglichung des Anderen abzulehnen (sie oder ihn als Person zu respektieren), bleibt längerfristig nur möglich, wenn die andere Person die gleiche Stellung einnimmt: "selbst zu diesem Willen zur Überwindung kann ich nur durch den Anderen gelangen, nur wenn der Andere, der meinen Gegenstand darstellt, die gleiche Bewegung wie ich vollzieht, allerdings in einer Weise, dass ich gleichermaßen sein wie er mein Gegenstand ist" (Patočka 1991b, 217).[3] Es gibt zwei Stufen oder Stadien dieser Beziehung, in der die endliche Gestalt – die meine sowie die des Anderen – überwunden wird.

1.2. Kampf

Dem Anderen begegnen wir zunächst in dinglichen Beziehungen, als Verdinglichte mit einem Verdinglichten. Zu dieser objektivierenden Restriktion werden wir durch verschiedene nähere sowie fernere Motivierungen verleitet, in letzter Instanz jedoch vom *Tod* motiviert: gerade den Tod nämlich schieben wir faktisch auf durch den utilitären Gebrauch der Dinge; dessen unausweichliche Ankunft verdecken wir vor uns durch unsere Selbstzerstreuung, in der stets neue Gegenständlichkeiten unsere Aufmerksamkeit beanspruchen. So hat sich der Tod "hinter unserem Rücken des Lebens [bemächtigt] und es, unter dem Vorwand seines Fortdauerns und der Wiederholung seiner Augenblicke, seines Inhalt entleert" (Patočka 1991b, 223). Gegen diese Objektivierung, diese "primäre Repression", ist jedoch eine Auflehnung möglich, die Patočka "Kampf des Erwachens" nennt (Patočka 1991b, 223ff.).

Man muss nun zuerst sagen: der Kampf kann auch – und das Erwachen muss sogar – ohne eine Beziehung zum Anderen gedacht werden. Mit Kampf ist zunächst die Aufleh-

---

[3] Zur Rolle der (des) Anderen in dieser sowie anderen Phasen von Patočkas Denken (siehe Karfík 2008, 71-81).

nung (des Einzelnen) gegen den Druck der objektivierenden Kräfte gemeint, eine *Umkehr* von üblichen verteidigenden Reaktionen auf die Gefahr des Todes zu einem von dieser Gefahr unabhängigen Handeln. Der Ausdruck "Kampf" deutet hier die Notwendigkeit an, den mit dieser Umkehr zwangsläufig verbundenen Widerstand zu überwinden:[4] die Umkehr setzt nämlich die schwierige Anerkennung der eigenen Sterblichkeit voraus, in deren Folge dann erst Handlungen möglich sind, welche nicht von dem Bedürfnis diktiert werden, den Tod wegzuschieben und zu verdecken.

Dies ist dann auch die Meinung des "Erwachens": es heißt, das Leben als etwas aufzudecken, das uns nicht nur gegeben ist, sondern das wir übernehmen und führen sollen – und zwar nicht beliebig, sondern gerade gegen die Neigung, durch Selbstzerstreuung in Gegenständlichkeiten den Tod zu verdecken und wegzuschieben; so zu führen, dass man sich nicht "in Abgewandtheit von sich selbst" vergeudet und zerstreuet.[5]

Der Ausdruck "Kampf" weist jedoch auch auf den wirklichen äußeren Konflikt (und somit auch den Anderen) hin. Gerade im faktischen Kampf entsteht die Gefahr des Todes; und bei dieser unmittelbarer Lebensgefahr kommt die Freiheit – die Fähigkeit, unabhängig zu handeln von der Notwendigkeit, das Leben zu erhalten – am deutlichsten zum Ausdruck. Hier also, im zwischenmenschlichen Kampf, wird die Verdinglichung des Anderen und unserer selbst überwunden; im Kampf auf Leben und Tod gewinnen wir das Bewusstsein dessen, dass wir und auch der Andere "kein Ding und überhaupt keine Objektivität" sind (Patočka 1991b, 217, Übersetzung modifiziert).

1.3. Hingabe

Das zweite und "tiefere" Stadium des Kontakts mit dem Anderen besteht für Patočka in der *Hingabe* (dazu und zum Folgenden siehe Patočka 1991b, 217).

---

[4] Daher sagt Patočka, dass *dieser* Umkehr *notwendig* der Kampfcharakter eignet. In der Sphäre der Selbstreproduktion des Lebens – vor der Umkehr – kann der Kampf hingegen durch eine andere, gewaltlose Tätigkeit ersetzt werden, die diese Selbstreproduktion besser verwirklicht (Patočka 1991b, 223).

[5] Wie an vielen anderen Stellen in Patočkas Studien treffen hier mehrere Gedankenlinien zusammen: die vom Bedürfnis, den Tod zu verdecken und wegzuschieben, diktierte Handlung – das Schweifen zwischen verschiedenen Tätigkeiten (vgl. Patočkas Ausdrücke "sich vergeuden", "sich zerstreuen") – die Abgewandtheit von sich selbst (d.h. wohl vom Bewusstsein der eigenen Freiheit und Verantwortung oder von deren bewusster Realisierung). Offenbar spricht hier Patočka *per negationem* über verschiedene Ebenen der "Ganzheit" oder "Einheit" des Lebens, die er dreißig Jahre früher thematisiert hat: Übernahme der Verantwortung für die eigene Lebensführung – Konzentration des Lebens auf Tätigkeiten, die den gewählten Motiven entsprechen – Wahl derjenigen Motive, die dem als höchsten erkannten Wert entsprechen (siehe Patočka 1937).

Zu einer tieferen Überwindung der Endlichkeit (…) kommt es hingegen dann, wenn ich mein Leben in den Anderen versetze, wenn ich nicht mehr die Bewegung der Rückkehr von ihm zu mir selbst vollziehe, sondern mich ihm hingebe. Ich werde durch die Entstehung des Anderen, genau wie er durch meine Entstehung wird. (ebd.)

Im Kampf wird die Ebene des Gegenständlichen überschritten: wir gewinnen das "negative" Wissen, dass wir kein Ding und keine Objektivität sind. In der Hingabe jedoch

eignen wir uns ein Bewusstsein von uns selbst als von etwas seinem Wesen nach Unendlichem an, von etwas (…), das außerhalb seiner selbst ein anderes Wesen zeugt – ein nicht bloß endliches, sondern ein nicht-objekthaftes. Ich rege dieses Wesen zu der gleichen Bewegung an, und es bleibt dadurch frei und nichtobjekthaft, dass es diese Bewegung an seinem Anderen – nämlich an mir – vollzieht. Ich manifestiere die Tatsache, dass ich nicht endlich bin, dadurch, dass ich es ganz dem Anderen gebe, der mir dafür das seinige gibt, in dem das meinige enthalten ist. (ebd.)

Auf dieses Moment kommen wir noch zu sprechen, kehren aber vorher kurz zum Kampf zurück.

1.4. Absolute Bedrohung

Wenn es einem Menschen gelingen sollte, wirklich *völlig* unabhängig zu handeln von der vorherrschenden Tendenz, sich den Tod zu verdecken und dessen Realität von sich fortzuschieben bzw., im Extremfall, sogar unabhängig zu sein von jeder Rücksicht auf die aktuelle Todesgefahr, dann tritt er, metaphorisch gesprochen, aus dem Rahmen dessen heraus, was durch diese Notwendigkeit gekennzeichnet ist, d.h. aber auch: er gerät außerhalb all der Sicherungen und der Geschütztheit, die das übliche Funktionieren bietet. So ist der Mensch einer Bedrohung ausgeliefert, die man – weil sein Überleben selbst bedroht ist – als absolut bezeichnen kann: "Die Bedrohung ist absolut, wenn sie alles erfasst, wenn nach ihrer Ausführung nichts mehr zurückbleibt" (Patočka 1991b, 224). Patočka meint wohl den extremsten Fall – eine Handlung, die ausgeführt wird, obwohl mit ihr die *Sicherheit* oder mindestens eine große Wahrscheinlichkeit des Todes verbunden ist. Gerade im Vergleich mit ihr kann er die Bedrohungen, denen sich ein Bergsteiger, Taucher, Kosmonaut, Akrobat aussetzt, als nicht-absolut bezeichnen, als solche, in denen "die Freiheit an die Tür klopft, ohne die Lawine bereits in Bewegung zu bringen," (Patočka 1991a, 141). Selbst in eine solche Unsicherheit *kann* man eintreten – und dies zeigt, dass man nach den Motiven der Handlung auch außerhalb der das Überleben sichernden Weltdinge fragen muss; dass auf der Erde und im Himmel "nichts ist, was der Existenz ihre letzte Stütze geben könnte, eine letzte Verankerung, ein letztes Ziel, ein letztes Warum" (Patočka 1991a, 140, Übersetzung modifiziert). Die Erde ist nicht jener feste Boden, als welcher sie meistens gilt. "Es 'ist' noch etwas anderes als das Spiel ihrer Erscheinungen und ihrer Wiederholung. Etwas ganz anderes als alles Seiende" (Patočka 1991b, 224).

1.5. Praktisches Transzendieren; das wahre Leben

Wesentliche Aspekte dieser Auslegung kennen wir bereits aus früheren Texten Patočkas: das Hinausgehen über das Gebiet des Gegenständlichen, ja des Seienden schlechthin, wodurch es überhaupt erst zum Ganzen wird (*Negativer Platonismus*); Transzendieren als Tätigkeit eines durch den Tod bedrohten Wesens, als Trotz gegen die Kräfte, durch welche der Tod seine "Macht" ausübt (*Ewigkeit und Geschichtlichkeit*).

Das Neue – außer der schon besprochenen Rolle des Anderen – besteht nun darin, dass das Transzendieren *praktisch* geschieht, durch ein *Handeln*, das sich nicht auf die gegenständlichen, seienden Stützen verlässt, ein Handeln, das seinen Wert nicht aus der möglichen Wirksamkeit in der Welt ableitet. Bislang bestand der Akt des Transzendierens meistens in einer Erweiterung oder Verschiebung der Aufmerksamkeit oder des Bewusstseinsinhalts, sozusagen in einem "itinerarium *mentis*", beziehungsweise in einer Haltungsänderung, die dazu notwendig ist (wie in der Bereitschaft, die Augen vor den nicht-manipulierbaren und bisweilen bedrohlichen Determinanten unseres Daseins nicht zu verschließen), und diese Umkehr führte erst nachträglich zu einer Änderung in der Lebenspraxis (zur Bildung eines Kanons des philosophischen Lebens u. ä.); diesmal besteht der Akt des Transzendierens selbst, sein Wie, in einer gewissen *Praxis*.

Durch unseren Verzicht auf eigene Interessen zeigen sich Himmel und Erde als das nicht-letztgültige, und "das Höhere" kann erscheinen:

> Die Erde und den Himmel in Frage zu stellen heißt jedoch, sich selbst zu opfern, damit etwas anderes 'sein' kann, damit Erde und Himmel nicht bloß sich selbst offenbaren, sondern damit sie Offenbarung des 'Höheren' werden. (Patočka 1991b, 224)

Durch das Ausschreiten in die Ungesichertheit gehen wir zugleich vom bloß gegebenen Leben über "zur Manifestation des wahren Lebens" (Patočka 1991b, 218); in diesem Ausschreiten zeigt sich, dass der Mensch imstande ist, auch jenseits der innenweltlichen Stützen aktiv zu sein, dass er fähig ist, frei in die "absolute Ungesichertheit" hinauszuschreiten, und dass darin das wahrhaft menschliche Leben besteht.

1.6. Hingabe an die Freiheit des Anderen

Einen eminenten Fall dieses transzendierenden Handelns stellt für Patočka, wie schon erwähnt, die Hingabe an den Anderen dar, denn gerade in ihr entdecken wir auf eine vorzügliche Weise unsere Unendlichkeit.

Es ist hier nicht der Platz, um die Rolle des Anderen in dieser Phase des transzendierenden Handelns genauer zu untersuchen, noch auch um die offenkundigen theologisch-Hegel'schen Wurzeln dieser Konzeption zu verfolgen. Angemerkt sei nur, dass der Autor mit dem Motiv der Hingabe an den Anderen wahrscheinlich ein Dilemma lösen wollte, in das er durch seine Auffassung des wahren Lebens geraten war: wahr sei das Leben, soweit es nicht von den Bedürfnissen beherrscht wird, die ihm unsere Sterblichkeit diktiert – aber zugleich, insoweit es nicht durch konventionelle Regeln des Handelns bestimmt wird (denn auch diese gehören zu den Gegenständlichkeiten, die das wahre Leben überstiegen hat; siehe Patočka 2011, 141-143). Zwischen den beiden kaum zu akzeptierenden Möglichkeiten, die noch übrig bleiben – zwischen der völlig leeren Willkür einerseits und einer neuen gegenständlichen Bestimmung andererseits –, wählt Patočka die Selbsthingabe an einen anderen Menschen: an ein konkretes Wesen, das stets in konkreten Umständen konkrete Existenzmöglichkeiten wählt, *das jedoch frei ist*, d. h. gegenständlich nicht definierbar. Das dem Anderen hingegebene Leben hat sich also wirklich aus jeder Bindung ans Gegenständliche gelöst, es bleibt nicht-verdinglicht, es lässt sich nicht endgültig definieren und ist daher in diesem Sinne un-endlich – es hat aber zugleich einen konkreten, positiven Inhalt; seine Un-endlichkeit ist keine uferlose Offenheit, die sich nie gezwungen fühlt, eine gerade offenstehende Möglichkeit abzulehnen, die aber schließlich auch nie einen Grund hat, sich für eine von den offenen Möglichkeiten zu entscheiden.[6]

1.7. Dominanz der Zukunft?

Bekanntlich hat Patočka die verschiedenen Lebensweisen ("Lebensbewegungen") durch die Dominanz einer je anderen Dimension der Zeit charakterisiert:[7] "Selbstverständlich trägt jede dieser Bewegungen die gesamte Zeitlichkeit in sich (...) In jeder von ihnen dominiert jedoch eine andere 'Zeitekstase', ein anderer Horizont" (Patočka 2010, 53). Die

---

[6] Im früheren Text 1991a sowie im späteren 1991d (diesem werden wir uns gleich widmen) geht Patočka einen Schritt weiter und zeigt, wie sich aus der Hingabe eine Gemeinschaft im Dienste des Seins ergibt. In dem erstgenannten Text werden sogar Himmel und Erde zur Offenbarung nicht bloß "des Höheren", sondern eines neuen, kommenden Reiches, des Reiches des Geistes und der Freiheit. Wie er sich die politische Verwirklichung dieser Gemeinschaft vorstellt, dazu siehe vor allem Patočka 1998b.

[7] Einen ähnlichen Versuch hat neuerdings, ohne auf Patočka explizit hinzuweisen, Petr Kouba unternommen (Kouba 2012). Seine zukunfts- und gegenwartsgebundenen Modi der Existenz entsprechen *grosso modo* der Auffassung Patočkas; durch die Dominanz der Vergangenheit wird der pathologische Modus charakterisiert. Koubas (und wohl auch Patočkas) Projekt stützt sich in seinem temporalen Aspekt auf eine spezifische Interpretation des 65. Paragraphs von Heideggers *Sein und Zeit*. Patočkas Charakterisierung der Lebensbewegungen durch die Dominanz einzelner Dimensionen der Zeit wird, soweit wir wissen, von der gesamten Sekundärliteratur zu diesem Thema übernommen, sofern es sich nicht um eine grundsätzliche Kritik handelt (wie bei Pavel Kouba 2007).

Wende von der Zerstreuung in den Dingen zum Bewusstsein unserer eigentlichsten Möglichkeit soll demgemäß auch eine Wende zur Dominanz der Zukunft heißen.

> Die Tatsache, dass auch die dritte Grundbeziehung zum Anderen eine zeitliche ist, geht aus ihrem Verhältnis zur Zukunft, zum Nichtsein, zum Tod (…) hervor. (Patočka 1991b, 225)

Weist aber diese Beziehung des Transzendierenden zum Nichtsein und zum Tod wirklich darauf hin, dass in seinem Verhältnis zur Realität nun die Zukunft und nicht mehr die Gegenwart dominiert? Ein Verhältnis zum Tod, also zur Zukunft, hat ja auch der in die Dinge zerstreute Mensch; er ist – gerade weil er seine Tätigkeit großenteils auf dessen Verdeckung ausrichtet – stark durch den kommenden Tod bestimmt. Wer sich seiner Lage im Ganzen bewusst ist oder wer sogar aktuell der absoluten Bedrohung standhält, hat zwar ganz gewiss ein diametral anderes Verhältnis zum Tod und zur Zukunft überhaupt, dies bedeutet jedoch weniger ein Übergewicht der Zukunft als vielmehr einen unterschiedlichen Zugang zu ihr – und einen unterschiedlichen Zugang zur Wirklichkeit als solcher: man ist bereit, auch die nicht beherrschbaren und eventuell bedrohlichen Faktoren des Lebens unverschleiert wahrzunehmen, seien sie noch künftig oder schon gegenwärtig.

Nicht manipulierbare und zugleich bestimmende Faktoren unseres Lebens liegen außerdem auch in der Vergangenheit. Patočka spricht vom Nichtsein, und dies steht zeitlich nicht nur "vor" uns, sondern liegt ebenso "hinter" uns. In diesem Sinne heißt es bei ihm etwa Ende der dreißiger Jahre: "Das Leben [wird] von *zwei* Abgründen begrenzt …, zwischen denen eine kleine Enklave seiner Ruhe wie eine kurze Pause besteht" (Patočka 1999, 97; Hervorhebung von J. F.). Liegt also der Unterschied zwischen dem transzendierenden und nicht-transzendierenden Leben eher in ihrem Zugang – einmal im entdeckenden, ein anderes Mal im verdeckenden – zu *beiden* Abgründen, nicht nur zum künftigen, sondern auch zum gewesenen?[8]

Und schließlich: der Unterschied zwischen dem Leben vor der Wende und nach dieser bestand darin, dass das erstere im Anderen eine Rolle, eine Funktion, in gewissem Sinne also ein Ding sah, das letztere eine Person; und auch der Unterschied zwischen diesen Seienden liegt eher in der Qualität oder in der *Art* ihrer Gegenwart und Zukunft denn in der Quantität oder dem *Ausmaß* des Bezuges auf die zeitlichen Dimensionen.

---

[8] Die Beschreibung der Probleme würde sich wohl merklich ändern, hätte sie den ersten Abgrund nicht aus der Sicht verloren. Das Bewusstsein, dass wir nicht waren und sind, müsste auch unsere Sicht der Tatsache ändern, dass wir sind und nicht sein werden; und auch das "bloße gegebene Leben" würde anders erscheinen – als ebenso ungenügend wie bewunderns- und mitfühlenswert, das Wegschieben des Todes dann als ebenso hoffnungslos wie verdienstvoll.

Trotz alledem hat die Rede vom "zukünftigen" Charakter des Transzendierens einen guten Sinn – nämlich dann, wenn wir bei aller Unangemessenheit der gegenständlichen Sprache doch die Natur dessen andeuten wollen, was "ganz anders als alles Seiende" ist und was sich beim Hinaustreten in die absolute Bedrohung zeigen soll. Eine Möglichkeit, etwas zu vergegenwärtigen und verständlich zu machen, was uns bestimmt und was dennoch "anders als seiend" ist, finden wir doch gerade in unserer Erfahrung mit der Zukunft: nie aktuell, aber immer reell; nie da, aber doch determiniert die Rücksicht darauf fast all unser Handeln; nicht seiend und auch nicht einfach nicht-seiend, sondern: künftig.

2. *Was ist Existenz?* (1969)[9]

2.1. "Ebenen des Lebens"; Selbstverlorenheit und Selbstsuche

Klarer als im vorangehenden Text werden in dieser Studie die verschiedenen "Ebenen des Lebens" ausgeführt, von der Ebene zufälliger Gegebenheiten bis zu derjenigen des Ich *sensu stricto*, d.h. der Ebene, auf der über "Selbstverlorenheit, Selbstsuche und zuweilen auch Selbstfindung des Menschen" entschieden wird (Patočka 1991d, 235).[10] Dieses Problem ist bereits in früheren Texten mehr oder weniger ausdrücklich benannt worden,[11] diesmal aber will Patočka diese Ebene erstens anschaulicher *entdecken* und den Abstieg zu ihr *demonstrieren*, zweitens detaillierter beschreiben.

Die Entdeckung geschieht dort, wo Patočka die biologischen, soziologischen und historischen Determinanten als Teile der Situation zeigt, in die "ich, mein eigenes gelebtes Leben, unausweichlich gerate, in der ich zu mir komme, um tatsächlich, durch Tat und Handeln nämlich, zu entscheiden und zu zeigen, dass ich bin und was ich bin"; wo er zeigt (gegenüber der naturwissenschaftlichen Haltung, die zur Einsicht neigt, ich *sei* meine Anlagen, Talente und Umstände), dass das sich entscheidende Ich kein weiterer Faktor auf derselben Ebene ist, dass er "hinter" oder "unter" diesen Determinanten liegt (Patočka 1991d, 236, Übersetzung modifiziert).

---

[9] Patočka1991d. In den Passagen, die unserem Problem gewidmet sind, deckt sich dieser Text mit dem Nachwort zur tschechischen Neuausgabe der Habilitationsschrift Patočkas aus der gleichen Zeit (Patočka 1990b).
[10] Patočka betont, dass das Suchen und Finden die verschiedenen Lebensebenen (also auch die des äußeren Handelns) "durchdringt"; wie jedoch seine folgende Auslegung zeigt, wird es *entschieden* auf der Ebene der empirisch nicht-fassbaren Freiheit.
[11] Patočka spricht über die menschliche Fähigkeit, "in verschiedenen Tiefen" zu leben (Patočka 1999, 96). Es geht nicht um verschiedene Arten oder Ebenen der "Einheit" des Lebens (siehe oben die Fußnote 5), sondern um die Ebenen des Lebens als solche.

Zur *Beschreibung* dieser Ebene dient dann eine zweifache Charakteristik der Beziehung des Menschen zu sich selbst; der Mensch verhält sich zu sich selbst in zweierlei Hinsicht anders als zu allem anderen. Erstens kann er nicht umhin, über sich selbst zu entscheiden. Gewiss, er kann auf die Entscheidung über diesen oder jenen Aspekt seiner Existenz verzichten; doch selbst dies ist ein Akt seines entscheidenden Ichs, selbst dadurch "führt" er im aktuellen Augenblick sein Leben und entscheidet darüber, wer er ist. Zweitens kann er auf sich selbst nicht "von außen" zugehen, er kann sich selbst als die hier und jetzt sich entscheidende Freiheit nicht zugleich beobachten (er ist "die einzige Sache auf der Welt …, die er nicht entdecken kann," Patočka 1991d, 236). Den gemeinsamen Zug dieser zweifachen Charakteristik bildet die Unmöglichkeit, *die* Distanz zu sich selbst einzunehmen, die der Prozess des gegenständlichen Erkennens voraussetzt. Selbstverlorenheit, Selbstsuche und Selbstfindung lassen sich daher nicht unbefangen feststellen, sollen sie nicht wesentlich verzerrt werden; es gilt, in ihnen Möglichkeiten *eigener* Lebensführung zu erkennen.

Dieselbe Ebene und vergleichbare Probleme (Nicht-Objektivierbarkeit dessen, was auf ihr vor sich geht; Bindung ans konkrete Ich; Notwendigkeit seiner aktiven Teilnahme und des Nachvollzugs der gemeinten Erfahrung) hat Patočka schon in einem Manuskript aus der Kriegszeit mit den Begriffen *Ernst*, *Unruhe*, *Interesse* und *Spannung* (Patočka 2007b, 53-57) beschrieben. Es ist jedoch augenfällig, dass im Vergleich mit diesen allgemeinen Ausdrücken, mit denen man *alles* Geschehen auf dieser Ebene des eigentlichen Ich charakterisieren kann, die Ausdrücke *Selbstverlorenheit*, *Selbstsuche* und *Selbstfinden* einen besonderen Moment unserer Existenz bezeichnen, nämlich den Moment ihrer *Bedrohung*: einen defekten Zustand, in dem wir uns befinden (hier mit der Metapher des Verlorenseins bezeichnet), ein entsprechend dringendes Bedürfnis, sich zu befreien oder die Lage richtigzustellen ("Selbstsuche") und die Möglichkeit hierin zu scheitern ("*zuweilen* auch Selbstfindung").

Die beiden ersten Ausdrücke können als verkürzte Neuformulierung des großen Themas von *Ewigkeit und Geschichtlichkeit* verstanden werden: in der Selbstverlorenheit (in den Texten aus der 60er Jahren meist als Selbstverlorenheit unter den Dingen verstanden) kehrt die bedrohliche Übermacht des Gegenständlichen zurück; in der (*aktiven*) Selbstsuche der Protest gegen diese Übermacht.

Die Bezeichnung "*Selbst*suche" erinnert uns weiterhin daran, dass das Transzendieren immer einen Weg zum Bewusstsein *unserer* Stellung im Ganzen bedeutet. Damit wendet sich die Aufmerksamkeit – im Vergleich mit dem oben interpretierten Text – wieder vom Anderen zum Ich: die Beunruhigung, die in der Beschreibung des Transzendierens die notwendige erste Phase darstellt, wird nicht durch die Objektivierung des Anderen hervorgerufen, sondern durch die eigene Selbstverlorenheit. In der Beschreibung der Wende selbst fehlt dann der Andere; der Kontakt mit ihm erscheint erst nachträglich, eher als eine Folge des Transzendierens:

> Die Reflexion ist ein Element des inneren Handelns, durch das ich die Verschlossenheit ... aufschließe für mich und für die Anderen. Deshalb ist die Existenz keine Isolation, sie führt vielmehr zur Kommunikation. Die Kommunikation ist kein beliebiges Mitteilen eines beliebigen Inhalts, in der Kommunikation sind wir jemandem ganz und gar geöffnet und ergeben. (Patočka 1991d, 240)[12]

2.2. "Zuweilen auch Selbstfindung"

Wie steht es nun mit dem dritten Motiv, mit der Selbstfindung, die nur zuweilen stattfindet, mit dem Motiv der Suche also, die nur in einigen Fällen an ihr Ziel führt? Außer in der Vorlesung *Leib, Gemeinschaft, Sprache, Welt*, wo eine andere Auslegung angedeutet wird (siehe unten), wird dieses Motiv in den hier zur Diskussion stehenden Texten auf eine Weise interpretiert, die in den früheren Texten Patočkas des Öfteren zu finden ist. Man kann wiederholt lesen, wie das anfängliche, unklare Bewusstwerden der Freiheit und des Ganzen zwar durch eine Unzufriedenheit, Beunruhigung u. ä. zum Ausdruck kommen kann, *ohne* jedoch zum wahren, radikalen Transzendieren zu führen – zum Protest gegen die Übermacht des Gegenständlichen *als solchen*, zum Hinausschreiten über das *Ganze* des Gegenständlichen, zum Bewusstwerden der Welt als des letzten, universalen Zusammenhangs, oder wie sonst das Transzendieren noch beschrieben wurde. Aus der Bindung an gewisse innerweltliche Dinge befreien wir uns oft durch die Bindung an andere; und in den *Studien zum Weltbegriff* schildert Patočka recht detailliert ein solches Verhalten, das die nicht-objekthaften Fernen nicht als eine Aufforderung begreift, alles rein Objektive zu transzendieren, sondern sich daraus immer nur weitere Objekte gewinnt (Patočka 2014, 89).

In all diesen Fällen ist das, wovon wir bedroht sind, die Gegenständlichkeit: diesmal nicht so sehr von "außen" als Übermacht der vergegenständlichenden Kräfte, die endlich zu unserem Tod führen; vielmehr eher von "innen", als unser Haftenbleiben an der Ebene des Gegenständlichen, als unsere "Zerstreuung" in die Seienden, denen wir in der Welt begegnen. Wenn wir uns selbst und unsere Situation verzerrt sehen, dann gerade wegen dieser Zerstreuung und dieses Haftenbleibens. Was dann getan werden soll, ist natürlich das Hinaustreten aus der Ebene des Gegenständlichen; und sobald dies geschieht, sobald wir dem Appell folgen und das Hinaustreten verwirklichen, kann es nur auf eine einzige Weise *scheitern* (wenn auch in verschiedenen konkreten Gestalten) – dadurch nämlich, dass es nicht konsequent genug ist, dass es also wieder bei einem Gegenstand stehen bleibt oder zu

---

[12] Zur Rolle des (oder eher: der) Anderen in diesem Text siehe oben Fußnote 6.

ihm abgleitet, so dass das Ganze des Gegenständlichen nicht wirklich überschritten wird. Dies war der Grund, warum Patočka einst "Religion" (Patočka 2007a) bzw. "Metaphysik" (Patočka 1988) kritisiert hatte: der Übergang aus einer gegenständlichen Ebene in ein Anderswohin, der Akt des Transzendierens also, werde in ihnen deformiert in den Unterschied zwischen zwei ontischen Ebenen, aus dem Transzendieren werde ein Transzendentes.

Und *darin* liegt nun auch der Grund, warum die Selbstsuche nur "zuweilen" erfolgreich ist, darin ist die Möglichkeit begründet, dass die Selbstsuche nicht zur Selbstfindung führt. Wir werden noch einer anderen Interpretation begegnen, dieser Text jedoch bleibt bei der Alternative, "uns [zu] finden und in unserem eigentlichen menschlichen Wesen [zu] verwirklichen" oder "uns im Einzelnen [zu] zerstreuen und [zu] verlieren" (Patočka 1990b, 261, Übersetzung modifiziert).

2.3. Welt, Sein, Offenbarkeit

Die Zerstreuung unter den Dingen verdeckt uns also meistens das Ganze unserer Situation, und aus diesem Zustand müssen wir uns befreien, "aufschließen" (zum Folgenden siehe Patočka 1991d, 238-241). Ein wesentliches Hindernis besteht in der Tatsache, dass wir uns oft das Ganze unserer Situation verdecken *wollen*: unter die Gestalten der Unwahrheit, aus der wir uns befreien sollen, gehören nicht nur die Nicht-Offenbarkeit und Illusion (die eine Sache von Mangeln und Störungen in physischen Organen oder psychischen Mechanismen sein können, also Ergebnis der "nicht-persönlichen", der Freiheit nicht unterliegenden Kräfte, etwas, was "mit uns geschieht"), sondern auch Verschlossenheit und Lüge (die wir immerhin in einem Maße *tun*, die in diesem Maße eine Sache unserer Entscheidung und Verantwortung sind).[13]

Es gilt also, die *Wende*[14] zum Bewusstsein unserer Stellung im Ganzen zu verwirklichen, einer Stellung, zu der auch unsere Situiertheit zwischen den Polen der Unwahrheit (im angedeuteten Sinne der Zerstreuung und Verschlossenheit) und Wahrheit gehört. Das Bewusstsein unserer Situation schließt dann das Bewusstsein ihres letzten Rahmens ein, den die *Welt* bildet: "Diese Wende wird also nicht von einem Verlust der Welt begleitet, sie ist im Gegenteil ihre wahre Entdeckung; diese Wende ist in gewissem Sinne weltlich" (Patočka 1990b, 256f., Übersetzung modifiziert).

---

[13] Vgl. Patočka 1991d, 240: Wir verhalten uns zu uns selbst wie zu einer "Aufgabe, die wir nicht gemeistert haben, die wir verschweigen und zerreden" (Übersetzung modifiziert).
[14] In diesem Sinne verwendet Patočka das Wort *Reflexion*: "Die Reflexion ist ein Element des inneren Handelns, durch das ich mich aus der Verschlossenheit – in welcher ich mir selbst, meiner Wahrheit, der Sicht auf mich selbst, so wie ich bin, auszuweichen suche – aufschließe" (Patočka 1991d, 240, Übersetzung modifiziert; vgl. dazu Kouba 2007).

Die als Entdeckung der Welt bezeichnete Wende wird auch als Hingabe an das *Sein* beschrieben; das Wesen der Wende kann also auch als Entscheidung beschrieben werden, die Wahrheit des Seins gegenüber der Macht des Seienden zu bevorzugen (dazu und zum Folgenden siehe Patočka 1990b, 266f.). Die Inkommensurabilität dieser Alternativen legt Patočka durch den "Mythos vom göttlichen Menschen" nahe, vom Menschen, der ganz in der Hingabe an das Sein und in dessen Licht lebt: sein Auftritt ist *ipso facto* ein Angriff auf das Selbstverständnis, das vor dem Ganzen unserer Situation sich verschließt und sich ausschließlich auf die Möglichkeiten der Beherrschung konzentriert; und ein Angriff auf die faktischen Kräfte, in denen dieses Selbstverständnis verkörpert ist. Weil ein solches Selbstverständnis in diesem Menschen (irrtümlich) nur einen Konkurrenten in der Weltbeherrschung zu sehen vermag, vernichtet es ihn; er muss jedoch zwangsläufig auferstehen, weil die Wahrheit von innenweltlichen Kräften nicht getroffen werden kann (auf diesen "Mythos" kommen wir noch zu sprechen).

Welt und *Sein* sind schließlich mit der *Offenbarkeit*, mit dem Erscheinen sinnverwandt: "weltzentriert" heißt auch "lichtzentriert" (Patočka 1990b, 266).[15] Die Wende soll daher zur Hingabe an das Sein führen, zum Sich-Einsetzen für die Offenbarkeit: das den eigenen Interessen, den hedonischen und utilitären Impulsen dienende Seiende wird zu einem solchen, "das sich dem Sein erschließt, das dafür lebt, dass die Dinge das sind, sich als das zeigen, was sie sind – und ich und die Anderen ebenso" (Patočka 1990b, 265).

2.4. Ein kleiner Rahmen für einen großen Mythos

All dies sind Facetten einer neuen Beschreibung des Transzendierens, die sich deutlich von den früheren Fassungen unterscheidet. Es seien nun die Hauptzüge dieser neuen Beschreibung zusammengefasst und ihre Spezifika hervorgehoben.

Die älteren Beschreibungen unterschieden sich darin, dass sie einmal die Aktivität, ein anderes Mal die Passivität des Menschen im Akt des Transzendierens betonten. Der Text, mit dem wir uns jetzt befassen, berührt eindeutig den aktiven Pol; er versteht diesen Akt als Werk unserer Aktivität; die Wende von der Verschlossenheit und Zerstreuung ist unser inneres Handeln. Der passive Moment (das Nachgeben gegenüber dem Zug der Ferne, der Faszination des Ganzen, dem Appell der Idee) rückt in den Hintergrund.

Wichtiger noch: im Vergleich mit den älteren Texten (einschließlich des oben analysierten) *verliert die Wende erheblich an Radikalität*:

---

[15] Diesem Gedanken liegt die (von Patočka auch anderswo thematisierte) Verwandtschaft der tschechischen Wörter *svět* (Welt) und *světlo* (Licht) zugrunde.

- Die Darlegung der Wende ist nun Teil eines neuen philosophischen Projekts, in dem die *ganze* Existenz – also das Transzendieren ebenso wie alle anderen menschlichen Tätigkeiten – mit *einem* Begriff interpretiert wird (nämlich mit dem der Bewegung). Die Wende, die das Transzendieren darstellt, kann also von den übrigen Aktivitäten nicht so radikal unterschiedlich sein; wenn Patočka sie mit anderen menschlichen Tätigkeiten in Zusammenhang bringt, dann betont er weniger ihre Andersheit als ihre Verwandtschaft: wie alles andere, ist auch die Wende eine Sache unseres Handelns, eine Modalität der Praxis.
- Die Gegenständlichkeit erscheint nicht *so* bedrohlich wie zuvor: sie bedroht uns nicht mehr als solche, sondern nur insofern, als unsere geistige Zerstreuung, d.h. unser fehlendes Selbstverhältnis und das geistige Aufgehen in den Dingen der Welt, unser "eigentliches menschliches Wesen" verdeckt.[16] Das Pathos des Appells, das Ganze des Gegenständlichen zu überschreiten oder gegen seine Übermacht zu protestieren, wird daher erheblich schwächer; wir sollen uns von der Zerstreuung als *unserer* falschen Haltung gegenüber den Dingen abwenden, nicht von den Dingen oder von der Gegenständlichkeit als solcher.[17] Die tödliche Übermacht des Gegenständlichen, die im Kampf gegen den Geist letztlich siegreich bleibt (so Patočka 2011), ist zu einer fehlerhaften *Interpretation* der physischen Wirklichkeit geworden, wodurch sie zwar weiter faktisch bedrohlich, aber grundsätzlich überwindbar scheint.
- Es findet sich hier nicht die Vorstellung einer *Idee*, die zu den Dingen ihr Nein sagen würde und uns als ein Appell diente, die Dinge zu überschreiten (wie im *Negativen Platonismus*); die Möglichkeiten des Überschreitens sind gerade *in* unserer Endlichkeit und Kontingenz gegeben:

Sich zu dem zu machen, was ich in Wahrheit bin, bedeutet einerseits, sich in dem anzunehmen, was ich in meiner Kontingenz und Endlichkeit, in meiner ganzen 'Schwere' und 'Unfreiheit', die mein Leben prägen, bin, andererseits aber *in dieser An-*

---

[16] Aus dieser geistigen Zerstreuung ergibt sich allerdings ein Selbstverständnis, das (dem Ganzen unserer Situation gegenüber verschlossen) nur die Möglichkeiten der *Beherrschung* sieht, und dies erzeugt dann die *faktische* "Übermacht des Seienden", die auch uns in die Zusammenhänge der beherrschten Seienden einreiht und uns dadurch *faktisch* bedroht. Diese Selbstzerstreuung und das aus ihr folgende Selbstverständnis sind jedoch – wie stark vorherrschend auch immer – nicht unüberwindbar.

[17] Es geht freilich um die Betonung verschiedener Aspekte eines und desselben Prozesses (denn wir ändern *immer* unsere *Haltung* zu den Dingen; uns von ihnen faktisch befreien können wir als leibliche Wesen natürlich nicht). Die früheren Beschreibungen haben das *Motiv* dieser Änderung betont, d.h. die Bestrebung, aus der Übermacht des Gegenständlichen sich zu befreien, die neue Beschreibung akzentuiert das *faktische Ergebnis*, d.h. den Wandel der Haltung.

nahme zugleich auch jenes Positive zu erkennen, welches erst möglich macht, dass das Leben etwas anderes ist als nur nichtige Leidenschaft, nichtiges Hangen an der Welt und ihren Gegenständen. *In diesem Hangen selbst*, in dem, wodurch es ermöglicht wird, ist die Möglichkeit enthalten, es zu überschreiten. (Patočka 1991d, 255, Übersetzung modifiziert, hervorgehoben von J. F.)

Unsere "eigentlichste menschliche Substanz und Möglichkeit" besteht gerade in dieser Doppelung, in unserem "Erdendasein, das zugleich eine Beziehung zum Sein und zum Universum ist" (Patočka 1990b, 261, Übersetzung modifiziert).

- Dem entspricht auch Patočkas Sprache: Es verschwinden starke, gleichsam anspornende Ausdrücke wie "Appell der Idee" oder "Kampf um die Ewigkeit"; es fehlt der radikale Begriff des *Chorismos*;[18] selbst darauf, was einer der früheren Texte als *Abgründe* benannt hat, wird hier bloß mit dem nüchternen Ausdruck *Endlichkeit* hingewiesen.

Kann man also von einem "allgemeinen Klima" reden, dann bewegt sich dieser Text in der Atmosphäre einer unverkennbaren Ernüchterung und Harmonisierung, einer Spannungssenkung, ja vielleicht einer Verkleinerung der Dimensionen – und zwar sowohl von "oben" als auch von "unten": Der Aufruf der Idee und der Kampf ums Ewige sind verstummt, und zugleich ist auch die bedrohliche Macht der Objektivierung zu einer reparabel scheinenden falschen Auffassung geschrumpft. Insofern werden die "Dimensionen" des Transzendierens reduziert; das Transzendieren, möchte man fast sagen, wird immanentisiert.[19]

Eines ist nun seltsam: die These von *Ewigkeit und Geschichtlichkeit*, nach welcher der Protest des Geistes gegen die Gegenständlichkeit zwar immer mit einer Niederlage endet, wodurch jedoch nicht sein *Sinn* verneint wird – diese These also gewinnt gerade in diesem "kleineren" und "harmonischeren" Kontext die emphatische Gestalt des "Mythos vom göttlichen Menschen" mit seiner zentralen Metapher der Auferstehung. Worauf will es mit dieser kräftigen Metaphorik hinaus? Das Gemeinte – die Inkommensurabilität von Wahrheit und Wirksamkeit, d.h. die Unmöglichkeit, die Wahrheit durch die faktische Wirksamkeit der Unwahrheit abzuschaffen – könnte ja auch mit einer Neuformulierung dessen zum Ausdruck gebracht werden, was Patočka weit früher (das Verhältnis zwischen Wirksamkeit und *Philosophie* betreffend) über den Tod des Sokrates gesagt hat: "Die Welt kann das Dasein des Philosophen annullieren – und siehe, Philosophie ist auf diese Weise in die

---

[18] Als Realisierung des *Chorismos* wird das Transzendieren bei Patočka 1999, 100 bezeichnet.
[19] Es liegt nahe, die Ursache darin zu sehen, dass Patočka sich diesmal an Aristoteles orientiert, nicht an Plato wie im *Negativen Platonismus* und teilweise auch in *Ewigkeit und Geschichtlichkeit*. Dagegen spricht aber die Tatsache, dass in den oben interpretierten Texten, die gleichwohl von Aristoteles inspiriert sind, keine ähnliche Restriktion zu sehen ist.

Geschichte eingegangen! Nichts zeigt besser, wie wenig adäquat dieses Mittel ist gegenüber der inneren Macht der Philosophie" (Patočka 2007a, 23).[20]

Was immer die Anwendung dieses Mythos über die Bedeutung von Patočkas Text besagt, es scheint klar zu sein, welche Folge umgekehrt dieser Kontext für die Bedeutung des Mythos hat. Sein Stoff ist offensichtlich dem Evangelium entnommen;[21] dieses erfährt also eine minimalisierende, radikal existentielle Auslegung, in welcher das Ereignis der Auferstehung Christi rein metaphorisch gedeutet wird – als eine Metapher dafür, dass ein ausschließlich auf Seiendes, auf Organisation und Macht beschränktes Denken, wie erfolgreich auch immer es sonst sein mag, nie die Wahrheit erreicht. Nur in dieser Interpretation (und nur hier) macht Patočka überhaupt die Auferstehung zum Thema; wenn er später auf die Ostergeschichte zurückkommt, dann bricht die Erzählung beim Ereignis der Kreuzigung ab.

3. Leib, Gemeinschaft, Sprache, Welt (1968)[22]

3.1. Integration der Endlichkeit

Auch in diesem Text trägt die Auslegung Züge einer gewissen Mäßigung:[23] Die Wende wird zwar als *Erschütterung* bezeichnet, als *Brechung der Herrschaft*, der wir bisher unterstanden; aber während früher der Zustand vor dem Transzendieren als eine verborgene Herrschaft des Todes gedeutet wurde, wird er hier als weniger bedrohliche "Herrschaft der *Erde*" bezeichnet (Patočka 1998a, 160f.; die Ausdrücke "Tod" und "Sterblichkeit" kommen in der ganzen Auslegung je einmal vor). Wo früher ein neues Reich sich offenbaren und eine Gemeinschaft im Dienste des Seins eintreten sollte, wo die Metapher

---

[20] Zu Patočkas philosophischer Deutung dieser Perikope und christlicher Motive überhaupt siehe Ludger Hagedorns Auslegung (Hagedorn 2014, 358-361).

[21] Nur scheinbar widerspricht dem die Tatsache, dass in Patočkas Mythos – im Unterschied zum Evangelium – der göttliche Mensch nicht im Namen der religiösen Autorität, sondern im Namen der "Welt" vernichtet wird, im Namen des auf Seiendes und auf Manipulation, auf Macht und Organisierung gerichteten Selbstverständnisses. In einem frühen Text (Patočka 2007a, 22f.) sagt Patočka, auch Religion verstelle dem Menschen den Weg zum wahren Transzendieren, sie verschließe ihn in der Welt der manipulierbaren Dinge; die religiöse Autorität, die im Evangelium den Tod Jesu (mit-)verursacht hat, kann also für Patočka zu den "weltlichen" Kräften gehören, ein Instrument des Verschließens ins Gegebene und Gegenwärtige sein.

[22] Dem gedruckten tschechischen Text liegen Aufzeichnungen aus der gleichnamigen Vorlesung (1968 vorbereitet, im WS 1968/SS 1969 vorgelesen) zugrunde. Der Text ist bislang nur ins Englische übersetzt worden (siehe Patočka 1998a).

[23] Entstanden etwa zur gleichen Zeit wie 1991d und 1990b (vgl. oben) teilt dieser Text mit ihnen eine gewisse Mäßigung der sprachlichen Emphase, die im Vergleich mit den Studien von Mitte der 60er Jahre (1991a; 1991b) deutlich wird. Die gemäßigte Diktion verdankt er vielleicht auch seiner Bestimmung für eine breitere Hörerschaft.

der Auferstehung notwendig war, soll diesmal eine weniger dramatische *Integration* der Endlichkeit in die Existenz geschehen (Patočka 1998a, 151 u. 160). Und die Wende selbst wird nur implizit beschrieben durch einen Vergleich der Zustände vor und nach dieser (Patočka 1998a, 159f.).

Das Leben vor der Wende ist also nicht dadurch gekennzeichnet, dass es unbemerkt vom Tod beherrscht wird, sondern – wie in einigen frühen Texten Patočkas – durch seine Zerstreuung in eine Reihe von Augenblicken. In diesen nehmen wir ausschließlich die Befriedigung oder Nicht-Befriedigung unserer vitalen Bedürfnisse wahr (das Leben ist "in einzelne Weilen des Glücks und Unglücks zersplittert", die erste Lebensbewegung) oder konzentrieren uns auf einzelne Beschäftigungen (die zweite Lebensbewegung). Alle diese Einzelheiten, denen wir uns widmen, sind offensichtlich endlich, sie hindern uns jedoch daran, *unsere eigene* Endlichkeit, die Endlichkeit unseres Lebens im Ganzen zu sehen (Patočka 1998a, 159f.).

Besteht dann das Leben nach der Wende darin, dass alles, was bisher übersehen oder unterdrückt wurde, "auf gewisse Weise in das Leben wiederum integriert werden soll" (Patočka 1998a, 151; zum Folgenden daselbst), so muss die Wende selbst, die in dieser Vorlesung eigentlich nicht beschrieben wird, in der Annahme des Übersehenen bestehen, in unserem Bekenntnis zu dem bislang Verdeckten – zu unserer Endlichkeit, zu unserer Situiertheit, zu unserem Erdendasein und unserer Sterblichkeit.

3.2. Zerstreuung, Verschließung, Hingabe

In den oben erörterten Texten hat Patočka eine Möglichkeit des Scheiterns des Transzendierens angedeutet: damit ist *nicht* die Möglichkeit gemeint, dass der Appell zum Transzendieren nicht erhört wird, dass unsere Zerstreuung unter den Dingen in uns keine Beunruhigung hervorruft usw. Diese Möglichkeit ist zweifellos gegeben, hier ging es jedoch um "Selbstsuche und zuweilen auch Selbstfindung": auch wo Selbstsuche sich ereignet, bleibt die Selbstfindung eine Eventualität, die nicht eintreten muss, und Patočka meint genau diesen Fall – dass das Transzendieren geschieht, schließlich aber scheitert.

Die meisten Texte deuten den Zustand als die Selbstzerstreuung in die Dinge und in ihr Besorgen, als ein Unwissen über unsere Situation im Ganzen infolge unseres Haftenbleibens auf der Ebene des Gegenständlichen (wenn die Gegenständlichkeiten einen Vorrangsinhalt unseres Bewusstseins bilden oder wenn sie für uns ein Modell und einen Maßstab der Realität darstellen, wenn nicht – im Grenzfall – die einzige Gestalt der Realität überhaupt[24]). Auch dieser Text bildet hierin keine Ausnahme, darüber hinaus fragt er aber nach "der *Wurzel* der Herrschaft der Erde in uns" (Patočka 1998a, 160, hervorgehoben von J. F; vgl. Patočka 1998a, 160f.). Wir sehen, dass die Herrschaft der Erde nicht unbedingt ist, es ist nicht undenkbar, sie zu erschüttern oder zu brechen. Was ist also die Bedingung, die sie ermöglicht und mit deren Aufheben sie fällt?

Im Voraus sei erwähnt, dass im Rahmen der Vorlesung Patočkas dies eine Randbemerkung ist, die nur für Illustration auf zwei geschichtliche Gestalten des Versuchs hinweist, "die Herrschaft der Erde in uns zu brechen", es ist keine Auslegung der eigenen Position des Philosophen. Dennoch können wir diese Sache nicht außer Acht lassen: Patočka kommt noch im fünften der *Ketzerischen Essays* darauf zu sprechen, wenn auch nur kurz, und vor allem ist sie für unser Thema relevant, insbesondere für das Spezialproblem des Scheiterns des Transzendierens.

Die beiden Beispiele Patočkas sind die buddhistische und die christliche Lösung der Aufgabe, die Gebundenheit des Lebens an das zu überwinden, was es von innen beherrscht. Der Buddhismus strebt das Erlöschen der Bedürfnisse selbst an, des "Durstes", der uns an die Erde bindet. Mit dieser Lösung, sagt Patočka, wird wirklich "die Wurzel selbst betroffen", zugleich aber verschwindet mit ihr das Verstehen, die einzelne Existenz, welche die Welt versteht. Das Christentum will dagegen die "Selbstverschlossenheit des einzelnen Ichs" überwinden, sein vergebliches Getrenntsein, seine Richtung auf sich selbst, seinen "Entwurf der Welt auf sich selbst hin", aus dem erst die fehlerhafte Haltung zu den *Dingen* erfolgt. So könnte die Herrschaft der Erde gebrochen werden, ohne dass das Verstehen und die Welt ihre Gültigkeit verlieren.

Das würde aber heißen, dass die "Selbstverlorenheit", die durch das Transzendieren überschritten werden soll, *nicht* in der Zerstreuung in die Dinge besteht, sondern in dieser Selbstverschlossenheit, in der Verkrümmung in sich selbst. Diese ist sicher mit der Zerstreuung kompatibel, keineswegs aber identisch, noch zwangsläufig verbunden: denn selbst die Freiheit eines Weisen, der die Zerstreuung überwunden hat, kann als "dämonisch" erscheinen, als Ausdruck eines fehlerhaften Willens zur Trennung und Verselbstständigung; das Gespräch der Seele mit sich selbst, ein vorzüglicher Weg Platons zur Einsicht des Guten, kann für die Seele gefährlich sein; worum es geht, ist die Überwindung der Selbstverschlossenheit, die selbstvergessene Liebe (Patočka 2010, 128). Das Transzendieren kann also nicht nur dadurch scheitern, dass es vom Wege abkommt oder vorzeitig stehenbleibt (dies waren die von Patočka kritisierten Fälle, wenn das Hinausschreiten über die Ebene

---

[24] Letzteres ist der Kernpunkt seiner Kritik am logischen Positivismus und Marxismus (vgl. Patočka 1988).

des Gegenständlichen wiederum bei einer Gegenständlichkeit landet), sondern dadurch, dass es gleich am Anfang sein Woher falsch identifiziert hat; dass die Bindung an Gegenständliches, die "Herrschaft der Erde", von der sich die Existenz befreit hat, nur ein Symptom der wahren Selbstverlorenheit war – der Selbstverschlossenheit, die selbst nach solcher Befreiung bestehen bleibt.

Wie gesagt, wird die christliche Lösung nur erwähnt als ein geschichtliches Beispiel und im Text der Vorlesung deutet nichts darauf hin, dass Patočka sich mit ihr identifiziert; seine oben angeführte Auslegung über die Hingabe an den Anderen könnte jedoch ohne weiteres ihre logische Fortsetzung darstellen.

Und im erhaltenen *Konzept* der Vorlesung ist es wirklich so: eine kurze Skizze der christlichen Auffassung der Erschütterung geht ansatzlos in eine (ebenso bündige) Auslegung des Transzendierens durch die Selbsthingabe über (Patočka 1995, 113). In der Vorlesung selbst (und unseres Wissens nach auch sonst bei Patočka) wird dieser Zusammenhang nicht explizit gemacht.[25] Könnten wir aber nicht vermuten, dass die "christliche" Auffassung – die Selbstverschlossenheit als das eigentlich zu Überschreitende – bereits in der früheren Auslegung der Hingabe stillschweigend wirksam war?[26]

Zusammenfassend kann man sagen: In der gewählten Textgruppe wird der Prozess des Transzendierens nicht immer in der gleichen Radikalität aufgefasst und nicht immer auf seine letzten Wurzeln hin befragt. Jedes Mal wird er aber als ein aktives Handeln geschildert, für das wir uns auf der Ebene einer nicht-objektivierenden Selbsthabe und Freiheit entscheiden; als ein nicht immer erfolgreicher Versuch, sich von der Zerstreuung und Selbstverlorenheit unter den Dingen zu befreien, sich unserer Stellung im Ganzen der Wirklichkeit bewusst zu werden und dementsprechend zu handeln.

Wir teilen nicht die These Patočkas, in dieser Konfrontation mit dem Ganzen dominiere die Zukunft über die anderen Zeitdimensionen; mit ihm jedoch sehen wir ein, dass zu dieser Konfrontation wesentlich auch die das Funktionale übersteigende Beziehung zum Anderen gehört – in der Gestalt des Kampfes und der Hingabe.

Sind wir bereit, in diesem Kampfe unabhängig von der bloßen Notwendigkeit der Lebenserhaltung zu handeln – halten wir also der "absoluten Bedrohung" stand –, so zeigen wir, dass wir uns nicht an die das Überleben sichernden Dinge der Welt klammern müssen; es werden damit metaphorisch Erde und Himmel in Frage gestellt und das Höhere, das

---

[25] Wiederum in einem ideengeschichtlichen Kontext hat Patočka die christliche Lösung – fast gleichzeitig mit der hier erörterten Vorlesung – genauer beschrieben (siehe Patočka 1987, 177 u. 184).
[26] Nach Ludger Hagedorn spielt dieser Gedanke in Patočka's Œuvre sogar eine noch weit wichtigere Rolle, als die von uns verfolgten Texte andeuten (siehe Hagedorn 2011, 258f.).

mehr *ist* als das Seiende, kann erscheinen. Auf diese Weise erscheint auch unser Leben nicht als bloß innerweltlich, sondern in diesem spezfischen Sinne als "un-endlich".

Dr. Jan Frei, Jan Patočka Archive, Center for Theoretical Study
of Charles University and the Czech Academy of Sciences, frei[at]cts.cuni.cz

Literaturangaben

Caputo, John D. and Scanlon, Michael J. (eds.). *Transcendence and Beyond. A Postmodern Inquiry.* Bloomington: Indiana University Press 2007.

Hagedorn, Ludger. "Beyond Myth and Enlightenment. On Religion in Patočka's Thought", in Ivan Chvatík and Erika Abrams (eds.). *Jan Patočka and the Heritage of Phenomenology.* Dordrecht-Heidelberg-London-New York: Springer 2011. 245-261.

Hagedorn, Ludger. "Kenosis. Die philosophische Anverwandlung eines christlichen Motivs bei Jan Patočka", in Staudigl, Michael und Christian Sternad (Hrsg.). *Figuren der Transzendenz. Transformationen eines phänomenologischen Grundbegriffs.* Würzburg: Königshausen-Neumann 2014. 349-366

Heidegger, Martin. "Vom Wesen des Grundes", in ders. *Wegmarken.* Frankfurt am Main: Vittorio Klostermann, 1976. 123-175

Karfík, Filip. *Unendlichwerden durch die Endlichkeit.* Würzburg: Königshausen & Neumann, 2008

Kouba, Pavel. "Le problème du troisième mouvement. En marge de la conception patočkienne de l'existence", in Renaud Barbaras (ed.). *Jan Patočka. Phénoménologie asubjective et existence*, Paris et Milano: Mimesis, 2007. 183-204.

Kouba, Petr. *Geistige Störung als Phänomen.* Würzburg: Königshausen & Neumann, 2012.

Patočka, Jan. "Existe-t-il un canon définitif de la vie philosophique?", in Raymond Bayer (ed.), *Travaux du IXe Congrès international de philosophie*, Vol. 10. Paris: Hermann, 1937. 186-189

Patočka, Jan. "Comenius und die offene Seele", in ders. *Kunst und Zeit. Kulturphilosophische Schriften.* Stuttgart: Klett-Cotta, 1987. 175-190.

Patočka, Jan. "Negativer Platonismus", in ders. *Ketzerische Essais zur Philosophie der Geschichte und ergänzende Schriften.* Stuttgart: Klett-Cotta, 1988. 389–431.

Patočka, Jan. "Die Natürliche Welt als philosophisches Problem", in ders. *Die Natürliche Welt als philosophisches Problem. Phänomenologische Schriften I*, Stuttgart: Klett-Cotta, 1990. 23-179 (=1990a)

Patočka, Jan. "Nachwort des Autors zur tschechischen Neuausgabe", in ders. *Die Natürliche Welt als philosophisches Problem. Phänomenologische Schriften I*, Stuttgart: Klett-Cotta, 1990. 181-269 (=1990b)

Patočka, Jan. "Zur Vorgeschichte der Wissenschaft von der Bewegung: Welt, Erde, Himmel und die Bewegung des menschlichen Lebens", in ders. *Die Bewegung der menschlichen Existenz. Phänomenologische Schriften II.* Stuttgart: Klett-Cotta, 1991. 132-143. (=1991a)

Patočka, Jan. "Natürliche Welt und Phänomenologie", in ders. *Die Bewegung der menschlichen Existenz. Phänomenologische Schriften II.* Stuttgart: Klett-Cotta, 1991. 185-229. (=1991b)

Patočka, Jan. "Der Raum und seine Problematik", in ders. *Die Bewegung der menschlichen Existenz. Phänomenologische Schriften II.* Stuttgart: Klett-Cotta, 1991. 63-131. (=1991c)

Patočka, Jan. "Was ist Existenz?", in ders. *Die Bewegung der menschlichen Existenz. Phänomenologische Schriften II*, Stuttgart: Klett-Cotta, 1991. 230-256. (=1991d)

Patočka, Jan. "[Leçons sur la corporéité]", in idem. *Papiers phénoménologiques.* Grenoble: Millon, 1995. 53-116.

Patočka, Jan. *Body, Community, Language, World.* Chicago-La Salle: Open Court, 1998. (=1998a)

Patočka, Jan. "Intellektuelle und Opposition", in *Report of the Center for Theoretical Study* 98, Nr. 07 (1998): 11-21 (=1998b)

Patočka, Jan. "Leben im Gleichgewicht, Leben in der Amplitude", in Hagedorn, Ludger und Hans Rainer Sepp (Hrsg.). *Jan Patočka. Texte – Dokumente – Bibliographie.* München /Freiburg: Hans Alber Verlag, 1999. 91-102

Patočka, Jan. *Some Comments Concerning the Extramundane and Mundane Position of Philosophy*, in idem. *Living in Problematicity.* Praha: OIKOYMENH, 2007. 18-28 (=2007a)

Patočka, Jan. "Das Innere und der Geist", in *Studia Phaenomenologica*, Vol. VII (2007): 50-68. (=2007b)

Patočka, Jan. *Ketzerische Essays zur Philosophie der Geschichte*, Berlin: Suhrkamp, 2010.

Patočka, Jan. "Eternité et historicité", in Jan Patočka. *Eternité et historicité*, Lagrasse: Verdier, 2011. 25-153.

Patočka, Jan. "Studie k pojmu světa", in Jan Patočka. *Fenomenologické spisy* III/1. Praha: OIKOYMENH, 2014. 70-173.

Staudigl, Michael und Christian Sternad (Hrsg.). *Figuren der Transzendenz. Transformationen eines phänomenologischen Grundbegriffs*, Würzburg: Königshausen & Neumann, 2014.

JASON ALVIS (Vienna)
"Scum of the Earth": Patočka, Atonement, and Waste

Abstract

Sacrifice, solidarity, and social decadence were essential themes not only for Patočka's philosophical work, but also for his personal life. In the "Varna Lecture" sacrifice is characterized uniquely as the privation of a clear telos, *as counter-escapist, and as sutured to a comportment of finite life that is non-causal and non-purposive. In his* Heretical Essays *a similar hope is expressed to extract meaningfulness from use-value, and to deploy a Socratic and Christian "Care for the Soul" that can counteract the decadences of our age. These interests and developments of the practice and notion of sacrifice point to Patočka's* double-hereticism, *both of the post-industrial age of technological advancement, and of what had become the unthought-through (and therefore taken for granted) of the Christian tradition. In both senses, his theory of sacrifice is not unlike that of St. Paul, who saw the necessity of counter-acting the decadence and pompousness of the Corinthians by calling them to become "scum of the earth."*

This helps reveal how sacrifice presumes, in general, an operative notion of waste, and this paper seeks to lend further understanding to the relation between solidarity and sacrifice by developing, from out of Patočka's own work, precisely how waste figures prominently in such a relation. Waste may be refused by merit of being deemed to have no value; waste can mark a layer of expenditure of using "something up" in a way that overlooks its societal surplus; and waste could depict whatever is, like a wasteland, uncultivable and barren. Waste then is employed in the essay as a heuristic tool for understanding how the normalization of the relation between solidarity and sacrifice is in need of being inverted, and how this inversion has consequences also for how solidarity can be considered in relation to atonement.

Keywords: Patočka, phenomenology, atonement, waste, heretiticism

1. Introduction

"Wasteland"
April is the cruelest month, breeding
Lilacs out of the dead land, mixing
Memory and desire, stirring
Dull roots with spring rain.
T.S. Eliot, 1922

Atonement is at-one-ment. What at first seems like banal word play indeed remains rooted in an etymology – *Atonen,* to be at-one (perhaps modeled on the Latin *adunare,* to unite), combines *ad* with *unum,* and (post 1300) concerns the melding of two parties into a unique social accord (*adunare*). Atonement eventually (from early 1500) depicted a condition or series of actions that resulted in fraternity, and in a more theological sense (from early 1600) became a matter of re-union or reconciliation after humankind's great wrongs due to a propitiation of the offended God.

One underlying preunderstanding that goes along with any understanding of atonement is that in order for any such reunion to occur, something must be laid to waste or sacrificed. The Hebrew *korban* is used in the Old Testament for sacrifice, and expresses the idea of an approaching or "bringing near" to a place of interaction with God in the temple – likely at an alter – via a ritual of "purification." In the Book of Isaiah the loss of meaning of the sacrificial slaughtering of animals is deeply bemoaned since atonement (*Zebah*) had become taken for granted, which led to a particular kind of political disorder the messiah-to-come eventually would restore. In the New Testament a radical shift is made in an understanding of atonement through shifting to the use of the word "ransom" (ἱλάσκομαι *hilaskomai*) – an atoning, propitiating, and forgiving sacrifice that makes for reconciliation of social bonds (Καταλλαγή, *katallagé*). Ransom covered the debt owed to God for contributing to evil[1] as Christ "came to serve, and give his life as a ransom for many." (Mark 10:45).[2] Christ's sacrifice amounted to the greatest waste or *expenditure* ever possible: God Godself (the irreducibly highest of values ever to be evaluated) is discarded vehemently from the social sphere. Early Christians thus stopped performing the tradition of animal sacrifice because they deemed it no longer necessary for solidarity and atonement (a scandal to the prevalent religious traditions).[3] The end of scapegoating is one thing that makes Christianity "the religion of the egress from religion." (Gauchet 1999, 40)

One could venture to suggest that the 20th century marks the return of forms of a religionless scapegoating – to destroy one individual for socio-economic grounds – but in a more effervescent, implicit, and culturally-embedded form. In every attempt to be no longer Christian, global capital has reinstituted scapegoating in a way that its mechanisms seek the benefit of its function while discarding the husk of religion and its hopes of sacrifice to strengthen social bonds. Although such a theory never was introduced by Jan Patočka,

---

[1] Compare here Isaiah 53:10 with Mark 10:45, especially the use of "in the place of many." See also Isaiah 43:3 for this understanding of "ransom" or *kÿper* in the context of other nations being given in exchange for Israel (also see Kim, 1983, 57).

[2] Cf. Hebrews 2:17: "For this reason [Jesus] had to be made like his brothers in every way, in order that...he might make atonement [*hilaskesthai*] for the sins of the people." Then in Romans 3:25, Paul claimed: "God presented him as a sacrifice of atonement, through faith in his blood." The verbs "propitiate" or "atone," *hilasterion*, are used by the apostle John, referencing Christ's death as an *hilasmos* (I John 2:2, and 4:10).

[3] For example, the rituals of Christianity – baptism and communion, e.g. – replace animal and scapegoating sacrifices. Paul claimed we are to no longer sacrifice in these ways. Jesus "cleansing of the temple" in the gospel of John was an act that began the process of reinstituting solidarity and communion.

anyone familiar with his work would not find it too surprising, as the interplay between sacrifice, solidarity, and a critique of modern European society remained essential for his work. Patočka enacted a kind of *double-hereticism*: First, he was a "heretic" of modern, industrial life in part because he drew attention to how society had taken for granted the role of sacrifice and taking-the-place-of-another. Patočka enacted an understanding of sacrifice that amounted to a paradoxical, non-economic, non-utilitarian, and counter-utopian vision of becoming a reject in a time of crisis instantiated by a certain industrialization of humankind. As a Czech dissident and original signatory of the Charter 77 civil rights movement in the 70's, his life was caught in the firefights of the post-world war amidst civil unrest and the struggle for liberation from Soviet occupation, and this first hereticism contributed to his becoming a philosopher not only *in a time* of crisis, but *of* crisis itself.

Second, he also was a "heretic" of the Christian tradition: here the theme of sacrifice again became a dominant one because he witnessed the radical attempt in the Czech Republic to extract Catholicism from its culture. In the 1940's he furnished a genealogy of this shift taking place in Europe more broadly (which he traced back to 15th century; c.f. Patočka 2006, 77), and ultimately concluded that there still remain "unthought-through" aspects of Christianity dispossessed of its religion "after the end of Christianity," with "sacrifice" figuring prominently among those forms of life in need of being thought-through (Hagedorn 2015, 10). In this sense he was a heretic of Christianity, for what called itself "Christian" had forgotten its core intelligibility – sacrifice. In the "Varna Lectures" Christian sacrifice is characterized as the privation of a clear *telos*, as in need of being distinguished from escapism, and as an experience in which the sacrifice is sutured to the sacrificee's mode of being. Christian sacrifice teaches that willing sacrificees care about a certain comportment of finite life itself that is non-causal, non-deterministic, and auto-resistant to playing by the rules of the industrial age in which we find ourselves still today.

These two, not so easily distinguishable hereticisms (of modern industrial life, and of the Christian tradition) coalesce perfectly in his two major tasks of *The Heretical Essays* – both to develop a new interpretation of "history" via a necessary distinction between purposelessness and meaningfulness, and to deploy a simultaneously Socratic and Christian "Care for the Soul" with the hopes of counteracting the societal pressures of decadence; pressures that have left us all placated and powerless to alter our own course in history. It is in this sense of being counter-decadent that his work is stunningly reminiscent of St. Paul's condemnation of the pompous and splintered Corinthians in needed of becoming the "scum of the earth" (I Cor. 4:13). They were called to become *peripsēma* (περίψημα,) – a scum that atones; an "offscouring" of dregs or filth by merit of being used-up or becoming a "waste" or rejection. This word *peripsēma* (like the grotesque remains of an exfoliation or shave) is used only once in the New Testament, and in this case points to the necessity of an *expiatory* sacrifice that, in its counter-decadence, is the core of atonement.

The goal of the remainder of this paper first is to introduce in greater detail Patočka's doubly-heretical notion of sacrifice, and second, to engage the notion of "waste" as a heuristic tool for contextualizing the "unthought" space between Christian sacrifice and solidarity today, in an age when western society thinks itself to have pulled the fish-hook of religion from its mouth. Despite any attempt to discard it, there is always a running theory of (at least quasi-religious) atonement and sacrifice that enervates a given society, and "waste" may help understand that relationship. Waste has varied definitions, as what is unused, unproductive, or unwelcomed and therefore cast from oneself or society. Traced to its Latin origination in *Vastus,* it concerns what is refused by merit of being deemed of no value, may mark a layer of expenditure of being-used-up, or may depict whatever is, like a *vast* wasteland, an uncultivable, barren, and open expanse.[4] Waste, at least from a more phenomenological interpretation, is a product of one's activity; as deemed *the-out-of-place* (c.f. Douglas 1966).

2. Patočka's Notion of Sacrifice in the Varna Lectures and Heretical Essays

2.1. Sacrifice and Modern Decadence

It is in regards to the overcoming of a kind of Christian abyssal devastation of sacrifice through which I want to interpret Patočka's theory of sacrifice in the Varna lectures. Many others (Hagedorn, Evink, Dodd, et. al.) have described in great detail the overall thrust of Patočka's notion of sacrifice, so reflection here will be limited and focused. Essential, it seems, is the way the Varna lectures end: "our imprisoned age must face itself," and sacrifice, a radical Christian sacrifice is *one key* to that. The epic of sacrifice so easily can be reduced to a hidden/implicit expectation within a given society. Today for example, industrial advancements have drawn so many to sacrifice themselves in everyday life, whether through enframement (Heidegger), computerization (Latour) machination (Lyotard), or technologization (Anders). Yet in every case, as each of the aforementioned thinkers attest, these activities are not germane to the genuine flourishing of human life, but

---

[4] "To waste away" is a temporal means of placating boredom in times of leisure. A "wasteland" is a barren place of death, lacking in vitality. "Wastes" are refuse and garbage often too emotionally offensive even to discuss. *Vastus* also can refer to *vaste* (Middle French, post 1500's), which characterizes what is immense, desolate, and unoccupied. The English word "De-vast-ation" unites these terms. Another word that is of etymological relation is effuse. From 1520's the Latin past participle adjective of *effuses* points to what is both "poured out" and to be vast, extensive, and broad".

rather benefit its proxy of technological apparatuses. These aspects of industrial life today embody empty, self-fulfilling, and vague themes of progress that shroud their most true functions, which are detrimental to the human good. It is in a similar vein that Patočka bemoans how sacrifice no longer is powerful in our time, and that whenever sacrifice does become a theme of engagement, it ends up economized in terms of resources. We once again succumb to retreating into technological language. Technology becomes the means by which the enlightenment of man gets overly conceived, as well as a bad-faith sublimation in response to the social-self reproach exacted via sacrifices and victims in waging wars.

A *true* understanding of sacrifice however, cannot be calculated in terms of power, is inherently paradoxical, and entails the radical experience of gain-via-loss in an inversion of power relations that involves a turning-away from the unproblematicity of "ordinary everydayness." Patočka endorses a particular form of Christian sacrifice as it differs from other religions of power, kingship, and authority-making. This kind of sacrifice is inherently social, in that neither no one person can embody it, nor one meaning underwrite it's motivity. Yet his theorization of Christian sacrifice is anti-telic in a way that also is anti-escapist, suturing the sacrificee to its lived, ontological modality. Christian sacrifice thus teaches that willing sacrificees care about a certain comportment of *finite life* itself that is non-causal, non-deterministic, and resistant to playing by the aforementioned rules of technological advancement. Finally, while some think Patočka does not draw sharp distinctions between "victims" and "voluntary sacrifices" (as neither the Czech *Obět,* nor the German *Opfer* make such differentiation), his work seems to necessitate a distinction, unabashedly valorizing the latter; the willing, volitional choice to sacrifice.

2.2. The Role of History

Patočka's best-known work *The Heretical Essays in the Philosophy of History* was an application of his dissident spirit to the core thought patterns of modern life in part responsible for the many atrocities of the 20th century. This work challenged many of the prevailing and accepted contradictions of his generation and culture in regards to history, such as the contradiction that history determines the past according to which we are inextricably bound to operate, yet that its annals are composed of the detailed descriptions of the acts of free subjects. He sought to arrive at a synthesis that honors both of these driving conceptions in order to allow social actors to be original/singular, yet in a way that retains social meaning on a macro-institutional level. Within a perhaps more phenomenological analysis, history is a matter of self-construal: histories, traditions, and narratives are in constant upheaval within consciousness, and trying to rely on a particular tradition or event is like "trying to hold on to the waves in a shipwreck." It is precisely this view of history that leads Patočka, in his 1952 essay "Time, Myth, and Faith" (Patočka 2015), to conclude that a *true* and free faith does not cling to an objective-relative meaning. The antinomy that generally goes unrecognized is that those who cling to myths and traditions seek with all of their energy a "pure origin", and in fact are clinging to but historically relativized meanings more in accord with a near-hedonistic escapism than with the teachings of Christ. Faith is opposed to such escapism, as the *very idea* of God has called the faithful *to realize* history, not simply be passive *subjects to* its many developments.

But this understanding of becoming radical shapers of history is a far cry from a call to become its superhero. Patočka's double-hereticism concerns the attempted reformation of both a secularized socialism, and a trenchant, Czech, cultural Christianity via a new understanding of myth as history itself. A flawed relation with history, in many respects, is at the core of the modern mind. Shaped against the backdrop of Karl Löwith's critique of teleological history in general and Christian eschatology in particular (Löwith 1957; cf. Hagedorn 2015), Patočka-the-phenomenologist understood how easily humans operate with the tendency to make the exception the rule; to integrate the truly outstanding into the naturalness of everyday life irrespective of such escapist views. Comparable to Arendt's view, the everyday absorbs how human acts are in fact given their purpose (not the other way around). Patočka remained disheartened by the fact that the majority of people's lives are spent either concerning themselves with their survival, or with the *forms* of everyday function that they have learned during this very survival process. For example, technology becomes an end in itself; work becomes a pleasure that fulfills our "orgiastic" drives for excitement; the *mysterium tremendum* is limited to the enchantment this world is capable of furnishing. The original synthesis of a new meaning of history at which Patočka sought to arrive ran counter to the modern insistence upon conflict and competition. His replacement or "heretical" understanding of history called upon, in the face of provocation, the revivification of a form of Christian "sacrifice" that grew from the solidarity of "the shaken" – those truly responsible persons who never forget the events that have shaped their lives, and therefore might respond to any crises that may befall them.

In addition to the profound and original meaning of Christian sacrifice, then, is the call to overcome the world. History only *is made* – it is not merely by observing or "knowing" (these highly enlightened means of more passive transcendental engagement) the truth, but rather by struggling for an inner historicity of the self. Christianity allows us not to be mere subjects of history, bound to the "information" given to its adherents from tradition and myth.[5] The present, decadent, "Post-Christian" era runs antithetical to what Patočka fashioned to be a synthetic, Christian-Socratic "care for the soul," which is a taking of "orgiastic" responsibility for one's own *Bildung* via radical individualization. If Christ has set one free, then this freeing perhaps is most importantly a freeing from political, cultural, and social imaginaries that seek to blackmail and entrap us. This freedom is from the metaphysical matrices (not unlike Adorno's "substitute images of the divine") that seek to govern every thought away from true care and responsibility via myth and the history of origination.

This furnishes an essential backdrop for a very particular observation about Christian life:

> the overcoming of everydayness assumes the form of the care for the salvation of the soul which won itself in a moral transformation, in the turn in the face of death and death eternal; which lives in anxiety and hope inextricably intertwined, which trembles in the knowledge of its sin and with its whole being offers itself in the sacrifice of penance. (Patočka 1996, 108)

Christianity's yet-to-be-thought and *unsurpassed* greatness is its propensity as a resource to overcome everydayness by promoting the caring about one's salvation from imminent death. This is enacted and engaged not by directly caring *for* oneself, but by sacrificing oneself in a way that the self-sacrifice in fact amounts to the soul's getting cared for.

3. Deepening a Theory of Waste via Patočka's Heretical Essays

This leads to the potential to exfoliate from Patočka's work some deeper reflection on the notion of waste, and this will be accomplished through four topoi.

3.1. History and Waste

A first reflection on waste points to a particular kind of insignificance one is called to attain in the act of sacrifice. The will to be significant is to be abandoned in the act, and the life of the truly Christian sacrifice, today, tends to be rejected automatically for it gets misunderstood (like religion in general) as insignificant. Religion often is deemed unimportant at worse, or it gets relegated to a private option at best, thus indirectly reinstituting its lack of importance. It is in this context that a reflection on "waste" might be instructive:

---

[5] See also Joas (2014) who questions this notion of optional, free-choice faith, which has set-off occidental reason on its individualistic, secular trajectories. Contemporary Christianity consequentially has led to a stark, often extreme individualization of belief, which in its secularized form is popularized according to petit-freedoms or, as Peter Sloterdijk once called them, "whims."

waste not only as what is passionately and willfully rejected, but also what is quietly dismissed to have no value, significance, or meaningful intelligibility. Even among the self-proclaimed "religious," the non-implicit and non-integrative conception of religious life leaves it in a precarious situation that leads to at least two possible outcomes: either it becomes insignificant (as just described) or it gets commandeered as an instrument. For example, even though Habermas quite recently has called for a "post-secular" society, the conception of religion within such a schema can amount to a pragmatic instrumentalization of religion as a tool for creating humans more moral. This inadvertently runs the risk of leaving religion as a second-order pawn to any purposive, social good.

Indeed, the contemporary rejections of Christianity today in this so-called "post-secular age" are far more inconspicuous and subtle, which makes such rejections in fact all the more dangerous: Christianity no longer is seen as being anything unique or of value on its own terms, but instead, in being instrumentalized, can but one tactic in achieving a purported social/political/moral *telos*. In other words, a post-secular acceptance of religion and the religious (so long as it and they are not "fanatics," of course) in contemporary society fact is a kind of rejection; namely, because it precludes from the very beginning the possibiliyt that it operates with a differential that makes any "real" difference on its own. In what seems to be a shift from secular to post-secular also comes a shift from outright rejection to implicit rejection. To channel Patočka here, such interpretations of religious life can be counteracted only when a radical sacrifice initiates a new selflessness whereby one is aligned with what has become in a given society insignificance or waste itself. "Christianities" must not succumb to their own instrumentalization towards a utopic vision; otherwise the sacrificing of oneself for another and the solidarity it creates does not get unrealized.

3.2. Solidarity with Meaninglessness

A second aspect of Patočka's *Heretical Essays* relevant to interpreting waste is the recognition that what is found meaningless is *precisely* that according to which the highest degree of intelligibility is accorded. For Patočka, "Human acts can be purposeless, yet be meaningful." (Patočka 1996, 54). Following Heidegger, the activity of making-sense or making-intelligible is a core human endeavor and the produced intelligibilities of such activity are irreducible to purposiveness. This is a counter-industrial meaningfulness, sense, or intelligibility. Contrariwise, within our present age, the societies in which we gain our present forms of meaning-making have led not only to a social understanding of how "purpose is causality raised up to the region of the meaningful..."; that is, to how meaningfulness has been reduced to purposiveness, but also to how *purpose itself* has become the ultimate meaning that in fact is incredibly *purposeless*! The result being that there is no purpose to purpose itself, yet the insistence (or obsession) with purposefulness today is affixed with a maximum meaningfulness. A certain determinism has found a social concubine in the synthesis between purpose and technology, which no longer only is a means, but has become an end in itself.

One problem here is that this kind of *telos-obsessed* thinking disregards and auto-rejects whatever is deemed to have *no purpose*. Its seeming inverse claim, which may amount to a more probing insight, reveals how we operate with the tendency to give the purposeful an ultimate meaningfulness in and of itself. And what is meaningful, we most always conclude, deserves attention, energy, and perhaps even adoration. In "man's search for meaning" (to reappropriate Frankl) one arrives at purpose itself, which in a decadent society often unknowingly gets raised to the status of a "value" and therefore ushered into the company of truth, beauty, or justice. As Patočka concludes, values are not purposes or goals, but rather indicative of the meaningfulness of what is formulated as "autonomous qualities," according to which we live as if they were universal (Patočka 1996, 55). We are the bestowers of meanings on things and – perhaps most importantly – it remains the task for man to be involved poetically in "bestowing meaning on the meaningless." (Patočka 1996, 57).

3.3. Meaninglessness and Waste

In another sense, meaninglessness is what presents itself as intelligible, yet is rejected on the grounds that it has no place in conscious life and is not deserving *attention*. Whatever is meaningless slips through our entirely "normalized" meaning-given conceptualizations of the world. This is entirely consistent with how Patočka ends his Varna lectures, claiming that "our imprisoned age must face itself" and that it now will take a radical Christian sacrifice to do so. Patočka bemoans how sacrifice is no longer powerful in our time, and that whenever we do recognize sacrifice it ends up economized in terms of resources (Patočka 2015, 20). The notion of sacrifice as such ends up getting lost once again in a technical and functional understanding of being.

Instead, sacrifice should be understood as precisely that which challenges these calculations and functions with a different form of life.[6] In a more prescriptive element, the Christian life lived (according to Paul's mandate to being scum of the earth) should involve

---

[6] For Patočka, today we flee from sacrifice and "into a technical understanding of being which promises to exclude this experience and for which there exists nothing like a sacrifice, only utilization of resources" and "Thus sacrifice represents a persistent presence of something that does not appear in the calculations of the technological world." (Patočka 1989, 337)

one's closer association not simply with the meaningless, but also those actions, places, and aspects of life that serve no utilitarian purpose in life whatsoever, and therefore are capable of being subversive in their enactment of *meaninglessness*. Here again an understanding of waste can help draw attention to the essential role the making-intelligible-of-meaninglessness might play.

3.4. The Care for the Soul

A final aspect of Patočka's work that bears significance for conceiving the role of waste within sacrifice is his version of the "Care for the Soul." To care for the soul is to reject any essentialist, never-differentiating *information* that hides under the guises of truth in myth, which amounts to *adequatio* or correctness. Instead, caring is born in an event to which one responds (e.g, St Paul's miraculous blindness and healing) by being "shaken" in a way that is powerful enough to shift the actor from being merely a passive observer and subject of history's movements, to becoming an alterer of them through a never-ending and dynamic inquiry and practice (Patočka 1989, 82).[7] These inquiries and practices enact a direct *devaluation* of what the world claims to value. They result in counter-cultural movements against what humans presuppose to be – by nature undebatably – good. These values range from climbing social ladders to attain better jobs, to keeping quiet and living unproblematically in a corrupt social state.

The care for the soul always entails a devaluing of how worth typically is attained, and it is in these regards that Christianity especially is instructive as the means of "devaluation of this world by a 'true' world, of life [and] will..." (Patočka 1996, 97) To devalue is to become subsequently rejected by the worlds' forms of decadence that enable what a society thinks to be a smooth, effortless, unproblematic, and carefree functioning. Patočka prophesied what he perceived to be a nascent and growing threat in Europe beginning in the 60's – we have begun a social "addiction to things" that only ends in "a decadent life, a life addicted to what is inhuman by its very nature." (Patočka 1996, 113, 97) Decadence goes hand-in-glove with increasing reliance upon the non-human. Instead, Christian life sutures the "care of the soul" to *melete Thanatou*, "care of death," which more accurately amounts to

---

[7] Regarding the constant movement of such caring especially under the Greek conception. Patočka also claimed that the soul "is the origin of movement, it can only be understood in movement. The movement of the soul in its most proper sense of the world is precisely *care for its very self*." (Patočka 2002, 124) Continuing, "The proper, positive care of the soul is somehow the concluding of something that is sketched into the nature of the soul, but is not always explicitly captured." (ibid.; see also Findlay, 2002)

"care of life." (Patočka 1996, 105) Under Patočka's theorization, this care of death/life/soul can only result in one's becoming a sacrifice for the lives of other's.

In particular, the Greek care for the soul is enriched by Christianity's adding to it an infinite, non-decadent care that at its core most simply *seeks to know what it does more fully*:

> the soul is by nature wholly incommensurate with all eternal being, that this nature has to do with its care for its own being in which, unlike all other existents, it is infinitely interested; and that an essential part of its composition is responsibility, that is, the possibility of choice and, in this choosing, of arriving at its own self – the idea that the soul is nothing present before, only afterwards, that it is historical in all its being and only as such escapes decadence. By virtue of this foundation in the abysmal deepening of the soul, Christianity remains thus far the greatest, unsurpassed but also unthought-through human outreach that enabled humans to struggle against decadence." (Patočka 1996, 108).

As it enriches the care for the soul via a radical sacrifice of the self, Christian life can slow down the grinding wheels of history in a way unique from other religious traditions.[8] As he put it in *Plato and Europe*, a Christian care of the soul is "disengaged from...Greek dialectic" and this has consequences for how it understands authority and acts in relation to dogmas that "are not considered as something to be accepted blindly" although "these dogmata have meaning." (Patočka 2002, 129) For Patočka Christian faith is the last hold-out in the struggle against social, political, and cultural decadence, but only in its renewed sense of sacrifice, that irreducible core of Christian life.

Since the care for the soul occurs paradoxically by abandoning self-interests, it is a care for the death and therefore life of others that motivates acts that help lift individuals from decadence. Decadent are those of us out of touch with our innermost *understanding* of the distinctions between functions, values, and meanings. And by merit of being distracted by that which has captured and held in stasis our "orgiastic" search for the *mysterium tremendum*, we remain trapped in a simultaneously kenotic and consumptive relation with the *forms* of utility themselves. Care for the soul offers a unique freedom from the authority of the historically evolved, social norms that order our lives, which tend to be marked by an economically oriented obsession with function. Means of overcoming such obsessions entails forms of relation whereby one is more attuned to what escapes the oversight of function, whatever within such a system is deemed an insignificant and meaningless waste.

---

[8] It is in this context that Hagedorn argues for how Derrida drew from Patočka in these regards in claiming that Europe must be emancipated from Athens and Rome in order to reach its full potential. Such a task can be accomplished only by being "fully Christian." (Hagedorn, 2015)

4. Waste and Sacrifice

It now becomes possible, via further insights from Patočka's Varna Lectures, to integrate more carefully the intelligibility of the role of waste in the relations between sacrifice and solidarity today. While there are many paths one could take in such an effort, there are three conceptual notions that I find most convincing when thinking about waste alongside Patočka's Varna lectures. Waste in this case can be thought and distinguished according to *Vastus'* three pronged distinction: devastation, expenditure, and wasted.

4.1. Devastation

Once a sacrifice occurs, it comes with a radical experience of mourning what has been lost. What could have been can be no more, and the future of possibility in this sense is wasted. If it is the case that, as Patočka suggests, "Those who thus sacrifice themselves do not avoid finitude, nor do they seek admiration on that account...", (Patočka 338, 1989) then it also remains true that one must go through finitude, and the abysmal reality that it would entail without reliance upon any escapist narrative (Re: Löwith). Christ on the cross was estranged from union with neither man nor God. This lonely devastation is given voice in the sense of abandonment: Christ's "Father, why have you forsaken me?" marks the experience of a certain vastness and emptiness, which gets expressed in terms of loneliness.

This points to how the sacrificee's life is one of a kind of devastation. The sacrificee does not come to expect a miraculous redemption in the act of sacrificing, or a form of "pay back" that would oblige a powerful God to bless the willing sacrificee. True sacrifice counteracts the hope to tap-into divine power for its own good, and to bring "this power under an obligation."[9] The lack of full divine activity for what at the time the sacrificee thinks to be good for him results in a kind of devastation of that for which a sacrificee somewhat naturally yearns – an exchange of goods for services. The sacrifice must be prevented from falling into economy by lacking a "return gift" or payment that would make for even a kind of enjoyment of the sacrifice. This could threaten to make for an easy sacrifice, the quality of which is not strained because there is a delayed gratification awaiting the sacrificee. The

---

[9] For Patočka "An understanding of sacrifice might basically be considered that in which Christianity differs from those religions which conceived of the divine always as a power and a force, and of a sacrifice as the activity which places this power under an obligation. Christianity, as we might perhaps think, placed at the center a radical sacrifice (…) and rested its cause on the maturity of the human being." (Patočka 1989, 338).

terror of devastation is part and parcel of the risk, faith, and abandon of sacrifice, which surrenders fairness, economy, and exchange.

4.2. Expenditure

It is in a similar sense that a willing sacrificee is not seeking recognition, completeness, or fulfillment, but (among other things) a certain unconditional and total accomplishment of giving in an indirect way. The sacrificee is not singularly focused upon one possibility of comportment but many, as the very notion of *directedness* often is inflected in causal or technological terms. In the place of this economy of directedness, the sacrificee yields to *something* beyond *some-things* so as to become implicit, incarnate, and integrated. The sacrificed-for is affirmed (which is not necessarily economical) in part because it calls for dedication as it retains the unique ability to not be appropriated economically in a totalizing instrumentalization. *This alone* would be something worthy of sacrifice.

Here one might be reminded of Bataille's notion of expenditure, which can point to both products of neoliberal waste (the bourgeois' buying and selling of useless adornment and jewelry, e.g.) as well as total abandonments of what one cherishes the most for a seemingly a-rational "cause." Bataille observed how Native American Potlatch festivals demonstrated a "general economy" whereby a competition is initiated to out-give other tribes excessively, riskfully, and wastefully (see Bataille 1991). One must "give it all away" to the point of wasting it. In this general economy "everything is put at stake" in a way comparable to Aztec scapegoating sacrifices, which are meant for a community to see its obsession with "restricted economy." Both readings reflect Bataille's tendencies to interpret the master/slave dialectic as an ultimately negating and abyss-leaping act in order to subvert economy.[10] Although Bataille's understanding has come under critique for an over-emphasis upon pure negativity, which counter-acts the gift of sacrifice (Derrida 1967), Bataille understood that a waste of expenditure is necessary in order for any sacrifice to take place.

---

[10] Countering Bataille, Derrida insisted on an aneconomical nature of the gift of sacrifice (see Derrida1967). In what would become decades of work on the gift, Derrida's language and conception of "economy" originates in a deconstruction of Bataille's general economy, which does not allow for a "resolution" or return to self-consciousness and ultimately, absolute knowledge the Hegelian dialectic insists upon. Bataille's exposition of economy fails because it ends in *absolute* negativity of death, and in "*abstract negativity*:" for "To rush headlong into death…one risks losing the effect and profit of meaning which were the very stakes one hoped to win." Bataille's excessive gift "can only utilize the *empty* form of the *Aufhebung*" (ibid.).

This helps qualify a definition of "waste" according to a certain logic of expenditure and excess. In abandoning economy, one relates with the "something" of sacrifice via an affective expenditure, and Patočka seems accurate to think that it is precisely the "cost" of the sacrifice that certainly is *not counted* in any typical sense. This is because, as he claims, sacrificees have an entirely different focus:

> In giving themselves for something, they dedicate themselves to that of which it cannot be said that it 'is' something, or something objective. The sacrifice becomes meaningful as the making explicit of the authentic relation between the essential core of man and the ground of understanding which makes him human and which is radically finite, that is, which is no reason for being, no cause, no force. (Patočka 2015, 21)[11]

This essential grounding is a kind of "weak" resistance that makes up the core of man and, especially in times of crisis, provides the motive to attempt the inversion of power relations. This is not unlike Gusdorf's (1948, 67) claim that "sacrifice puts us in the presence of a 'paradoxical' form of exchange," and inherently subverts power relations by an expenditure that counteracts what is straightforward and economical.[12]

4.3. Wasted

This leads to a third reflection upon waste as the experience of oneself-as-wasted. For Patočka, today we flee from sacrifice and "into a technical understanding of being which promises to exclude this experience and for which there exists nothing like a sacrifice, only a utilization of resources" and "thus sacrifice represent a persistent presence of something that does not appear in the calculations of the technological world." (Patočka 1989, 337). The soul of Europe has lost touch with its deeper enervation, and sacrifice is a non-telic means of restoring frayed social bonds. Sacrifices are irreducible to causes and fall outside the jurisdiction of utility and usefulness. In a sacrifice, there can be no praise of the input/output register (Lyotard).

To become "a waste" is to be subjectivized according to a non-cultured space that is radically held in place by a certain *hyper-naturalness*. By opening oneself up to death, and

---

[11] Patočka employs a late-Heideggerian ontology, one where the relation with being as Dasein becomes a matter of dynamism that matches the "not-hereness" of Dasein. Dasein, like the gift, is never "here," and Patočka then applies this to sacrifice. One does not sacrifice for some "thing" but for that which already exceeds what one thinks to be the motivity or *telos* of the sacrificed.

[12] Sacrifice is an a priori structure within the affirmation of personal life, and one remains caught between the economic and counter-economic. Earlier, Gusdorf claims that "sacrifice is the realization of a kind of economy between man and the gods, but the economic sense of this economy masks in reality a deeper sense." (Georges Gusdorf 1948, 86)

to the non-ordinariness of life, one commits the *most natural act* (the natural, the unconditioned, and the uncultured here all are related) of living by yielding oneself truly to what one lives for. In the case of a willing sacrificee, one likely knows that eventually their sacrifice *will be forgotten*, and this amounts to the experience of being wasted: the sacrificee is to be cast from the social norm, is not to be re-integrated into the whole, and is not to be saved or her dignity restored. Yet it is in this role of being-sacrifice that today one might perform the role of being a de-socializing, sliding signifier (not unlike the Aztec or Native American practices) in the registers of economical calculation and industrialization. The sacrificee may find consolation in being – as Patočka knew all to well – an embodiment of social waste that issues the persistent call for a re-evaluation *not simply of all values* as Nietzsche so eloquently sought, but of a society's *non-values*: of what it rejects and is willing to not save or die for.

5. Scum of the Earth

These reflections on waste hopefully remain irreducible to a straightforward *negativity* through which one must persevere in order to achieve some positive social outcome. Sacrifice is not a *direct affirmation of the negative*, a "tarrying with the negative," or even a dialectic of negation and affirmation. Patočka's reflections go deeper than these tendencies by pointing to atonement as the key for solidarity via (as interpreted throughout this essay) a radical relation with waste. Despite the sacrificees' attitude of ambivalence necessary towards an instrumentalized social outcome, she must heed the warnings that the lives of early Christian martyrs present in their imitation of Christ's sacrifice. For the sacrifice to have any productive outcome (again, beyond any hopes of utility) it still needs to have some affirmative return to that which was sought for atonement. If Christianity is to offer anything radical for today it must challenge its economically oriented predicates that so often easily ensnare it. Far too often theories of Christian atonement presume a certain Divine economy with penal justice as the principal and overarching means. Instead Christ atoned for any further needs of scapegoating and paying penance. Yet it occasionally gets presumed falsely that sacrifice (along with scapegoating) also is to be discarded from Christian practice. However, a true sacrifice can protest against our "technical understandings" of everyday life, and it indeed can teach "our outwardly rich yet essentially impoverished age to face itself." Patočka's renewed, Christian/Hellenistic understanding of sacrifice involves an "abysmal deepening of the soul" that employs a dedication to being-wasted so as to defect from the ever-widening reach of technologization and its fraying social bonds.

In this article[13] I have had no other pretense than to reveal some of the ways an understanding of waste might thicken a conceptualization of the relation between solidarity and sacrifice. The relation between sacrifice and solidarity generally is presumed to operate pragmatically: one sacrifices for whomever one already has solidarity, fraternity, or friendship. In other words, this kind of sacrifice is a natural, if not evolutionary product of such solidarity. This would mean that there is very little that is special about sacrifice, as it is not so incredibly difficult to sacrifice oneself (a parent protecting a child for example) for someone with whom a bond already has been established. Instead, given the a-telic and waste-oriented qualifications of sacrifice to which this paper has drawn attention, such a pragmatic, if not utilitarian understanding of this sacrifice/solidarity relation needs to be corrected. Patočka's understanding of Christian sacrifice (the sacrifice to end all scapegoating as well as any telic orientation), alongside an understanding of how waste figures into its operations, points us to how sacrifice comes ontologically prior to solidarity, namely because solidarity must be prevented from becoming an end or purpose, by which *sacrifice would be reduced to a mere means.*

Instead, the inverse seems more accurate: solidarity should be predicated upon sacrifice. This necessity hopefully also draws attention to the role of waste in the inversion of power relations Patočka underscored. The three-fold qualification of waste (wasted, expenditure, and devastation) and its aforementioned description highlight this paradoxical value of sacrifice, and may help prevent sacrifice from reverting to instrumentality. Recognizing the role of waste within sacrifice helps take it one step further so as to prevent "solidarity" from becoming a telic end of the sacrifice. If it become a telic end, then once again, sacrifice takes on a purpose of function. Waste, as closely related to the "Unconditioned" may serve a divine function by de-culturing such tendencies. This helps remove sacrifice from being but a means of achieving some (seamlessly weaved and implicit) *ideal* of a perhaps false understanding of solidarity as a form of social balance.

Indeed, if one accepts the aforementioned inversion of the solidarity/sacrifice relation, then this also calls for another understanding of solidarity. It is not merely the tranquil, beautiful soul of a peaceful social relation. Instead, it should be seen more like an *atonement,* one that has has gone through the experience of forsakenness in a way that the natural flow of the will to "exist unproblematically" (Patočka 1996, 13) is suspended. As Patočka understood, solidarity, like atonement must overcome its being presumed synonymous

---

[13] This article was conceived and written with the generous support of two research grants from the Austrian Science Fund (FWF). It was conceived within the framework of the project "The Return of Religion as a Challenge to Thought" (I2785) and concluded in the project "Secularism and its Discontents: Toward a Phenomenology of Religious Violence" (P 29599).

moreso with an "unproblematicity" and the many persistent *demands* of our carnal and mundane livelihood. And this is one reason why sacrifices must also be embedded culturally in order to atone for our technological decadence that pays no attention to the affects of waste or "non-values." St. Paul's call to become "scum of the earth" is perhaps more relevant today than it ever has been. Yet it is perhaps only when 1) reason runs aground, 2) technologically decadent means of everyday life are suspended, and 3) the escapisms that so easily entrap our theological imaginaries are placed at bay that a sacrificee might find her identity finally where it belongs: between purposelessness and infinity.

Dr. Jason W. Alvis, Institut für Philosophie, Universität Wien,
jason.wesley.alvis@univie.ac.at

References

Bataille, Georges, and Roburt Hurley. *The Accursed Share: An Essay on General Economy*. New York: Zone Books, 1991.

Derrida, Jacques, and Alan Bass. "From Restricted to General Economy: A Hegelianism without Reserve." in *Writing and Difference*. Chicago: University of Chicago Press, 1967.

De Warren, Nicholas. "The Gift of Eternity." in Ludger Hagedorn and James Dodd (eds.). *The New Yearbook for Phenomenology and Phenomenological Philosophy*. Volume XIV, London: Routledge, 2015.

Douglas, Mary. *Purity and Danger: An Analysis of Concepts of Pollution and Taboo*. London: Routledge, 1969.

Findlay, Edward. *Caring for the Soul in a Postmodern Age: Politics and Phenomenology in the thought of Jan Patočka*. Albany: SUNY Press, 2002.

Gauchet, Marcel, and Oscar Burge. *The Disenchantment of the World: A Political History of Religion*. Princeton, NJ: Princeton University Press, 1999.

Girard, Rene. *Violence et sacre*. Paris: Grasset, 1972.

Gusdorf, Georges. *L'expirience humaine du sacrifice*. Paris: PUF, 1948.

Hagedorn, Ludger. "Christianity Unthought," in Ludger Hagedorn and James Dodd (eds.). *The New Yearbook for Phenomenology and Phenomenological Philosophy*, Volume XIV, London: Routledge, 2015.

Joas, Hans. *Faith as an Option*. Stanford CA: Stanford University Press, 2014.

Löwith, Karl. *Meaning in History: The Theological Implications of the Philosophy of History*. Chicago: University of Chicago Press, 1957.

Patočka, Jan. *Andere Wege in die Moderne: Studien zur europäischen Ideengeschichte von der Renaissance bis zur Romantik*. Hrsg. Von Ludger Hagedorn. Würzburg: Königshausen und Neumann, 2006.

Patočka, Jan. *Heretical Essays in the Philosophy of History,* trans. Erazim Kohák. Chicago: Open Court, 1996.

Patočka, Jan. "The Dangers of Technicization in Science according to E. Husserl and the Essence of Technology as Danger according to M. Heidegger," in Erazim Kohák (ed.). *Jan Patočka: Philosophy and Selected Writings*. Chicago: University of Chicago Press, 1989.

Patočka, Jan. "The Dangers of Technicization in Science according to E. Husserl and the Essence of Technology as Danger according to M. Heidegger (Varna lecture, 1973)," *The New Yearbook for Phenomenology and Phenomenological Philosophy*, Volume XIV, Special Issue: "The Philosophy of Jan Patočka", edited by Ludger Hagedorn and James Dodd. London: Routledge, 2015. 13-22.

Patočka, Jan. "Time, Myth, and Faith" in Ludger Hagedorn and James Dodd (eds). *The New Yearbook for Phenomenology and Phenomenological Philosophy*. Volume XIV, London: Routledge: 2015.

Patočka, Jan. *Plato and Europe*. Stanford CA: Stanford University Press, 2002.

CHRISTIAN STERNAD (Leuven)

The Force of War.
Max Scheler and Jan Patočka on the First World War

Abstract

The First World War was both an historical and a philosophical event. Philosophers engaged in what Kurt Flasch aptly called "the spiritual mobilization" of philosophy. Max Scheler was particularly important among these "war philosophers", given that he was the one who penned some of the most influential philosophical writings of the First World War, among them Der Genius des Krieges und der Deutsche Krieg. *As I aim to show, Max Scheler's war writings were crucial for Jan Patočka's interpretation of the First World War in the sixth of his* Heretical Essays. *However, the importance of Scheler's war writings goes far beyond the First World War for Patočka, since they offer Patočka a far-reaching interpretation of the 'excessive' character of the 20th century. As I will show through the example of Max Scheler, the German war philosophers succumbed to a dangerously romantic conception of "force" – and it is this ominous force, which Patočka takes to lie at the root of the increasingly excessive character of the 20th and 21st centuries.*

Keywords: Scheler, Patočka, war, force, sacrifice

1. The Force of the War, the Forces of War

"I came to see World War I (…) as the great seminal catastrophe of this century – the event which (…) lay at the heart of the failure and decline of this Western civilization" (Kennan 1979, 3) – this is American Historian George F. Kennan's famous assessment of the importance of the First World War as a world-historical event. This statement might seem outdated at the beginning of the 21st century, after two terrifying World Wars, the unimaginable genocide of the Holocaust, a Cold War that pushed the entire world to the brink of nuclear self-annihilation, and countless irreconcilable regional conflicts of ever-increasing intensity. However, the intention behind the statement was to show that the historical event of the First World War had profoundly changed the way in which Europe – and subsequently the world –

---

[1] The research leading to these results has received funding from the European Research Council under the European Union's Seventh Framework Programme (FP7/2007-2013) / ERC grant agreement n° 617659 (GRAPH).

perceived itself and, further, that it was precisely the First World War that brought about a world-historical change by setting the course for the excessive nature of this century.

The First World War can be seen as a starting point of the catastrophes to come. The violent deaths of previously unimaginable numbers of people in the battlefields, the first use of bio-chemical weapons like mustard gas, the first machines like tanks and airplanes as new agents of war, the sheer endless stalemate of trench-warfare, the novel experience of attrition warfare, psychopathological phenomena such as "shell-shock", the thousands of mutilated soldiers returning from the front, the slow collapse of the difference between the battlefield and the homeland, the total mobilization of material and psychological resources – all of these features called for individual and collective responses for which there was no roadmap. Hence, intellectuals of all disciplines responded to this genuinely new event in their own ways.

Philosophers too reflected upon the importance and consequence of this world-historical event. The events of the war were accompanied by a surprising, and previously unprecedented, philosophical engagement. In particular, German philosophers like Rudolf Eucken, Max Scheler, Ernst Troeltsch, and many others wrote books, essays, articles, countless pamphlets, and held public speeches and talks to defend the national cause and the war effort in general (Lübbe 1974, Flasch 2000, Bruendel 2003, Sieg 2013, Hoeres 2014). These philosophers soon realized that this war was being fought on two very different battlegrounds where very different weapons were being used. They conceived of this war not so much as an historical-political event of fighting forces in the battlefield, but instead as a philosophical war, i.e. a genuinely spiritual event upon which hung the fate of all humankind. This spiritual event followed very different rules than the war that took place on the "real" battlegrounds. For the first time in history, philosophers became soldiers equipped with pen and paper as weapons (*Kriegsdienst mit der Feder*[2]), fighting in a war of ideas, of culture, of values – a "spiritual mobilization" (Flasch 2000), as the German historian Kurt Flasch has aptly described it.

This spiritual warfare mobilized not only philosophers, but also their philosophical concepts as such, which underwent crucial reinterpretations and left a decisive imprint on 20th century philosophy.[3] Basic philosophical ideas, such as life & death, community, sacrifice, spirit, value, culture, and many others became irrevocably tainted or even thoroughly corrupted by the experience of this first total war. From among these many concepts, I will focus on one peculiar concept, which remains ominous but at the same time ubiquitous; namely, the

---

[2] This expression stems from the philologist Theodor Birt (quoted from Bruendel 2003, 11).
[3] Domenico Losurdo has shown this remarkably well in the case of Heidegger and the First World War (see Losurdo 2001).

concept of "force". As mentioned above, one can find a strangely romantic fascination with the idea of force in the work of German war philosophers. It is the Czech philosopher Jan Patočka who, in the 1970s, returned to this concept in his *Heretical Essays* and interpreted the 20th century *itself* as war, and did so by means of the concept of force or, as he writes, the "transvaluation of all values under the sign of [force]." (Patočka 1996, 124)[4]

The First World War unleashed forces of a hitherto unparalleled and unknown scale. It mobilized every single aspect of European life that was possible to mobilize: Weapons, ammunition, equipment, food, medicine, troops, infrastructure, to name only the most important among them. More importantly, it mobilized people – materially and psychologically. People – soldiers in particular – became forces, fused into the unity of a single force, and became a part of a mobilization of massive proportions. In his famous *Die totale Mobilmachung* (Jünger 1993) from 1930, war veteran Ernst Jünger tried to retrospectively express and describe the uniqueness of this mobilization of forces in the First World War. For him, only a "power of cultic origin" (ibid., 124) could have achieved what he calls a "total mobilization" (ibid., 125), i.e. a mobilization that leaves no potential force untapped and that fuels the energy of war like an erupting volcano (ibid., 123).

Materially *and* psychologically – the latter category is one of the defining elements of the transformation in warfare that emerged. The First World War was an event that mobilized the masses, the force of the masses, and the forces within the masses. Rudolf Eucken, the German philosopher and Nobel Prize laureate, emphasized in his speech *Die sittlichen Kräfte des Krieges* that this war, although destined for bloodshed and destruction, could awaken the slumbering forces that would not have arisen in times of peace (Eucken 1914). Furthermore, he tried to draw attention to how the war unites forces that otherwise lie disconnected from one another. In his view, war binds all of these particular forces together, creating one single force, which by its accumulation exceeds the mere sum of its parts. This force is not only a material force, but an "inner strengthening"[5] (*innere Kräftigung*) (Eucken 1914a, 166) that

---

[4] The English translation by Erazim Kohák often greatly differs from the Czech original. In this particular passage, Patočka uses the word *síla* (force) and not *moc* (power). This is important to mention since there is a terminological difference between 'force' and 'power' in Patočka. Furthermore, the words for 'force' (síla) and 'violence' (násilí) stem from the same root. It is therefore important to listen to the relation that force and violence uphold in the Czech, since this brings force and power into an interesting relationship with Scheler's thought, where power has to control violence. Patočka uses a very similar train of thought in *Plato and Europe*. I am thankful to Daniel Leufer for pointing this out to me.

[5] The English language does not convey the proximity of *strengthening* and *force* like the German language does. In German, these two words share the same root: *Kraft* and *Kräftigung*. Hence, the force of war leads to an inner strengthening, but it is also this inner strengthening that makes the fighting forces more forceful.

arises with the war, so that this inner strengthening justifies this particular (German) war (cf. Hoeres 2004, 447-449).

The Germans were not alone in their fascination with the conception of a force that accumulates, renews and even transcends itself. On the French side, Henri Bergson characterized the warfare in terms of the force that either wastes or renews itself (*la force qui s'use et celle qui ne s'use pas*). In distinguishing between material and moral forces, Bergson sought to show why the enemy, Germany, would inevitably run out of force, since it only "worships brute force" (Bergson 1915, 46), i.e. material force. The force that renews itself, however, is the moral force which is kept alive by ideals – ideals which, in Bergson's opinion, Germany did not possess, or at least did not foster: "The energy of our soldiers is drawn from something which does not waste, from an ideal of justice and freedom." (ibid., 46) Taking up Bergson's idea of the nature of the war, one would have to conclude by mathematical principle that France will win the war against Germany. When all material forces are depleted, it is France's moral force that would rule over the lack of moral force in Germany. A simple or even oversimplified equation perhaps, but an equation which is nevertheless based upon the guiding principle of force which seems to define the essence of the conflict in Bergson's opinion.

One of the most interesting and crucial aspects of these conceptions of force is that this ominous force is simultaneously both bound and not bound, to human restraint. It is perhaps another defining aspect of the First World War that this relationship between human might and the might of force itself shifted dramatically out of alignment. Viewed from the perspective of the 21st century, the First World War seems to be the first event involving a dramatic loss in control that, over the course of the 20th and 21st centuries, would repeat and amplify itself, reaching its apex in nuclear brinksmanship. This force, which is idolized and worshipped in the writings of these philosophers during the First World War, became something that leaves the 21st century trembling in fear. The engagement with the force of war in this sense resembles a child playing with fire – unleashed by a deep fascination for yet unknown might, and followed by a frantic search for control and containment. Taking up Eric Hobsbawm's narrative of "the age of the extremes" (Hobsbawm 1995), this fire might have never stopped and kept on burning throughout the course of the 20th and 21st centuries.

2. Max Scheler I: The Excess of Force

Max Scheler's war writings are among the most important and most influential writings of the First World War. In fact, Scheler's case is unique in the history of philosophy since he was the first philosopher ever appointed by the ministry of foreign affairs (*Auswärtiges Amt*) for war propaganda (Flasch 2000, 106). During the first years of the war, he wrote several important essays, including the especially influential: *Der Genius des Krieges und der Deutsche Krieg* (Scheler 1986). In this essay, Scheler attempts to give a philosophical justification of war in general and for the German war cause in particular. However, not all of his war writings are affirmative of the war. As Zachary Davis has shown in his article *The Values of War and Peace* (Davis 2012), Scheler undergoes a dramatic shift in perspective and deeply regrets his previous "mobilization" for the German war cause (Flasch 2000, 103-146). In his later writings, he explicitly turns against his belligerent writings and he reevaluates and defends the philosophical concept of peace and pacifism, which he had previously discarded so enthusiastically.

Scheler's *Der Genius des Krieges und der Deutsche Krieg* is one example of how the idea of force permeates war writing. This is manifest in his use of many expressions ranging from "force" and "forces" to several interesting and more sophisticated composite notions, like "force of will" (*Willenskraft*) and "force of sacrifice" (*Opferkraft*), etc. In his view, war becomes the means to bind and release the forces accumulated throughout the course of history – Scheler here speaks of a "uniting force of war" (cf. Scheler 1982, 76) a notion to which I shall return later. Although this understanding of war as an agent within history tens in a rather mythical direction, Scheler shows that war is something that can only occur in and is hence bound to human realms. Furthermore, he explicitly turns against the idea that war itself is nothing other than an expression of the conflicts of rivalry, already evident in the animal kingdom. In his opinion, human conflicts are entirely different since these human conflicts are always spiritual in their essence, even though they show themselves to be brutally material at times:

> That any similar forces are at work here and there, that of course is certain. But only when these forces enter into an interaction with the conscious and reasonable spirit, through whose possession the erect vertebrate becomes the 'human being' within history, only then can they generate these phenomena.[6] (ibid., 14)

Against the fashionable deterministic philosophical positions of his time (Darwinism particularly), Scheler argues that "Human things like war and labor can never be fully understood by biological laws; because the new factor of spirit is added."[7] (ibid., 34). Here, it is important to note that Scheler emphasizes this "new factor of spirit". At first glance, this seems to be an

---

[6] "Daß irgendwelche gleichartigen Kräfte hier und dort wirken, das freilich ist gewiß. Aber erst indem diese Kräfte mit dem bewußten, vernünftigen Geiste zu einem einzigartigen Zusammenspiel treten, durch dessen Besitz das aufrechtgehende Wirbeltier erst zum 'Menschen' der Geschichte wird, erzeugen sie jene Erscheinungen." (All quotes from Scheler are translated by the author, C.S.)

[7] "Menschliche Dinge wie der Krieg und die Arbeit können niemals vollständig aus biologischen Gesetzen begriffen werden; denn der neue Faktor 'Geist' kommt bei ihnen hinzu."

innocuous statement that only serves the purpose of a terminological differentiation. If one takes the consequences of this into account, then this means that by definition, every war – not just the First World War – is a spiritual war in its essence. If one connects this to the very specificity of the so-called "spiritual mobilization", and its respective war philosophies (especially *The Ideas of 1914*), it becomes clear that there cannot be any other war than a spiritual one, at least in Scheler's view. Therefore, it is also not surprising that Scheler attributes a creative principle to war, i.e. that war is a principle in history which fosters the spiritual development of humankind, insofar as war is something both spiritual and also deeply human. In his opinion, it is only through conflict that humankind can drive itself further and higher in its spiritual development.

Scheler's fierce rejection of peace, and of Kant's concept of "eternal peace" especially, is partly based on this logic. Scheler proceeds under the assumption that war is something primordial which, as a force, runs through the course of history. As such, it shapes history and fosters its developments. Peace, in turn, is regarded as the universal halting of this movement. In Scheler's view, the concept of eternal peace is even something "reactionary" since it entails that humanity accepts the current state as a universal state and closes itself off from history's future development. As such, it is the most backward idea in the philosophy of history. The strong rejection of eternal peace, and also Kant *per se* as Domenico Losurdo (Losurdo 2014) convincingly shows, is a common feature of German war philosophy and is particularly evident in the *Ideas of 1914*. Werner Sombart, in his book *Händler und Helden* (Sombart 1915), provides the most provocative case, since he even pities old Kant for his "sad writing" on eternal peace, which does not show the great philosopher Kant, but only the "small-minded Kant from Königsberg; grief-stricken, creased and disgruntled over the death of Lampe."[8] (ibid., 93)

In Scheler's opinion, peace is only the temporary bracketing of a more fundamental state of war that runs throughout history.[9] As such, it transforms the force of conflict into various more implicit forms of social conflict in times of peace, something which is not recognized as being a part of this one fundamental force. Scheler's critique of capitalism (Scheler 1982, 36) goes so far as to state that capitalism is only another form of warfare in which individuals are permanently set against each other. The error, therefore, would be to call this state of affairs peace, since it is just a more wisely concealed form of permanent conflict that, fur-

---

[8] "Die traurige Schrift des alten Kant über den 'Ewigen Frieden', in der nicht der große Philosoph, sondern nur der über den Tod Lampes vergrämte, gnittrige und verärgerte Partikulier Kant aus Königsberg zu Worte kommt, bildet die einzige unrühmliche Ausnahme."

[9] This of course is reminiscent of Heraclitus' conception of war as "the father of all things" (Diels/Kranz, 22 B 62).

thermore, inhibits the possibility of real conflicts and the subsequent historical, political, and spiritual changes that would arise therefrom.

As indicated above, Scheler holds that war is something specifically and properly human, "eigentümlich Menschliches" (ibid., 14). This idea, however, shifts to various degrees and it is not entirely clear whether man has power over war or war has power over man in the end. This is especially the case when he argues that war is the dynamic or guiding principle of history. War, then, becomes itself a force within history that puts man under its spell. As Scheler says, "War is the dynamic principle of history as such"[10] (ibid., 19). The limitation of human power could not be expressed more clearly as in the following statement where war figures as the return to a creative source, one that shapes humanity's activity and fate:

> "Every war is the return to the creative source out of which a state even emerged; diving into the mighty source of life from where the great borderlines are drawn wherein human fate and activity will range furthermore."[11] (ibid., 19-20)

In Scheler's opinion – and in the opinion of many other phenomenologists who reflected on the First World War, as Hans Rainer Sepp has shown in his article *Die Grenze der Solidarität* (Sepp 2014) – war contains the force necessary to give rise to meaning as such and meaningful structures of the life-world in particular; it gives meaning first and foremost to social entities, such as states, communities, shared values, etc. With special regards to Europe, Scheler argues that the war shapes an idea of community that could not arise otherwise. For him, it is a general rule that war is the "strongest force in history to build states, peoples and nations" (*stärkste staaten-, völker- und nationenbildene Kraft der Geschichte*) (ibid., 39). With special reference to the First World War, he argues that the task of "welding together the Western European nations to a kind of unity and solidarity, for which we yet lack a name, might be reserved for this outrageous war"[12] (ibid., 39-40). Hence, in his opinion, the war has an unparalleled "uniting force" (ibid., 76) and figures as a "builder of community" (*Gemeinschaftsbildner*) (ibid., 280) that can generate a new form of unity and solidarity, something which could not arise in any other way.

---

[10] "[D]er Krieg [ist] das dynamische Prinzip [...] der Geschichte".
[11] "Jeder Krieg ist Rückkehr auf den schöpferischen Ursprung, aus dem der Staat überhaupt hervorging; Untertauchen in die mächtige Lebensquelle, aus der heraus die großen Grenzlinien bestimmt werden, in der sich menschliches Geschick und Betätigung fernerhin bewegen kann."
[12] "[S]o ist es also diesem unerhörten Kriege vielleicht vorbehalten, die westeuropäischen Nationen zu einer Art der Einheit und Solidarität zusammenzuschweißen, für die uns noch der Name fehlt." Although the concept of solidarity does not gain any more theoretical substance in Scheler, one could draw connections to Patočka's concept of the "solidarity of the shaken" in the 6th Heretical Essay: "the solidarity of those who are capable of under standing what life and death are all about, and so what history is about." (Patočka 1996, 134)

This holds especially true for the people sacrificing their lives for the well-being of the German nation. His notion of the "force of sacrifice" (ibid., 99) captures the thought that the act and ideal of sacrifice radiates a force that is essential to the communal existence of the German people. The centrality of the idea of sacrifice is, of course, not something limited to Max Scheler's thought as almost all war philosophers reflect on it. This can be easily seen in the simple fact that almost every war book is dedicated to the soldiers, friends, sons & daughters, et al. who participated in the war in any way.[13] What is specific to Scheler's view of sacrifice is that he divorces it from the idea of exchange. On the contrary, Scheler tries to think about a form of sacrifice that is given, and which does not receive anything in return. The soldier who dies at the front for his fatherland cannot get anything in return. The massive death of soldiers at the front for the German Fatherland also greatly exceeds any logic of exchange. On the contrary, Scheler thinks that the sacrifice has a meaning in itself and that it bridges the gap between the contingent act of sacrifice and the eternal sphere of values.[14] Scheler holds that the soldier's sacrifice is an act that gives birth to new values, values that integrate themselves in the development of the pantheon of values. Since values have an eternal form, this means that soldiers, in their contingent act, touch the life of the eternal, even feel the "breath of eternity" (*Anhauch des Ewigen*) (ibid., 85). The significance is that the act itself, as an act, points towards the eternal sphere of values; moreover, the act of sacrifice becomes a symbol of these values. In this sense, it can be easily seen how this conception of the sacrifice contains a force, or even becomes a force itself, which goes against traditional forms and theories of sacrifice.

---

[13] Sombart's *Händler und Helden* commences with the dedication: "To you, the young heroes out there facing the enemy." (Sombart 1915, III). Rudolf Eucken dedicates his *Die Träger des Deutschen Idealismus* to his sons: "To my dear sons Arnold and Walter who both stand in battle." (Eucken 1916, 7) In a later print of his book, he would adapt his dedication to his sons "who stood in battle." (Eucken 1916/1919, 7). Scheler dedicates his book "To my friends in the battlefield." (Scheler 1917, 8). Ernst Haeckel dedicates his book not only to the soldiers, but also to the bereaved, and declares: "The income of this writing is determined by the author for the support of the bereaved of the German soldiers who sacrificed their lives and domestic happiness to the salvation of the fatherland and the preservation of the international law." (Haeckel 1915, 4) Hence, the cultural importance of the idea of sacrifice cannot be overstated.

[14] This is precisely the point at which his war writings become connected to his masterpiece *Der Formalismus in der Ethik und die materiale Wertethik*, written around the same time as his war writings (Scheler 1966). Another short, but insightful, piece that adds to the puzzle is his essay *Vorbilder und Führer*, which explains the very ways in which idols and leaders are carriers of values who contribute to the objective hierarchy of values (Scheler 1957). In this example, the soldier would fall into the category of the "hero" and hence would foster "vital values". Furthermore, German Historian Ulrich Sieg shows in the second chapter of his book *Geist und Gewalt* how the philosophy of values had a high peak in philosophical and public discourse after the two assassination-attempts on Kaiser Wilhelm I. by Max Hödel and Karl Nobiling in 1878. (Geist 2013, 19-57)

3. Max Scheler II: The Adjustment of Force

Before the war had even ended, Scheler became very critical of his own war writings (like many other German philosophers in the so-called *Ideenwende 1916/1917*). In a lecture from 1927 entitled *Der Mensch im Weltalter des Ausgleichs* (*Man in the Era of Adjustment*) (Scheler 1976a/Scheler 1958), Scheler introduces the idea of "adjustment". Apart from the speech's theoretical ambition, this text constantly returns to the First World War and situates the concept of adjustment against the background of the war. Scheler argues that Europe now finds itself in a severe crisis, following the tragedy of the First World War. This first global war was not only an historical event but is, for him, the most decisive moment in the history of humankind (Scheler 1958, 103). In his view, this war is the watershed between an old age and a new one. The old age was an age of the steady rise of partial-particular forces (ibid.) in conflict: The Peasant wars, the English and the French revolutions, the small German and the Great Russian revolution. The First World War, however, ushers in a new age, given that it is the "first truly common experience" (*erstes wirkliches Gesamterlebnis*) (ibid.). Scheler even argues that this first total experience is the beginning of the history of humankind (ibid.) – it is the beginning of humankind, since it is the first event that bundles all of the partial-particular forces into one common total-experience of force (ibid., 104). All of the particular peoples, in their particular yet different life worlds, are fused into one gigantic total experience in which humankind experiences itself as one for the first time. Since this is a remarkable passage in his speech (in which he even refers to Rudolf Eucken), I will quote it in full:

> The last epoch was essentially one of growing tensions which kept becoming more particularized, the epoch of the 'growth of forces,' as Rudolph Eucken called it. This trend was relatively seldom interrupted by violent revolutionary processes which released tension, such as the Peasant Wars, the English and French revolutions, the little German and the great Russian revolution. However, the most general formula applicable to the incipient era; the era of a *universal release of tensions* in human relations, is, it seems to me, that of the *adjustment of forces*. It is, at the same time, an era in which man once again relies on his living spirit and heart and tries to become the *master* of demonic powers which had become *centers of attention* after being unleashed by the last epoch. His purpose is to make these powers serve the salvation of humanity and the meaningful realization of spiritual values. (ibid., 103-104)

In Scheler's writings on the war, one can see that he interprets the First World War as an event of force. It is not only the accumulation but also the release of force that are so unprecedented in this war. However, Scheler became so fascinated with the force of war that he became its dupe, something expressed remarkably well by the quote provided at the beginning of this article. In his late text on *Man in the Era of Adjustment*, he comes to terms with this former demonic spell of force and argues that the coming age will be an age of the global adjustment of the particular forces that, only a few years prior, drove humankind into the yet unparalleled catastrophe that was the First World War. His late speech, therefore, can be seen as a sober realization of his previous intoxication with the idea of force during the First World War. As such, Scheler might be one of the few cases of a former war philosopher who underwent a philosophical demobilization, which Davis showed in detail (see Davis 2012).

However, one has to mention that Scheler's prophecy for the coming age did not come true; the First World War was followed by an even more catastrophic Second World War which then passed into a Cold War in which, for the first time, humankind as a whole came close to self-extinction.[15] Given this, it seems reasonable to ask why this anticipated age of adjustment did not take place.

Somebody who thought about the nature of this coming age was Jan Patočka. Scheler's influence on Patočka is significant and directly observable in a couple of texts that refer to Scheler explicitly. These references are a testament to the fact that Patočka read Scheler's writings extensively throughout his life. These works by Patočka include *Plato and Europe* (Patočka 2002), the *Séminaire sur l'ère technique* (Patočka 1990), but also a lesser known text with the title *Max Scheler. Versuch einer Gesamtdarstellung* (Patočka 1999), which was written on the occasion of the Czech translation of *Die Stellung des Menschen im Kosmos* (Scheler 1976b). This relatively unknown piece is interesting because in it Patočka sets out to achieve the rather ambitious task of introducing the Czech reader to Scheler's thinking in its entirety. In the passages where Patočka addresses Scheler's philosophical engagement in the First World War, it is somewhat surprising to find a rather warm appraisal of Scheler's infamous war writings:

> Although belligerent and erroneous without doubt, these reflections do not lack depth and are full of observations which even under different circumstances retain their validity – among them especially the book *Die Ursachen des Deutschenhasses* which has not lost its interest, even today.[16] (Patočka 1999, 342-343)

---

[15] The two philosophers who were most preoccupied with this coming age under the permanent threat of nuclear self-annihilation were Karl Jaspers in *Die Atombombe und die Zukunft des Menschen* (Jaspers 1957) and Günther Anders in *Die Antiquiertheit des Menschen* (Anders 1956), *Endzeit und Zeitenende* (Anders 1972), and *Hiroshima ist überall* (Anders 1982).

[16] "Zwar kampfeslüstern und zweifellos in die Irre gehend, lassen sie aber doch die Tiefe nicht vermissen und sind voll von Beobachtungen, die auch unter veränderten Vorzeichen Gültigkeit behalten – dazu zählt vor allem das Buch über die Ursachen des Deutschenhasses, das bis heute nichts an Interessantheit verloren hat." (translated by the author, C.S.)

4. Jan Patočka I: The Metaphysics of Force

In the 6th essay of his *Heretical Essays in the Philosophy of History*, Jan Patočka thinks about the First World War and its consequences for the historical and spiritual situation of present-day Europe – and consequently for the Western world in general. In his view, the First World War was the "decisive event in the history of the twentieth century." (Patočka 1996, 124) It bore witness to an unprecedented unleashing of forces that set the course for the excessive wars to come. In his opinion, the Second World War and, subsequently, the Cold War only repeated this (potential) excess of force, but with an ever-increasing intensity – for Patočka, the difference between these wars is a only a quantitative and not a qualitative matter. Although his observations in the *Heretical Essays* only hint at the possible ramifications of the nuclear arms race of the Cold War, the *Séminaire sur l'ère technique* follows these questions in greater detail. There, it becomes evident that humankind has entered a new ontological era under the threat of total self-annihilation (cf. ibid., 114).

His use of the seemingly innocent notion of "force" does not draw attention to itself in this context, and yet this idea of force unfolds into a surprising complexity of ideas that, in the end, results in a dark and even "mythological" (ibid., 116) use of the word. In short, Patočka's remarks raise the question of whether this force is something that remains bound to the realm of man or whether this force is something that takes man into its own realms. Furthermore, Patočka characterizes humankind's struggle in the 20th century as a struggle between the "forces of the day" and the "forces of the night" (ibid., 6th essay). Yet, it is not entirely clear whether these forces are part of this one mythical force; also unclear here is whether these forces become part of the human sphere or not.

The more frequent and terminologically consistent use of force in Patočka begins in the 5th heretical essay where Patočka raises the question of whether technological civilization is decadent or, worse, destined to decay. After speaking about the constitutive role that religion – here Christianity specifically – plays, as being the most powerful upsurge against decadence, he combines his analyses on the orgiastic with later analyses of the First World War. In direct reference to Ernst Jünger's *Totale Mobilmachung*, he argues that it is precisely war that enables the "release of orgiastic potentials which could not afford such extremes of intoxication with destruction under any other circumstances." (ibid., 114) Taking up his former analysis of religion, the orgiastic grows out of a lack of distance and a deep fascination with that which transcends the realm of everydayness. The orgiastic is enraptured with the exceptional, "where something more powerful than our free possibility, our responsibility, seems to break into our life and bestow[s] on it meaning which it would not know otherwise."[17] (ibid., 99) This connection between technological civilization, religion, and the First World War is not obvious at first glance. However, in Patočka's opinion, both religion and the experience of the front in the First World War commit man to a form of transcendence that could not be achieved by any other means.

Patočka's understanding of force is deeply connected to the Heideggerian understanding of technology (Heidegger 1977). His answer to the question of whether technological civilization is decadent depends upon the idea that technology only offers "substitutes where the original is needed." (Patočka 1996, 117) Technology, and the civilization that obeys its laws, leads to man's profound alienation and converts reality into a means through which everything is calculable, mobilizable, and is to be used for any given purpose. Since everything is turned into a force, these partial forces contribute to a rule of a force which is unbound from human control and, hence, seems untamable: "It generates a conception of a force ruling over all and mobilizes all of reality to release the bound forces, a rule of Force actualized through global conflicts." (ibid., 117) At this point, Patočka's understanding of technology functions as an indirect key to understanding his ominous use of force: Technology, or as Heidegger himself would call it the "enframing" (*Ge-stell*) (Heidegger 1977, 19ff.), turned reality into partial forces that for any given purpose are calculable, mobilizable or are transformed into, in Heideggerian terminology, the "standing reserve" (*Bestand*) (ibid., 17). This turns man into the grand accumulator of force, but also integrates him into this force, a station through which force passes:

> It seems as if humans have become a grand energy accumulator in a world of sheer forces, on the one hand making use of those forces to exist and multiply, yet on the other hand themselves integrated into the same process, accumulated, calculated, utilized, and manipulated like any other state of energy. (Patočka 1996, 116)

Hence, we can now answer one of the questions we poased above: man is the master of force, but at the same time is also a slave to force. In a very dense paragraph, Patočka states that man has lost his relation to being and instead becomes a force himself in the age of technology, in his social being first and foremost. Being itself has been broken down into partial forces and, as such, being has been converted into a force; however, man has also become "a gigantic transformer, releasing cosmic forces accumulated and bound over the eons." (ibid., 116)

---

[17] For an investigation of Patočka's interpretation of religion between the sacred and the profane, between responsibility, irresponsibility and the orgiastic, see also Sternad 2015; concerning the question of religion and Europe, see Sternad 2016.

Since man is so immersed into this world of forces: "Force is the Highest Being which creates and destroys all, to which all and everyone serve." (ibid.116)

To return to the 5th heretical essay's initial question, technological civilization is decadent because in this framework, man has lost his relation to being. Instead,

> force manifests itself as the highest concealment of Being which [...] is safest where it is exposed to view in the form of the totality of what-is; that is, of forces that organize and release one another, not excluding humans who, like all else, are stripped of all mystery. (ibid., 117)

Nevertheless, this relation to being does not seem to have been lost for good. Instead, Patočka emphasizes: "Hidden within Force there is being which has not ceased to be that light which lights up the world, though now only as a malevolent light." (ibid., 117) Here again, Patočka's thoughts fall in line with the Heideggerian idea that concealment is never just a concealment, but is deeply related to its unconcealment, i.e. the unconcealing concealment or, vice versa, the concealing unconcealment. Taking these thoughts and combining them with his interpretations of the First World War, the consequences are quite staggering: Although the First World War is situated in a technological world, and is as such a technological event, the forces released by the war transcend the realms of this technological framework. In other words, the release of forces through the war could bring being into light. This is precisely the moment when his interpretation of the writings of war veterans Ernst Jünger and Teilhard de Chardin come into play, since their front experiences seem to be the apt depiction, in Patočka's view, of a man who has overcome himself in the trenches.

5. Jan Patočka II: The Forces of the Day and the Forces of the Night

This is the point at which Patočka's narrative of the "metaphysics of force" (ibid., 116) is divided into two governing principles: "the forces of the day" and "the forces of the night." (ibid., 6th essay) The forces of the day obey the law of technology. They are the principles by which the world is governed through reason, although this reason is understood as an instrumental form of reason. The logic of the day has turned reality into forces at man's disposal and, hence, is part of the mobilization, which in the war, according to Ernst Jünger, became *total mobilization*. In Patočka's view, the First World War is an event that clearly depicts the logic of the day:

> It is the forces of the day which for four years sent millions of humans into hellfire, and the front line is the place which for four years hypnotized all the activity of the industrial age which a participant of the front, Ernst Jünger, called the age of [...] total mobilization. (ibid., 125)

The term "total mobilization" designates the process in which every force becomes a means to an end yet to come. Although Jünger used this description to show the uniqueness of the First World War, Patočka goes beyond Jünger to show that the First World War was only the inception of a whole new century that was to be characterized by this permanent total mobilization. As Patočka shows, total mobilization in itself has no end, since it transforms every force into a standing-reserve waiting for its application. Against Jünger, Patočka argues that: "War as the means of releasing Force cannot end." (ibid., 132) Instead, the substantial difference between war and peace vanished, since peace is also characterized by a total mobilization of forces that inhibit the potential outbreak of war. For Patočka, this war showed something different, i.e. that it is precisely the forces of the day, the instrumental logic of reason that did not end the war, but "mutated into something peculiar which looks neither quite like war nor quite like peace." (ibid., 119)[18]

Patočka's provocative claim, or perhaps indictment, at the beginning of the 6th essay is that we did not yet fully understand the significance and essence of the First World War. This war set something in motion that we tried to understand by means of old concepts from the 19th century, concepts which were defined by the reason and the logic of the day. To quote Patočka:

> The First World War provoked a whole range of explanations among us, reflecting the effort of humans to comprehend this immense event, transcending any individual, carried out by humans and yet transcending humankind – a process in some sense cosmic. We sought to fit it into our categories, to come to terms with it as best we could – that is, basically, in terms of nineteenth-century ideas. [...] [But] all approached war from the perspective of peace, day, and life, excluding its dark nocturnal side. (ibid., 119-120)

However, and this is decisive for the trajectory of the 6th heretical essay, there is also what Patočka ominously calls "the forces of the night". The forces of the night are what slip through the firm grip of technology, mainly because of their non-instrumentality. The reason for getting into this extensive conversation with Teilhard de Chardin and Ernst Jünger is because there is a sacrifice at the front which does not belong to the day's rational calculation anymore. Patočka differentiates between two forms of sacrifice: on the one hand, the relative sacrifice is that which belongs to the realm of trade and calculation. It is instrumental in the

---

[18] It is indeed surprising to read a remarkably similar depiction of this permanent mobilization in George Orwell's *Nineteen Eighty-Four*. In the last chapter of the second part, Winston reads the ominous forbidden book by Emmanuel Goldstein, the supposed leader of the resistance. In this book, Goldstein explains the genesis of the hyper-totalitarian state and age in which Winston finds himself (Orwell 2008, Part Two, Chapter IX). It is very likely that Patočka knew Orwell's *Nineteen Eighty-Four*.

sense that one gains something for the offer. Absolute sacrifice on the other hand – which Patočka equates with the experience of the front – is something completely different:

> The front-line experience [...] is an *absolute* one. Here, as Teilhard shows, the participants are assaulted by *an absolute freedom*, freedom from *all* the interests of peace, of life, of the day. That means: the sacrifice of the sacrificed loses its relative significance, it is no longer the cost we pay for a program of development, progress, intensification, and extension of life's possibilities, rather, it is significant *solely in itself*. (ibid., 129-130)

This *solely in itself* means that it leaves behind the logic of the day, the logic of mutual exchange and calculability. In absolute sacrifice, man gives itself for something, which is nothing, or to accentuate it differently: no-thing. It is precisely this setting itself free from relationality that achieves this absolute form of freedom. (cf. Sá Cavalcante Schuback 2011)

The idea that guides Patočka's thoughts here is that of an eschatology of sacrifice that breaks with the logic of the force. The only thing that overrules force is absolute sacrifice, since it escapes the logic of the day. The sacrifice of giving oneself for nothing, for no-thing, can no longer be converted into a force. Hence, it is only the logic of the day that prolongs the war without end. "War as the means of releasing Force cannot end." (Patočka 1996, 132) Instead, absolute sacrifice amounts to a suffocation, an implosion of force, since man rejects his role as the accumulator of force, denies to force the use of his being, and declines to be its conveyor. This act certainly points to this twofold relation that man maintains with force or, vice versa, that force maintains with man. Force can only manifest itself through man and man can only be empowered through force. To return to the metaphor used above, one can say that there is no need to play with fire, but the deep fascination of touching something that exceeds the ordinary force of man is so intriguing that it sets in motion this vicious spiral towards destruction and self-destruction.

6. Conclusion

The First World War was a unique event in the history of the 20th century insofar as it introduced a new kind of warfare that radically broke with all means of war employed by that point in history. This new warfare introduced a potentially endless war that could only end through complete exhaustion and attrition. In the hellfire of the trenches, humankind was confronted with a new force that far exceeded the control of political diplomacy. Instead, political diplomacy was turned into a fragile balance of forces in which peace was no longer the lasting absence of war, but only the temporary suspension of war. The Cold War's nuclear arms race made it all too clear that the mere absence of gunfire cannot be considered to constitute true peace. To this day, this situation has only changed in degrees, not in principle.

Missiles are pointed at almost every country on earth. The frightening system of MAD (*Mutually assured destruction*) guarantees that nobody attacks first without facing the consequence of self-annihilation in almost the same instant.

Max Scheler and Jan Patočka were confronted by dark aspects of the 20th century and responded in their own ways. Although their situations were dramatically different, they both seemed to believe that man's complex relation to force was key to understanding the excessive nature of the previous century. Many philosophers, and other intellectuals of all kinds, were fascinated with this idea of force in the First World War; they fueled its fire by means of enthusiastic speeches and writings, and looked forward to the advent of a new beginning of history. As both Scheler and Patočka, showed, this truly was the beginning of a new age with which we still wrestle today.

Scheler had his moment of painful realization, even undergoing a conversion of sorts, upon realizing that this spiritual mobilization was without end. Interestingly, Scheler clearly saw his dangerous fascination with force and proposed a counter-concept meant to reorient humankind towards a global adjustment of conflicting forces. Although Scheler admits that this idea describes nothing peaceful *per se*, it still leads to the hope that humankind will realize itself in a higher form of being that he calls not the "Übermensch", but the "Allmensch" (Scheler 1958, 101-102). His death in 1928 prevented him from seeing the future events of the 20th century and it also prevented him from the sad realization that this old age of increasing particular forces did not end with the First World War; it only continued in increasingly violent outbursts of force over the remainder of the 20th century.

Jan Patočka had the fortune, or bad luck, to have been born after Scheler and, hence, witnessed what Scheler could not have foreseen. In the middle of the Cold War, and under communist oppression, Patočka takes up these ideas again and reflects upon the century's excessive nature. For him, the First World War was also the decisive event in the history of the 20th century and introduced an incalculable force into history with which man had to struggle. Unlike Scheler, Patočka does not see an age of adjustment on the horizon. On the contrary, Patočka seeks a way to break through force precisely at the place of its clearest expression, i.e. trench warfare, as depicted in Ernst Jünger and Teilhard de Chardin. In these accounts, Patočka outlines an implosion of force that rejects force's domination over man. In other words: where Scheler saw hope in a global adjustment of force, Patočka sought an implosion of force in the *locus* of its greatest excess.

The example of the concept of "force" shows an unsurpassed mobilization of philosophy during the First World War. What it also shows is precisely how the First World War was not only a historical, but also a philosophical event that left a crucial imprint on the philosophy of the 20th century and maybe even the 21st century. The connection between Max Scheler and Jan Patočka is so rich because they both responded to events that were almost impossible to respond to, both by using this ominous concept of force. What we can take from their analyses is not so much their interpretations of the events of their time, but rather the crucial insight that the 20th century gave birth to forces which far exceed humanity's capacity to control them. This is especially obvious in the mobilization of the masses, but also in the technology that goes into warfare today. Hence, what we can learn from these devastating examples is to be aware of the seeds and the growth of all kinds of mobilization and to avoid, by all means, fighting against force with force. To quote Patočka one last time: "Whither do such perspectives lead? War as the means of releasing Force cannot end." (Patočka 1996, 132)

Dr. Christian Sternad, Husserl-Archives, Centre for Phenomenology and Continental Philosophy, KU Leuven, christian.sternad[at]kuleuven.be

References

Anders, Günther. *Die Antiquiertheit des Menschen. Band 1: Über die Seele im Zeitalter der zweiten industriellen Revolution.* München: C.H. Beck, 1956.
Anders, Günther. *Endzeit und Zeitenende. Gedanken über die atomare Situation.* München: C.H. Beck, 1972.
Anders, Günther. *Hiroshima ist überall.* München: C.H. Beck, 1982.
Bergson, Henri. "The Force which wastes and that which does not waste," in idem. *The Meaning of the War.* London & Edinburgh: Ballantyne Press, 1915. 41-47.
Bruendel, Steffen. *Volksgemeinschaft oder Volksstaat. Die "Ideen von 1914" und die Neuerung Deutschlands im Ersten Weltkrieg.* Berlin: Akademie Verlag, 2003.
Davis, Zachary. "The Values of War and Peace. Max Scheler's Political Transformations." *Symposium* Vol. 16, Nr. 2 (2012): 128-149.
Diels, Hermann, and Walther Kranz (eds.). *Die Fragmente der Vorsokratiker.* Zürich: Weidmann, 1985.
Eucken, Rudolf. *Die sittlichen Kräfte des Krieges.* Leipzig: Verlag von Emil Gräfe, 1914.
Eucken, Rudolf. "Der Krieg und die Philosophie." *NuS*, Vol. 151 (1914a): 166-170.
Eucken, Rudolf. *Die Träger des Deutschen Idealismus.* Berlin: Ullstein, 1916.
Flasch, Kurt. *Die geistige Mobilmachung. Ein Versuch.* Berlin: Alexander Fest Verlag, 2000.
Haeckel, Ernst. *Ewigkeit. Weltkriegsgedanken über Leben und Tod / Religion und Entwicklungslehre.* Berlin: Verlag von Georg Reimer, 1915.
Heidegger, Martin. *The Questions Concerning Technology and Other Essays.* New York & London: Garland Publishing, 1977.
Hobsbawm, Eric. *The Age of Extremes. 1914-1991.* London: Abacus, 1995.
Hoeres, Peter. *Krieg der Philosophen. Die deutsche und die britische Philosophie im Ersten Weltkrieg.* Paderborn et. al.: Ferdinand Schöningh, 2004.
Jaspers, Karl. *Die Atombombe und die Zukunft des Menschen.* München: Piper, 1957.
Jünger, Ernst. "Total Mobilization," in Richard Wolin (ed.). *The Heidegger Controversy. A Critical Reader.* Cambridge / London: MIT Press, 1993. 119-139.

Kennan, George F. *The Decline of Bismarck's European Order. Franco-Russian Relations, 1875-1890.* Princeton: Princeton University Press, 1979.
Losurdo, Domenico. *Heidegger and the Ideology of War: Community, Death, and the West.* Amherst: Humanity Books, 2001.
Losurdo, Domenico. *Von Hegel zu Hitler? Geschichte und Kritik eines Zerrbildes.* Köln: Papyrossa, 2014.
Lübbe, Hermann. *Politische Philosophie in Deutschland: Studien zu ihrer Geschichte.* München: Deutscher Taschenbuch Verlag, 1974.
Orwell, George. *Nineteen Eighty-Four.* London: Viking, 2008.
Patočka, Jan. "Séminaire sur l'ère technique," in idem. *Liberté et sacrifice.* Grenoble: J. Millon, 1990. 277-324.
Patočka, Jan. *Heretical Essays in the History of Philosophy.* Chicago & La Salle, Illinois: Open Court, 1996.
Patočka, Jan. "Max Scheler – Versuch einer Gesamtdarstellung", in idem. *Texte, Dokumente, Bibliographie.* Freiburg/München: Karl Alber, 1999: 338-396.
Patočka, Jan. *Plato and Europe.* Stanford: Stanford University Press, 2002.
Sá Cavalcante Schuback, Marcia. "Sacrifice and Salvation: Jan Patočka's Reading of Heidegger on the Question of Technology," in Ivan Chvatík and Erika Abrams (eds.). *Jan Patocka and the Heritage of Phenomenology.* Dordrecht: Springer, 2011: 23-38.
Scheler, Max. *Der Genius des Krieges und der Deutsche Krieg.* Leipzig: Verlag der Weißen Bücher, 1917.
Scheler, Max. "Vorbilder und Führer", in *Schriften aus dem Nachlass. Band 1: Zur Ethik und Erkenntnislehre.* Gesammelte Werke, Vol. 10. Bern: Francke, 1957. 255-344.
Scheler, Max. *Philosophical Perspectives.* Boston: Beacon Press, 1958.
Scheler, Max. *Der Formalismus in der Ethik und die materiale Wertethik. Neuer Versuch der Grundlegung eines ethischen Personalismus* (Gesammelte Werke, Bd. 2). Bern: Francke, 1966.
Scheler, Max. "Der Mensch im Weltalter des Ausgleichs", in *Späte Schriften.* Gesammelte Werke, Vol. 9. Bern: Francke, 1976a. 145-170.
Scheler, Max. "Die Stellung des Menschen im Kosmos", in *Späte Schriften.* Gesammelte Werke, Vol. 9. Bern: Francke, 1976b. 7-182.
Scheler, Max. "Der Genius des Krieges und der Deutsche Krieg", in *Politisch-Pädagogische Schriften.* Gesammelte Werke, Vol. 4. Bern: Francke, 1982. 7-250.
Sepp, Hans Rainer. "Die Grenze der Solidarität. Der Erste Weltkrieg und die Phänomenologie." *Tijdschrift voor Filosofie* Vol. 76 (2014): 761-793.
Sieg, Ulrich. *Geist und Gewalt: deutsche Philosophen zwischen Kaiserreich und Nationalsozialismus.* München: Hanser, 2013.
Sombart, Werner. *Händler und Helden. Patriotische Besinnungen.* München/Leipzig: Duncker & Humblot, 1915.
Sternad, Christian. "Specters of the Sacred: Jan Patočka, Or: The Hidden Source of Jacques Derrida's 'Phenomenology of Religion'." *New Yearbook for Phenomenology and Phenomenological Philosophy*, Vol. 14 (2015): 287-299.
Sternad, Christian. "Religion jenseits von Mythos und Aufklärung. Edmund Husserl, Jan Patočka, María Zambrano und Jacques Derrida über das geistige Erbe Europas." *Metodo. International Studies in Phenomenology and Philosophy,* Vol. 4(1) (2016): 151-179.

MARTIN KOČÍ (Prague)

The Experiment of Night:
Jan Patočka on War, and a Christianity to Come[1]

Abstract

In the wake of the present-day crises, social conflicts and growing divisions, Patočka's reflections on war and totalitarianism appear abiding. Moreover, the enigmatic language, which Patočka uses, especially in his late Heretical Essays, *sounds provoking and paradoxical. This article elaborates on the hypothesis that Patočka's reflections provide us with something more than a historical analysis interpreting the wars of the 20th century, and the 20th century as a war. I will argue that Patočka finds an intrinsic link between modernity, as a particular mode of being, and war and totalitarianism as unavoidable consequences of such a mode of being. To describe this situation, Patočka puts forth the dialectic of the light of day and the darkness of night. Paradoxically, in a somewhat mystical turn, Patočka gives preference to the night as the driving force of transgressing modern logic and the defective mode of modern being which throws crowds to the hell-fire of modern warfare. Against this background, this paper will present an innovative reading of Patočka's reflections as a specific search for an adequate spiritual response to the discontents of modernity. I will suggest that the trajectory of Patočka's thought can be read through the lens of a particular philosophy of religion, even though Patočka never elaborated on this avenue explicitly. Thus, I will propose that Patočka's thought opens up the possibility of reconsidering a heretical idea of Christianity that is coming after Christianity.*

Keywords: Jan Patočka, Christianity, modernity, war, totalitarianism

---

History has known many wars. All of them were bloody, ugly and left uncountable numbers of victims. Nevertheless, the 20th century, the presupposed time of fullness, the kairos of rational modernisation and technical evolution, has changed the way we think about war. Modernity has transformed the perception of the world and humanity due to the machinery of modern warfare. Against this background, Patočka writes the last of his *Heretical Essays* entitled "The Wars of the 20th Century and the 20th Century as War", which Paul Ricoeur characterises as "frankly shocking". Ricoeur was shaken because the content of Patočka's essay, as he writes, focuses on 'the dominance of war, of darkness and the demonic at the very heart of most rational projects of the promotion of peace' (Ricoeur 1996, viii). Experimenting with the experience of night underlines this paper.

---

[1] This article is a part the research project "Christianity after Christendom: Paradoxes of Theological Turns in Contemporary Culture" PRIMUS/HUM/23 (funded by Charles University, Prague).

The enigmatic tenor of Patočka's reflections is best captured in his thought-provoking words concerning the status of modern warfare.

> The first world war is the decisive event in the history of the twentieth century. It determined its entire character. It was this war that demonstrated that the transformation of the world into a laboratory for releasing reserves of energy accumulated over billions of years can be achieved only by means of wars. Thus it represented a definitive breakthrough of the conception of being that was born in the seventeenth century with the rise of mechanical natural science. (Patočka 1996, 124)[2]

If we were going to analyse Patočka's reading of the 20th century and its wars, we would need to examine the following three points. First, Patočka interprets modern warfare *historically* as the fight between the idea of imperial Europe and the idea of a revolutionary break with this status quo. Interestingly, he places Germany and the Central Powers on the side of a revolutionary attack on the status quo represented by the Allied Powers. In this respect, Patočka is inspired, on the one hand, by the German historian Fritz Fischer's thesis that Germany deliberately triggered the First World War (Fischer 1961), and, on the other hand, by his own analysis of the modern technical rationalism which he names as the revolution of scientification. Second, Patočka provides us with a reflection on the war as a global social change, a decisive moment of recent history, which remodelled Europe, and, in fact, the entire world. In this respect, the war is interpreted as an outburst of modernity (negative interpretation) and, at the same time, as the fire that purges and opens up possibilities of something new to come (positive interpretation). Third, Patočka formulates the philosophical reflection of the front in terms of the existential drama of individual human beings. The focus on the experience of the front is based on records by the Jesuit Teilhard de Chardin (1965), who confessed that the war was an encounter with the Absolute, and the German writer Ernst Jünger, who famously captured the modern spirit behind the warfare, for example, in his book *Der Arbeiter* (1932) and the essay *Die totale Molbimachung* (Jünger 1930, 9-30).

These three facets usually delineate the framework of discussion about Patočka's thought-provoking interpretation of war and its consequences. Dozens of studies elaborate on the above-mentioned trajectory and it is worth mentioning that some of the best are collected in the special issue of *Studia Phaenomenologica* "Jan Patočka and the European Heritage" from 2007 and the *New Yearbook for Phenomenology and Phenomenological Philosophy* (published in 2015) dedicated to Patočka, especially on the themes of *Religion, War and the Crisis of Modernity*. Although the present study builds on the previous schol-

---

[2] I have modified and corrected Kohák's English translation which reads the sixteenth century while Patočka's original reads the seventeenth.

arship, its goal is to open up a new perspective on reading Patočka's enigmatic thoughts related to the ideas of war and the darkness of night.

The main claim of this paper argues that Patočka provides us with something more than a historical analysis interpreting the wars of the 20th century, and the 20th century as a war. I will argue that Patočka finds an intrinsic link between modernity, as a particular mode of being, and war and totalitarianism as the unavoidable consequences of such a mode of being. To describe this situation, Patočka puts forth the dialectic of the light of day and the darkness of night. Paradoxically, in a somewhat mystical turn, Patočka gives preference to the night as the driving force of transgressing modern logic and the defective mode of modern being which throws crowds of people into hell-fire. Against this background, this paper will present an innovative reading of Patočka's reflection on war (and totalitarianism) as a search for an adequate spiritual response to the impasse of modernity. Furthermore, I will suggest that the direction of Patočka's search makes sense from the perspective of a particular philosophy of religion, even though Patočka never elaborated on this avenue explicitly. Thus, I will argue that one of the most paradoxical and shocking consequences, to recall Ricoeur's evaluation once again, of Patočka's thought is the reconsidering of a particular path of spiritual thinking, namely a heretical idea of Christianity that is still to come.

1. The Discontents of the Light of Day

The interpretations of the cruel bloody events of the last century are numerous, different and contradict each other in offered explanations. However, they all have one thing in common. Their shared denominator is, in Patočka's wording, the perspective of *the day, the life and the peace* (Patočka 1996, 120). In this respect, the rivers of blood and rotting bodies are interpreted as an ugly but necessary price for a better world. Casualties and victims become heroes who laid down their lives for peace. This interpretation of the consequences of war as the necessary price for peaceful wellbeing is, in Patočka's opinion, untenable and scandalous. Instead of the perspective of the day, Patočka provocatively invokes the darkness of the night.

> It is the demonic of the day which pretends to possess all in all and which trivialises and drains dry even what lies beyond its limits. [...] The grandiose, profound experience of the front with its line of fire consists in its evocation of the night in all its urgency and undeniability. (Patočka 1996, 127 and 129, transl. modified)

How can Patočka's mystical tone phrased as the conflict between *the day* and *the night* be explained? And why is it the darkness of night that should interest us more than the dawn of the day?

The metaphor of the day evokes the light and the light turns our attention to the Enlightenment. From the Cartesian *clare et distincte*, modernity advances the idea of bringing clearer light into the world. The narrative of progress promises a constant evolution in this respect. Patočka claims that the gradual process from the mathematisation of nature, through thinking *more geometrico,* to the techno-scientific rationalism of late modernity produces a massive reservoir of forces. Warfare puts this potential in motion. "It is the forces of the day which for four years sent millions of humans into hellfire" (Patočka, 1996, 125). In other words, Patočka seems to suggest that the front, total mobilisation, the machinery of mass-killing and uncountable casualties is the result of the enlightened reason of modernity.

The promise of modernity initiates the project of peace and a better life based on the progressive rationalisation of humanity and society. Thus, modernity is knowledge and more knowledge brings a brighter future for everyone. What is meant here by knowledge is the force of *techné* – a technical comprehension of nature supposedly allowing its absolute control – creating "a perfectly functioning thoughtlessness" (Myšička 2004, 197). Indeed, despite its orientation to the gain of knowledge, one of the consequences of the modern spirit, as Heidegger often reminds us, is the pause of thinking. This is caused due to the illusion that 'modern man' marches toward a paradise. However, the accumulation of (technical) forces attained on this path leads neither to paradise, nor to rational and peacefully society, but to the tragedy of warfare. The tragedy is re-narrated and presented as an eschatological struggle for the future. And the future, in this respect, is nothing less than the end of all wars and the ultimate instalment of eternal peace: a bright prospect, indeed. Yet Patočka ironically points out that the aims of peace are, in fact, perpetuating war aims (Patočka 1996, 125). This calls for an explanation. But first we need to listen to Patočka himself.

> The war against war seems to make use of new experiences, seemingly acts eschatologically, yet in reality bends eschatology back to the 'mundane' level, the level of the day, and uses in the service of the day what belonged to the night and to eternity. (Patočka 1996, 127)

The demonic of the day, as Patočka calls the situation of late modernity, does not fade away with the last shot on the front. The eschatological war continues in totalitarian hegemony of the second half of the century of wars. The fight for tomorrow's progress proceeds, even though there is no open front.

The warfare of totalitarian hegemony is cold and hybrid. Thus, Valérie Löwit reads Patočka's last *Heretical Essay*, which is our main concern here, as his contribution to the study of totalitarianism, notwithstanding that he does not mention the term in the course of the entire text (Löwit 1997). Löwit remarks that, for Patočka, totalitarianism is not only a political regime. Rather, it is a general tendency of modernity. Why? As we have seen above, a key feature of the modern spirit is gaining knowledge. And the purpose of knowledge is not, as it used to be in the preceding historical epochs, to discover wisdom but the mastery of things. In this sense, Patočka sees modern epistemologies as the deviation from the traditional metaphysical questioning that is based on the wonder in front of that what is. The consequence of the modern development is the loss of the very question of being human. And it is in this respect when Patočka actually comes close to Hannah Arendt and her groundbreaking analysis of totalitarianism not only as a political, but also a philosophical problem.

Arendt opens her provocative study on *The Origins of Totalitarianism* with an alarming warning: 'The totalitarian attempt at global conquest and total dominion has been the destructive way out of all impasses' (Arendt 1973, viii). In other words, totalitarianism is an effort to solve crises, overcome uncertainties and answer questions, in Patočka's wording, by means of shedding the light of day on all problems. According to Arendt, the totalitarian hegemony pursues its goals by way of, at first sight, negligible confusions and substitutions. For example, the responsible action is exchanged for obedient behaviour, political power is turned into a force pushing through planned goals, rationality and rational reflection are confused with argumentation and, consequently, truth is replaced with a logical coherence (Arendt 1973, 475-477). An unavoidable consequence of all this is the remodelling of the human condition. Instead of the philosophical tradition which stresses the self's *relation* to life, that is, a constant questioning of life's meaning, the situation of totalitarianism turns the goal of human life into a sheer survival which is presented as the *absolute value*. What is at stake here is aptly formulated by Patočka's own characterisation of a totalitarian society, which he describes as a deceptive portrayal of human life longing for its self-preservation. And this illusion of life lived as a lie sacrifices many for 'bonum (malum) futurum' (Patočka 2006, 426).

A totalitarian logic and the rule of the day, in the name of an even brighter future and peace, is the cruellest form of war 'appealing to the will to live and to have'. As such, Patočka continues, this is 'the terror that drives humans even into fire-death, chaining humans to life and rendering them most manipulable' (Patočka 1996, 133). To put it bluntly, a constant threat of physical oppression and also psychological intimidation, often directed at the most vulnerable places, or just a tacit agreement about 'live and let live' in relative comfort in the sun which is brought by the day, make totalitarianism a prolongation of the war agony of the 20th century.

The relentlessness of the day turns our eyes to the night. For Patočka, Teilhard de Chardin is the one who mystically shows that the night—the front and the war—contains a sort of absolute freedom which has been lost for the day. The night has the power to reveal the depth of being, something which is difficult to realise against the background of the techno-scientific rationalism of our modern, all too modern minds. What kind of reasoning is behind this line of thought, which may be—with Ricoeur—described as frankly shocking? Peter Trawny clarifies this enigmatic train of Patočka's thoughts (Trawny 2007). Drawing inspiration from Jünger, who expresses the experience of the front in a less mystical tenor than Teilhard, Patočka seems to argue that warfare is a natural state of modernity due to its totalitarian character. Totalitarianism is a new metaphysical principle of modernity: the organisation of work and life, scientific knowledge, the government and, of course, war; this all has the contours of total control. To use the above-mentioned idea of Arendt, modern totalitarianism is the way out of all impasses. This means no room for questions because everything has been already answered.

In consequence, the human being is considered to be an object, a raw material (*Rohstoff*) usable and mis-usable for anything, including the fight against war. For Patočka, this is the adequate description of the situation of the day because it demands from particular persons their deaths for purposes stated by others. Now, how is it possible, against the background of the above mentioned absurdity of the war, that a heretical idea hatches out from this? A shocking idea that the war has another side, perhaps a positive one which manifests something important, is something we should not omit.

2. Blessing the Darkness of Night

Patočka delves into the night. Heraclitus is his guide in its depths. 'At the dawn of history, Heraclitus of Ephesus formulated the idea of war as that divine law which sustains all human life' (Patočka 1996, 136). Thus, Patočka thinks of war from the perspective of *polemos*—conflict—which has its positive side. Through this lens, war is not a totally rational means with an absolute irrationality of ends, as it appears to be in modernity due to its need to enlighten everything and everyone. War is not for *something*. The Heraclitean perspective presents war as the situation where one stands in front of *nothing*. This is the experience of the front, that is, the engagement with something that is no-thing. And precisely in this, Patočka discovers a constructive, positive element coming out of the negativity of war (Patočka 2002, 373).

Polemos reveals the opposition between the totality of life in modernity and the search for meaning, questioning the meaning of being in front of nothing. The absoluteness of the day forces out the consciousness of one's own finitude. This means that the awareness and anxiety of being-towards-death is displaced and substituted with an emphasis on bare life and its preservation at whatever cost. The night of war is the break-even point and a dramatic upheaval which unveils modernity's rational, all too rational, and enlightened illusions (Trawny 2007, 393-394).

The point of Patočka's turn to the night is to overcome modernity as a total mastery of (bare) life, which has lost its energising power of questioning. Patočka explains the notion of the night in his fragment with the working title *The Way Out from the War:*

> This deliberate emphasis on the *Night, death and war* is not a penchant for irrationality. Rationalism which may be endangered here is the rational *escapism* in which find refuge all the weaknesses of human beings declining to the snare of *bare* life. The argument of the Night, war and death is directed against this *bare* life without depth and absoluteness. (Patočka 2002, 490)

And as Patočka adds, the night is not driven by *force* but has the *power* to awake, that is, 'the power of spiritual authority' (Patočka 2002, 490). Patočka's unusual, one would say heretical account of modern warfare provokes dissenting opinions on the matter. For example, Catherine Chalier in "On War and Peace" expresses her disappointment at Patočka's glorification of war as the force of the night (Chalier 2002). Furthermore, she disagrees with placing Heraclitus on a pedestal of western thinking for his *polemos*. According to Chalier, reading the war through the lens of Greek ontology leads Patočka to the interpretation of war as if it were a beautiful harmony of cosmic forces, as it is expressed in the works of Teilhard. After all, she adds, how can one understand war as the disclosure of meaning?

Indeed, the war is a rotten fruit of modernity, as Patočka says. However, Chalier repudiates the preference of an ontological perspective and favours an ethical one. Performing a Levinasian gesture, Chalier suggests that war urges us to see the face of the other and to assume the responsibility for the other instead of individual immersion in the consciousness of being-towards-death (Chalier 2002, 38-39). In other words, what war reveals is primarily not one's finitude but the fragility of the other, which lays foundations for an ethical life and thus meaningful being in the world.

To deal with this criticism, two points must be made. First, it is an undisputable fact that Patočka draws inspiration mostly from ancient Greek philosophy and thus, for instance, in comparison to Levinas, he really seems to neglect other sources of European tradition, such as the (Hebrew) Bible and religion. Nevertheless, and this is the problem with Chalier's interpretation, it would be a fatal mistake to identify Patočka's use of 'Greek ontology' with the supposition of a static ready-made conception of the world, through which

Patočka reads modern warfare. In fact, Patočka's choice of Heraclitus, a pre-Socratic figure, shows his attraction to a kind of philosophy, which questions all-too-easy metaphysical, static concepts. Patočka enhances philosophy, which challenges harmonious portraits and totalitarian pictures of the whole, including an image of war as a complex harmony of cosmic forces. Heraclitus' *polemos*, contrary to Chalier's critique, is the place where disharmony, problematicity, and thus questioning reveal themselves.

The second point to be made concerns the meaningfulness and meaninglessness of war. For Patočka, the experience of the front itself does not give a new meaning of life. Myšička reminds us that the front, in Patočka's opinion, is an absurdity par excellence and as such it shows *nothing,* no thing. War and the totalitarian hegemony of the 20th century is a step out of *something* into *nothing* (Myšička 2004, 199-200). Hence, the question of meaning arises against the horizon of the front and war. However, the place—*locus*—of the manifestation of the question of meaning is not the agent of this question itself. It is always a concrete human being who is shaken and (re)discovers the urge of questioning because of his experience of upheaval, which interrupts the ruling of the day. In short, Patočka is far from any glorification of war. He says that 'war is senseless as a nihilistic war and only provides the best opportunity to find the other' (Patočka 2002, 500).

The core idea of Patočka's 'frankly shocking' reading of warfare can be expressed in four points: (1) enemies stand on the same side of conflict (*polemos*) because 'they' are thrown into the same turmoil as 'we' are; (2) the project of the day, that is, the idea of progress and emancipation, does not necessarily postulate more meaning than the reality of the night; (3) those who engage with war experience upheaval, which enables them to conduct the *epoché* from the aims of the day and to find something that is no-thing; (4) this no-thing, manifested in the darkness of the night, reveals itself as an unimaginable possibility of being (Patočka 2002, 501).

> Thus the *night* comes suddenly to be an absolute obstacle on the path of the day to the bad infinity of tomorrows. In coming upon us as an *insurmountable* possibility, the *seemingly* transindividual possibilities of the day are shunted aside, while this sacrifice presents itself as the authentic transindividuality. (Patočka 1996, 130-131)

This needs to be unpacked in more detail and explained in less metaphorical language. It seems to me that the notion of sacrifice can illustrate the meaning of Patočka's reasoning in a more practical way.

The night rehabilitates the notion of sacrifice as something essentially non-technical and absolute. For Patočka, sacrifice breaks with the logic of modern warfare and the logic of modernity. The rule of the day sends millions of souls to die for peace, the progress of humankind, and a better world based on the technology of rationalism, humanism, etc.

However, these totalitarian projects are not about authentic sacrifice but only leave victims. Patočka carefully distinguishes between the notion of victim and the notion of sacrifice because his native Czech language uses for both the same word: *oběť*. Patočka plays with the enigmatic meaning of the word, which is difficult to capture in English. For him, the victims (*oběti*) of the day, offered (*obětování*) for the dawn of tomorrow, urge sacrifice (*oběť*) which bears witness to the truth transcending bare life. Marc Crépon rightly senses two senses of sacrifice in Patočka while he is commenting on the dark tone of the philosopher (Crépon 2007). The victim is used and scapegoated, freely or forced, for the ideology of the preservation of life. Conversely, sacrifice is the absolute experience, from which there is no way back, breaking the calculus of techno-scientific modernity. Sacrifice reveals the idea of truth, uncovers the pressing question of meaning. Only in the night is light shed on this *absolute freedom* of sacrifice (Patočka 1996, 129-130). Is it a mere coincidence that the sun set and darkness came over the whole land, as if it were night, during Christ's crucifixion? (Cf. Mt 27:45; Mk 15:33; Lk 23:44).

The idea of sacrifice, in its relation to the dialectic of the light and darkness, drives us in close proximity to religion, specifically to a particular philosophy of spiritual being in the world. In the following section, I will elaborate on this thesis, which might be considered to be "frankly shocking" in the context of Patočka's thought.

3. Transgressing Everydayness

Although the 6th Heretical Essay is the most famous text where Patočka deals with the tension between night and day, the dialectic itself is introduced much earlier. For example, in the essay "Life in Balance, Life in Amplitude" from 1939, Patočka distinguishes the philosophy of day, on the one hand, and the philosophy which experiments with the experience of night, on the other (Patočka 2007). Life in balance stands for the former, whereas life in amplitude is the expression of the latter.

The philosophy of day, in Patočka's opinion, corresponds with the axioms of modernity. Its goal is to ground being in harmony and balance. It promises full enlightenment and emancipation from uncertainty. It brings progress, clarity, logicality and the absolute rationality of all means; in short, the rule of the daylight. The consequence of this philosophy is, according to Patočka, a total organisation of life, that is, a life without disturbing questions, a life of unproblematic everydayness.

The second philosophical approach, which Patočka favours, rejects such a totalisation of human life within clearly the delineated borders of a fully enlightened system. In contrast, Patočka claims that "man [sic!] appears to be most human [...] where the seemingly fixed form of life is scattered and where everything problematic, unsteady and extreme, which is hidden under the surface of normal living, is recovered" (Patočka 2007, 32). However, this philosophy of the human being prefers the darkness of night over the bright sky of the day.

Patočka deliberately chose to experiment with the night because this experience withdraws the human being from a plain life of balance and everydayness. The upheaval and crisis opens up the path of life in amplitude. The philosophy of amplitude breaks with the drab world of boredom, which Patočka associates with the words of Voltaire's Candide: 'cultiver son jardin' (Patočka 2007, 33). Patočka never left this idea of transgressing the everydayness of plain life behind. For example, in the last study completed during his lifetime, "On the Masaryk Philosophy of Religion", he addresses the same problem, although he uses a different vocabulary (Patočka 2015b). Against the background of the question of the meaning of being-in-the world, and taking into account Heidegger's distinction between being and beings, Patočka interprets the realisation of ontological difference as the breaking point with the boredom of everydayness. Patočka's question, in fact, tackles the problem of whether the meaning of being can be found outside a life in history, that is, somewhere in a world of eternal ideas which will shed light on everything there is, or whether the meaning and the search for it is something indissociably related to particular human lives. In other words, the point of a broad discussion, which reviews mainly the thought of Kant and Dostoevky (despite the name of Masaryk in the title of the essay), can be summarised as dealing with the conflict between the idea of a given meaning on the one hand, and a never complete and constantly sought meaning on the other. Figuratively, and continuing in Patočka's language game, the light of everydayness makes visible only beings (including the disclosure of their meaning) which are present-at-hand. However, what really matters in one's life is the embracing of being as an event (*Seinsereignis*) which gives itself in the darkness of *nothing*. What seems to be a trait of the 'frankly shocking' nihilism in Patočka's thought is rather the opening of a deep existential drama. It is against the background of the confrontation with the nothing of finitude where the difference between things and persons, which are no predetermined things, appears. The whole problem, as Patočka sees it, is about the question of undecidability 'beforehand.' This emphasis on the open (hi)story of every individual being leads Patočka to the position which embraces the uncertain darkness of night over accepting the light of everydayness because uncertainty is also freedom.

Now the question is: What is wrong with the life of everydayness? Why would the philosopher want to disturb us from the ordinary life and its pleasant tranquillity?

By way of addressing these questions, we touch upon the crucial aspect of Patočka's argument about war as an outburst of the enlightened modernity. For Patočka, war, as European humanity experienced it in the 20th century, is a horrifying force of the day because it constrains the human being to less than it is in its capacity and even its vocation in-the-world. Uncountable victims of war laid their lives down for the illusion of peace, that is, life in balance. For Patočka, the problem is not that someone would like to live a life in balance. The problem is that human freedom, understood as a vocation to become more than human seems to appear, is substituted for the deception of a life in balance, that is, in a plain acceptance of forces of the day that urge humanity to march on the path of progress towards a bright paradise of balance and life equilibrium. This is the crucial problem that Patočka identifies in the modern mode of being, which he analyses under the rubric of *Gestell* (borrowed from Heidegger). The danger of enframing is overly technical reasoning and, in consequence, the instrumentalisation of everything (Patočka 2015a, 15). Modern war stands as a perfect example for its total character which is possible due to technical enhancement. Suddenly, human beings become numbers. It applies both to the soldiers to be 'used' in the battlefield and also to the casualties and victims of the warfare and its side-effects. To paraphrase a horrifying saying: the tragedy of one's death turns into statistical information about the death of many.

In other words, for Patočka, the modern condition sheds light on everything, makes everything visible and pretends that all that appears in focal points is possible to master. However, in consequence, for the deemed fullness of appearance, the appearing itself is obscured (Dangers, PP). Patočka illustrates this with the disappearance of authentic sacrifice. In his opinion, the modern mode of being oriented towards the mastery of things, the total control of everything and the radicalisation of rationalism suppresses the breakthrough of sacrifice. In fact, sacrificial acting, within the logic of *Gestell*, is turned into usable means for certain purposes (Patočka 2002; 2015a).[3]

Nevertheless, *Gestell* as this transformation of one's attitude to the world has also another side. Next to pointing out the fulfilment of the technical age, and its potentially tragic ends, it announces the possibility of something new arising, that is, the reconsideration of being in its difference from beings.

In this respect, the human being is more than he appears. Humans are called to freedom and the experience of the front is the *locus* where this vocation manifests itself, and where an individual being is able to rediscover it. Thus, the negativity of night turns out to be something positive. It reveals that the authentic vocation of the person is to transcend everydayness and to live in amplitude.

---

[3] I have elaborated on the notion of sacrifice in Patočka elswhere (anonymised, 2017).

War, after all, is the most extreme expression of embracing freedom. In his essay on the philosophy of amplitude from 1939, Patočka mentions another agent of this disturbing yet, in his opinion, deeper mode of being: namely, Christianity. It has been successfully argued elsewhere that his reflection on Christianity accompanied Patočka throughout his entire professional career (Vesely 2013). What kind of Christianity Patočka has in mind becomes clearer when we look at his later works (Patočka 2015a; 2015b).

Patočka commits a heresy against both rationalism and fideism in Christianity. Against Kant, who is extensively discussed in "On Masaryk's Philosophy of Religion", Patočka does not postulate regarding another world where rewards follow good deeds. Patočka's Christianity does not know any second—better—world above this world and its history. It is Christianity which is not escaping from this dark world to the bright light of eternal ideas or postulates regarding practical reason. In short, Patočka's Christianity does not know an absolute external meaning which is given, present, and to be accepted (Patočka 2015b, 408). Hence, Patočka turns Christianity upside down because he does not postulate a complete concept of Christianity which would demand conformity as the ultimate aim of human life. Or, as Hagedorn reminds ourselves, the concept of Patočka's Christianity does not reckon with individual immortality, a revealed transcendent God, or a God as a postulate of reason (Hagedorn 2011, 257). On the contrary, Patočka thinks about Christianity in terms of the event of being, or to put it better, as a possibility where a difference appears between manipulable beings and being. This Christianity does not need any externally given meaning and does not preach any fixed meaning to come either. The point is 'the coming' itself which is related to particular human beings. Again, the play between light and darkness is behind this way of reasoning. The bright world of eternal ideas is put aside in order to concentrate fully on being-in-this-world which is not just a thing among other things and, in this sense, concerns *no-thing*.

The whole thing can be translated into the conflict between the metaphysical and the phenomenological attitude towards Christianity. Patočka, who obviously favours the latter, suggests not to meditate on the grounding of the meaning of the world and existence but points out the problematicity of being-in-the-world and existential shakenness of all relative meanings.

> By exhibiting phenomena of relative and convulsing meaning, phenomena such as the conversion of the significance of life where, in the apparent loss of meaning, one finds something unshakable as a path toward the projection of *new possibilities of life*, which are not properly speaking already given, but which only can and must be conceived. (Patočka 2015b, 130; italics author)

These new possibilities are a solid ground which appears against the background of the experience of being shaken. Christianity informs about this originary human vocation—the call to being—because Christianity 'rested its cause on the maturity of the human being' (Patočka 2015a, 22).

Thus, coming back to the pre-war essay from 1939, according to Patočka, Christianity is the philosophy of amplitude for its attentiveness to the depth of life which includes both dealing with pain and transcending everydayness. In other words, Christianity knows about the experience of night which is an indispensable part of human life and it also knows that this experience is not just to be overcome but enables humans to become more than they appear. Christianity seeks to break into the depth of the human experience of being in the world. And for Patočka, the crucial aspect of Christian attitude is that it does not enclose human experience in its finitude. In Patočka's wording: 'The essence of humanity is not to feel fulfilled by finitness' (Patočka 2007, 41). Or, to formulate it positively, Christianity throws one into the love of eternity (De Warren 2015).

Conclusion: A Spiritual Thinker of a Christianity after Christendom

We have started with war and ended up with religion. Moreover, Patočka is presented, perhaps unexpectedly, as a spiritual thinker *sui iuris* of unsettling life in amplitude. Although the Czech philosopher explicitly resists a reading which would associate 'something mystical' with his dialectics of the night and the day, it is an indisputable fact that the experience he refers to in relation to the front and warfare in his late works is an extremely important line of thought decipherable already in his earlier texts. And these reflections are explicitly related to Christianity. I take this discovery as an invitation to elaborate upon this thought-trajectory and to verbalise something which Patočka never did himself.

It is clear that the Christianity Patočka has in mind does not simply correspond with the mainstream understanding of this religion. However, at the same time, the reference to Christianity touches something that is a part of tradition. Let us meditate on this unusual reading of Patočka for a moment.

The idea of amplitude, that is, the call to life, which is not encapsulated in finitude, is, in fact, a Christian idea. Patočka even lists some examples from whom he draws this inspiration: Pascal, Kierkegaard, and Dostoevsky are prophets of a Christianity that is still to come (Patočka 2007, 40). Patočka sides with these figures on the edge of heresy, when looking from the traditional Christian standpoint, and thus shows that the title of his *Heretical Essays* pertains not only to his interpretation of war but has a multiple meaning.

Of course, Christianity can also be the agent of life in balance and, in this sense, the ground of everydayness. Perhaps, this is the mainstream manifestation of Christianity in its long history. Analogously to the tension between the light of day and the experience of dark night, there is a Christianity, which gives comfort, however, at the price of the total organisation of life, and a Christianity which gives access to unsettling and disturbing experiences. The latter is Patočka's, as well as our interest here.

> If we want truth, we are not allowed to look for it only in the shallows, we are not allowed to be fascinated by the calm of ordinary harmony; we must let grow in ourselves the uncomfortable, the irreconcilable, the mysterious, before which the common life closes its eyes and crosses over to the order of the day. (Patočka 2007, 39)

These words summarise the reasons behind Patočka's opting for the experiment of night. The truth of being reveals itself in limited situations such as the experience of the front in the midst of total destruction. This is the inspiration drawn from Teilhard de Chardin's records. This is what Christianity bears witness to. However, I suggest that we can even move a step further. Patočka offers a radical reinterpretation of Christianity after the end of the Christian era.

"Christianity after Christendom" or a "Christianity to come" as a spiritual response to modernity and its defective modes of being is, in Patočka's conception, outside the sphere of the theological. Although Patočka alludes to some biblical topics, such as sacrifice (2015a), the story of the God-man (2016, 115-180), and conversion (1996, 75), he transposes their message for our—modern—context, his intentions differ from any apologetical aims. The crux of sacrifice is not the person of Christ but a challenge addressed to every human being; the call of conversion is not meant as a turn from unbelief to faith. Rather, it is the expression of an ever-present existential drama turning around a life in balance and the possibility of a life in amplitude; the concept of incarnation, if we can associate this theological term with the discussion of Patočka's philosophy at all, is not about the descent of the transcendent God to the world but must be understood as the event of being (*Seinsereignis*). Ludger Hagedorn aptly reiterates Patočka's vision:

> Gott ist mit den Menschen, aber ganz anders als es die traditionelle Vorstellung will, anders als in der 'theologischen Öde'. Er ist mit uns in einer grundsätzlich sinnproblematischen Welt. [...] Er wird erfahren als die Fraglichkeit dieser Welt, als die Fähigkeit zur Transzendierung dieser Welt in der Aufgabe aller singulären Interessen und Bindungen. Gott ist *in* der Geschichte, ist 'die lebendige Hoffnung auf Weltumkehr.' (Hagedorn 2014, 363, in reference to Patočka 2002, 450ff.)

For these reasons, for example, Veselý argues that we find in Patočka a tragic Christianity *without* the Christian proprium (Veselý 2013). Some theologians would perhaps agree, although the question whether theology in its contemporary (phenomenological) turn can find inspiration in Patočka's reinterpretations remains open for further discussion.[4] It seems to me, however, that Patočka's discussion on war contributes to, and also makes visible, the reality of his – philosophical – project of Christianity after Christendom (Patočka 2015a, 22).

It is clear that in its orientation towards the future, this Christianity has no prescribed patterns of development. On the contrary, it contains a moment of surprise. However, the question is how to move beyond the metaphor of destabilising night? What is the content of unexpected surprises delivered by Christianity to come? Looking from outside, this form of Christianity appears as truly embedded in history, free from the possession of knowledge about the next things to come. In other words, the Christianity, which is coming after the end of Christian era, does not follow any pre-given, pre-designed pattern of development. Internally, Christianity is not so much about the content of belief, meant as the adoption of opinion about things such as the existence of God, heaven, rewards for the good, etc., but as a mode of being in the world and, which is crucial, a mode of *thinking* about the world, history and human existence. To use Patočka's vocabulary, this being *qua* thinking is living in questions and problematicity, which are not seen as obstacles but as thought-provoking engines and paths to realise the depth of the entirety of life in the world and in history. And going beyond this disturbing language, the project of Christianity after Christendom offers a spiritual response to the tragic outburst of modernity. This response does not consist in turning to the creed as a sort of deposited knowledge. Rather it turns to thought patterns, known to traditional Christian intellectual structures and, at the same time, allows interruptions coming from the future.

My response to the above-mentioned criticism about Patočka's void Christianity *without* Christianity would be that it misses the point because it seeks to delineate a positive content of this Christianity, consisting of propositions, arguments and opinions to be adopted or rejected. Patočka's project of the Christian *after*, however, concerns the structural element of being Christian. In other words, the 'after' does not refer to a consecutive time, that is, to a progressing Christian entity exchanging one of its forms for another, that is, a more enlightened and rational one. The 'after' points out the internal experience of transgressing something we have called everydayness, or what might be called boredom, or a

---

[4] I think particularly of the representatives of the so-called theological turn intentionally dwelling in the borderlands of theology and philosophy: Jean-Luc Marion; Emmanuel Falque, John D. Caputo.

life in balance, that is, a life without questions, which also means a life without a future. Christianity bears witness to this existential experience; however, this experience is surely not restricted to Christians. At one point in the *Heretical Essays*, Patočka talks about the experience of being shaken. The experience of those who go through a liminal situation, for example, war and totalitarian oppression. Christianity is, in a way, an institutionalisation of this movement of life and the background against which it is important to creatively live through this experience.

Patočka describes the experience of being shaken as the moment when certainties tremble, the defence of plain life is not enough, and history is interrupted by a greater force, which Patočka surprisingly calls, 'something divine' (Patočka 2002, 403). However, this is not any attempt to Christianise the Czech philosopher or even to claim that this unknown divine force is the Christian God. What Patočka has in mind is the break of transcendence in a particular (hi)story of the person. Yet this transcendence does not come from elsewhere but from within history. Only from history and within history is it possible that something new will come. This is the experience of being shaken.

But is it possible to withstand it? How can one live with the certainty of absolute uncertainty? For an individual, this is perhaps too demanding. This is the reason for introducing the concept of *the solidarity of the shaken*, that is, the interpersonal aspect of the experiment of the night.

Christianity, on which I elaborate against the background of Patočka's reflections, incorporates this interpersonal aspect. Moreover, Christianity in its constant coming, in its pondering of the 'after' is capable of finding value in the experience of the shaken. By way of internalising the darkness of night, that which seems as unsettling at first sight becomes something positive and a community building agency. And it appears as the community guarding being against its reduction to plain everydayness and the satisfaction with a life in balance. As Patočka remarks, the solidarity of the shaken is the community of those who understand the conflict between the slavery of finiteness and the freedom of transcendence: of those who are willing to engage with a problematic, shaken (sinnerschütterte) meaning of the world.

The suggestion of Christianity after Christendom is not meant as an apology for a supposed redemption (*das Rettende*) from the power of the day and its blinding light. Rather, I understand this Christianity as a potential advancement of Patočka's main concern, that is, not to be fulfilled by finiteness. Christianity is experienced in experimenting with the night. What war reveals in a rather brute way, Christianity delivers by way of internalising the experience of being shaken. Moreover, Christianity institutionalises the interpersonal element of this experience, which is something Patočka calls the solidarity of the shaken.

It is obvious that such a Christianity is not simply present-at-hand but still coming. Nonetheless, an important message of this *heretical* Christianity is that even from the negativity of night there is stemming out of it something positive: namely, the love of eternity without escaping from the peculiar realities of history. It is doubtful whether this conclusion will have any impact on theology and mainstream-lived Christianity. On the other hand, it would be a failure of philosophy not to see the potential, which is embodied in Christian thought-patterns. Patočka committed himself to exploring these paths, despite entering the edge of heresy.

Dr. Martin Kočí, Centre of Theology, Philosophy and Media Theory at Charles University, Prague, martin.j.koci[at]gmail.com

References

Arendt, Hannah. *The Origins of Totalitarianism*. London, New York: Harcourt Books, 1973.

Chalier, Catherine. "On War and Peace". *Parallax* Vol. 8, Nr. 3 (2002): 34-44.

Crépon, Marc. "La guerre continue: Note sur le sense du monde et la pensée de la mort". *Studia Phaenomenologica* Vol. 7, Nr. 1 (2007): 395-408.

De Warren, Nicolas. "The Gift of Eternity," in *The New Yearbook for Phenomenology and Phenomenological Philosophy*, vol. XIV, "Religion, War and the Crisis of Modernity", A Special Issue Dedicated to the Philosophy of Jan Patočka, ed. by Ludger Hagedorn and James Dodd. London: Routledge, 2015. 161-180.

Fischer, Fritz. *Griff nach der Weltmacht: Die Kriegzielpolitik des kaiserlichen Deutschland 1914/1918*. Düsseldorf: Droste, 1961.

Hagedorn, Ludger. "Kenosis: Die philosophische Anverwandlung eines christlichen Motivs bei Jan Patočka," in Michael Staudigl, and Christian Sternad (eds.). *Figuren der Transzendenz: Transformationen eines phänomenologischen Grundbegriffs*. Würzburg: Köningshausen & Neumann, 2014. 349-366.

Hagedorn, Ludger. "Beyond Myth and Enlightenment: On Religion in Patočka's Thought". In *Jan Patočka and the Heritage of Phenomenology: Centenary Papers*. Edited by Erika Abrams and Ivan Chvatík, Dordrecht: Springer, 2011. 245-262.

Jünger, Ernst. *Der Arbeiter: Herrschaft und Gestalt*. Hamburg: Hanseatische Verlagsanstalt, 1932.

Jünger, Ernst. "Die totale Mobilmachung" in *Krieg und Krieger*. Berlin: Junker und Dünnhaupt, 1930. 9-30.

Löwit, Valérie. "Evropa a původ totalitarismu u Hannah Arendtové a Jana Patočky," *Filosofický časopis* Vol. 45, Nr. 5, (1997): 796-814.

Myšička, Stanislav. "Dvacáté století jako váýlka u Jana Patočky". *Politologica. Acta Universitatis Palackianae Olomucensis* Vol. 3 (2004): 193-203.

Patočka, Jan. *The Natural World as a Philosophical Problem.* Translated by Erika Abrams. Evanston: Northwestern University Press, 2016.

Patočka, Jan. "The Danger of Technicization in Science according to E. Husserl and the Essence of Technology according to M. Heidegger," in *The New Yearbook for Phenomenology and Phenomenological Philosophy*, vol. XIV, "Religion, War and the Crisis of Modernity", A Special Issue Dedicated to the Philosophy of Jan Patočka, 2015a. 13-22.

Patočka, Jan. "On Masaryk's Philosophy of Religion," in *The New Yearbook for Phenomenology and Phenomenological Philosophy,* vol. XIV, "Religion, War and the Crisis of Modernity", A Special Issue Dedicated to the Philosophy of Jan Patočka, 2015b. 95-135.

Patočka, Jan. "Life in Balance, Life in Amplitude" in *Living in Problematicity*. Edited by Eric Manton. Praha: Oikoymenh, 2007. 32-42.

Patočka, Jan. "K záležitostem Plastic People of the Universe a DG 307" in S*ebranné spisy Jana Patočky, vol. 12. Češi I: Soubor textů k českému myšlení a českým dějinám.* Edited by Karel Palek, and Ivan Chvatík. Praha: Oikoymenh, 2006. 425-427.

Patočka, Jan. *Sebranné spisy Jana Patočky, vol. 3. Péče o duši, III: Kacířské eseje o filosofii dějin; Varianty a přípravné práce z let 1973-1977; Dodatky k Péči o duši I a II.* Edited by Ivan Chvatík, and Pavel Kouba. Praha: Oikoymenh, 2002.

Patočka, Jan. *Heretical Essays in the Philosophy of History.* Translated by E. Kohák. La Salle, IL: Open Court, 1996.

Ricoeur, Paul. "Preface to the French edition" in Jan Patočka, *Heretical Essays in the Philosophy of History*. Translated by E. Kohák. La Salle, IL: Open Court, 1996. vii-xvi.

Teilhard de Chardin, Pierre. *Écrits du temps de la guerre: 1916-19.* Paris: Grasset, 1965.

Trawny, Peter. "Die Moderne als Weltkrieg: Der Krieg bei Heidegger und Patočka". *Studia Phaenomenologica* Vol. 7, Nr. 1 (2007): 377-394.

Veselý, Jindřich. "Jan Patočka a křesťanství". *Studia Philosophica* 60 (2013): 63-84.

PHILIPPE MERLIER (Limoges)

Patočka, the meaning of the post-European spirit and its direction

Abstract

The Europe that was born from Plato's "care for the soul" can today no longer be recognized; it has been replaced by the self-management of the economic EU. How can we now come back to a Europe concerned about its soul, the others, and the world, reinventing itself as a new nation? Jan Patočka's thoughts on post-Europe can show us the way.
Starting from some clarifications on the definitely European initial meaning that Patočka detects in Socrates' "care for the soul", the purpose of this article is to examine what in this European spirit can be saved in the post-European age, and to what extent a "European nation" can still make sense. This analysis leads us, building on the visionary texts written in the seventies by Patočka, to rethink the possibilities of a reformation of European reason, and a métanoïa of Post-Europe.

Keywords: Jan Patočka, care of the soul, reason, Europe, Post-Europe

If one were to characterize Europe with the use of an organic metaphor, one might feel tempted to state that the soul of Europe is located in Greece, its heart is in the Czech Republic – the only country on the old continent that remained a democracy in 1938 – and its two lungs are in France and in Germany. I dreamt of Europe reverting to its ancient Greek roots: care for the soul, concern for the others and the world, universal, luminescent reason. I dreamt of a social-minded Europe that would have implemented its project of perpetual peace and united its states around liberty, responsibility, equal dignity of all human beings and solidarity of all its citizens. With Robert Schuman I thought: "Europe will not be made all at once, or according to a single plan. It will be built through concrete achievements which first create a de facto solidarity." (Schuman 1950) I thought that Europe would urgently require a cosmopolitan solidarity built on the rights of man and that the political will to work out a European constitution could not but be based on such a solidarity, which "will have to be widened to encompass all citizens of the Union, so that, for example, Swedes and Portuguese will be ready to vouch for one another." (Habermas 2006, 87)

Instead of that, nothing else is common to the European community as it has been built than a market economy, its currency and its finance. And, out of some incredible irony of History, Greece is the first country that was on the verge of leaving that monetary Europe. The economic Europe has been constructed regardless of the intellectual, cultural, ethical and political Greek foundations of Europe. That Greece should be the first country to reject the economic Europe, like some graft that does not take, is actually quite understandable. After all, what is left in "common" in the so-called European "community"?

The Europe that was born from Plato's care for the soul can no longer be recognized. The age of the post-Europe described by Jan Patočka is underway. Moving away from the line drawn by Schuman and Delors to wander, the Europe we longed for quickly vanished. Can the identity of Europe be content with an economy without *oïkouménè*? Can it remember *Europa* and come back to its first principles? Will we, who are Europeans from the old continent fallen down from our Greek cradle, manage to come to life again and reinvent *dēmokratia*? How can Europe be founded again? Under what conditions can an European "nation" arise?

The care for the soul of the spiritual Europe has been replaced by the self-management of the economic Europe. How can we now come back to the European "thing itself", to a Europe concerned about its soul, the others and the world, reinventing itself as a new nation? The project of a European nation, both *theoria* and *praxis*, both a "regulative idea" (Husserl) and a practical construction arising out of a philosophy of action, has to be worked out at fresh expense. Jan Patočka's thoughts on post-Europe can show us the way.

Thus, starting from some clarifications on the definitely European initial meaning Patocka detects in Socrates' "care for the soul" (I), our purpose is to examine what in this European spirit can be saved in the post-European age and to wonder to what extent a "European nation" can still make sense (II). This analysis leads us, building on the visionary texts written in the seventies by our phenomenologist philosopher, to wonder why and how European reason can be reformed. Can we hope for a *métanoïa* of Post-Europe?

1. European care for the soul

In its Socratic meaning, the soul is what bears the inner determination of man. "The soul decides for itself and, to that end, it has a power of its own – the knowledge of truth and of the good." (Patočka 2017)[1]

Caring for the soul is first healing a mind torn between two *logoï,* at worst a mind that contradicts itself without being aware of it, and consequently says nothing (*ouden leigein*), is meaningless. "Socrates' approach in his care for the soul is determined by this tendency to find out an inner trouble, signaled by a logical or linguistic antagonism and hidden by the hypertrophia and the sclerosis of an inconsistent self." (ibid.) Therefore, the

---

[1] It is our own translation into English as for all texts by Patočka.

first step of the therapeutics is elenchtic -the refutation of the absence of problematicity in everything related to the things of the good. Moreover, the Socratic care for the soul starts with "tracing out the limit," with the famous Delphic *gnôthi seauton*, the "know thyself" showing humans their limit (know you are only humans don't go into *hubris*, don't pretend to be gods). Caring for the soul begins by drawing the limit between what humans know and what they do not know.

Only *sophrôn* humans know what they know and what they do not know. But is self-knowledge just possible? That is the whole subject – an aporia – of Plato's dialogue *The Charmides* and "Socrates has no theoretical certainty at all about the construction of self-knowledge. The problem European metaphysics has been constantly dealing with from Aristotle to the most recent thinkers is set out here for the first time." (ibid.) *The Charmides* deals with the very topical problem of the relationship between science (*épistémè*) and wisdom (*sophrosunè*), and we know all too well how our modern society wrongly tends to take the technician expert for a sage.

To Patočka, self-knowledge is a two-sided problem, one side "is inner concentration under the influence of the healing *logos*," the other is the humble knowledge humans should have of their personal limitation. The Socratic care for the soul then unfolds through two pedagogical forces, dialectics and irony. In *L'Europe et après* Patočka points out that with Democritus, and even more with Plato, the care for the soul works in a questioning frame of thought which takes the form of "accounting through reason" (*logon didonaï*) including "the certainty there will be no closure" – the endless movement of an "inquiring logos" constantly looking for foundations. (Patočka 2007, 104-105)[2] Such a gaze into what is, wisely avoids hubris. It is built on "the renunciation to any claim to hold the truth" on the being and "care for the soul compels humans to look for what is good, to start seeking out some evident clarity on everything they think, say and do." (ibid. 112)

That shows how strong the demand for responsibility is with this care for the soul. Only this conception, specific to the "open soul", can show humans they are not given beings, "but beings who need to be borne." (ibid. 218) To the closed subjectivity, everything seems given in advance: humans, the Earth, living beings, objects, values, etc. However, what Greek history and philosophy have tried to understand is precisely the problematicity of the world of life – which, as far as it is concerned, is never given as a theme, as we have all known since Husserl. Originally, Europe means "a gaze into what is", according to Patočka. However, twisting the meaning of it, Europe gradually made a bad use of its re-

---

[2] All the subsequent references to Patočka and quotations come from his last texts, from the beginning of the seventies to his death, are from the compendium *L'Europe après l'Europe* (Patočka 2007).

sponsibility, so to speak: Europe set itself "a demand for universal responsibility which explains to a certain extent that European mankind may have taken its form of life for that of the whole of mankind." (ibid., 235) Its tutelary presumption to want to account for the others as for itself, on all levels, political, theological, economic and scientific, made it lose its aura. (We will come back to that, supra II).

For the time being, let us briefly recall the description Patočka gives of the three aspects of Plato's care for the soul[3]:
- as an onto-cosmological project, care for the soul, as a driving principle, is a gaze into what is, extended to the whole being;
- the second aspect has to do with the political project of a state refounded in spirit with the soul as its structure (*The Republic*);
- care for the soul as self-knowledge, deepening the inner life of the soul, its relationship to the body and to intercorporeality -the soul is here conceived as the structure of appearing.[4]

The third aspect refers to the problem of *The Charmides*, as we have seen. But the problem of the European spirit is precisely that it no longer seems able to reach self-knowledge:

> The curse of the European spirit (…) is that, full of itself, it is unable to understand the others and consequently does not know itself either. It has found out a host of efficient means to become the master of the world, but all have also been used – as we now see after the fall of Europe – for the purpose of self-destruction. Europe as a hegemonic power no longer exists. (Patočka 1990, 211)

Once the diagnosis is made, and even before considering whether there is a possible therapy, what are the reasons for the disease the European spirit suffers from?

2. From the European spirit to a post-European nation

To Patočka, the specificity of European spirituality is the will to found the gaze into what is, on the one, the universal and the inner and social knowledge of the human soul. Its historic failure lies in the *outer* path of its hegemonic conquest and its imperialistic aspiration. From now on Europe must take the *inner* path opening up to "the becoming-world of the world of life." (Patočka 2007, 40-44) The European spirit first aimed at irenic universal reason; it distorted this aim and turned it into a warlike, arrogant, and intrusive exportation

---

[3] See especially the paragraphs 9 to 12 in Patočka 2007.
[4] "The soul is not only the fact that there is the being but also that the being appears, that there is a specific, constant and irreducible structure of its manifestation." (ibid., 129)

of its universalism. This exportation was carried out violently: through colonialism, through its unilateral political vision of democracy (its mono-democratism), through its ultraliberal economic expansion imposing overconsumption as a way of life, through its "technoscienticism" and through its neglect of classical "humanities". Patočka describes this phenomenon clearly: "the spiritual dissolution" of Europe was achieved by the development of technosciences, "the decadent culture of subjectivism", the decline of "languages and the classics which were the spiritual cement of any Europeanity." (ibid., 46-47)

The 17th century rationalism and science have gradually replaced metaphysics and religion. Eventually, their ambition to determine the whole Real and to subdue nature gradually imposed the *Gestell* gaze. Science as "a domineering form of knowledge which wants to include the whole of nature in its theory only appeared in Europe." (ibid., 227) In spite of the historical conflicts that opposed science and religion, "the spirit of European Christianism was to subject nature to men's practice by a new rationality at the service of one's fellow human being." (ibid., 228-229)

But then, what can enable the European spirit to revert to its original will ? If the care for the soul makes sense within the community, and if Plato's analogy between the soul and the community has limits of its own, the problem identified by Plato still remains and must be revived in seeking for "the specific meaning of the new community in combining intellectual distance and courageous commitment." (ibid.) In other words, the European spirit can only find itself again and be vivified through the alliance between *sôphrosunê* and *andreia*.

For instance, can we be wise and courageous enough to conceive a European "nation"? To speak of a European "nation" in the sense of a common *identity* would require that a majority of the inhabitants of Europe "feel" European. A president of Europe and a passport (for lack of a "European identity card") would be necessary but not even sufficient. Only a real community of the activities of the mind, that is to say culture and education, could give European peoples a national identity. "The spirit, as it advances towards its realization, towards self-satisfaction and self-knowledge, is the sole motive force behind all the deeds and aspirations of the nation. Religion, knowledge, the arts and the destinies and events of history are all aspects of its evolution. This, and not the natural influences at work upon it (as the derivation of the word *natio* from *nasci* might suggest) determines the nation's character" (Hegel 1975, 56).

In this age of deterritorialized flows, the notion of a European "nation" would imply conventional and ideal borders rather than natural and national ones. A European people can only exist through an activity of the mind giving it its singularity. This spiritual activity is made up of the Greco-Roman heritage, the legacy of Judaism through Christianism and

Islam, the humanist values of the Enlightenment and the democratic model with its values of liberty, equality, solidarity and secularism *(laïcité)*.

Admittedly, some geographic limits can be devised for Europe: the Atlantic border in the west, the icy Arctic Ocean with Iceland in the north, the Ural River in the East – since orienting Europe is giving it some Orient of its own – and the Mediterranean Sea in the south, with cousins – Morocco, Algeria, Tunisia, and Turkey- connecting with European institutions as associated countries. But European borders cannot be internal, that is "interiorized". There can only be borders *for* (*European*) *interiority* if they are idealized.[5]

Without that condition, "national borders would not be capable of securing (or trying to secure) identities, would not be capable of marking the threshold at which life and death are played out (in what in Europe is called 'patriotism')" (Balibar 2002, 94). Does the very idea of European patriotism (a non-economic one) make sense? Is it even to be desired? It is possible to conceive a nation without a homeland, whose unity is nevertheless secured by European defense and a European army. Habermas warns us: "The solidarity of citizens is shifted onto the more abstract foundation of a 'constitutional patriotism'. If it fails, then the collective collapses into subcultures that seal themselves off from one another." (Habermas 2001, 74)

What could a European "nation" be?

The European nation cannot be an international economic alliance, as is the present European Union, which citizens not only fail to appropriate but denigrate, being only sensitive to its harmful effects and remaining blind to the benefits it brings them regionally. The economic union confused the origin of Europe and its end: under the pressure of globalisation, it took for *the* beginning what could be *a* finality. "It is for us... to put some flesh on the Community's bones and, dare I suggest, give it a little more soul (…) You cannot fall in love with the single market." (Delors 1989)

The European nation cannot either be an empire, in the sense of a post-national sovereign state, which annexes old nations in the context of Europeanism or under the pretext of universalism. Nor should it be an unprecedented capitalistic financial empire, and certainly not a patchwork of old Nation-States closed in on their particularism and their nationalism as in the 19th century. Its unity cannot be reduced to the sum total of its inward-looking parts.

Instead, the European nation could be a federation of the United States (or united regions) of Europe, whose citizens would at last share the sense of a common cultural identity – the one that recognizes differences in cultures-, with a conclusive territory whose borders

---

[5] This decisive wording dates back to Fichte's *Addresses to the German Nation* (1807) as put it Etienne Balibar (Balibar 2002, 94).

would be redefined and with common foreign and defence policies. Then the main task of the European nation would decidedly be to wipe out misery on its own soil:

> A day will come when bullets and bombshells will be replaced by votes, by the universal suffrage of nations, by the venerable arbitration of a great Sovereign Senate, which will be to Europe ...what the Legislative assembly is to France... it is the object to which I shall always direct myself – the extinction of misery at home, and the extinction of war abroad. (Hugo 1849, 11)

We are still very far from the aim Victor Hugo called for. Let us come back to what, according to Jan Patočka, would enable the spirit of present Europe -that is our Post-Europe- to come to itself.

3. Can we hope for a metanoïa of Post-Europe?

Is there any chance for Europe to return to itself? Such is the essential question raised by Patočka, who already in 1970 perceived that Europe would have to discuss "with the cultural traditions that gave the European idea a necessary factual basis. These traditions have so far been considered as dead and meaningless, but we will have to learn to take them seriously." (Patočka 1990, 212) Europe can only be revived by transforming itself through otherness. To this end, it must give up the all-embracing, even totalitarian pretense of its rationality:

> If Europe, as Husserl thought, means rationality, if rationality is synonymous with universality, there was a contradiction in claiming and keeping rationality as the exclusive property of Europe. The end of Europe may have a positive meaning. European rationality, which is unifying, may launch a bridge which will make it necessary to take seriously and think without preconceived ideas what is exactly furthest from us. (Patočka 2007, 212-214)

The Czech philosopher considers this salutary possibility with caution. Is Europe ready to open itself to multiethnic rationality? Patočka points out that Husserl's *Krisis* has already mentioned "the urgent task of deepening the foundation of European rationality, which is the only way to make it possible to have a genuine discussion with all the living traditions of the world of life *in concreto*." (ibid.) This deepening of European reason implies going out of subjectivism and its tendency to become absolute, in order to find the way to transcendental intersubjectivity. Its historical spirituality cannot be reduced to scientific and technical rationalisation: "as soon as it is extended to the reason expressing itself in ethical life, poetry, art, and religion, there is no reason why traditions quite different from our European one could not be allied to rational motives." (ibid., 210) Indeed, there are forms of logic, modalities of human reason different from those we practice in Europe: we have to understand how they express themselves in non-European traditions in order to deepen the dialogism between them and us. Europe's task is to build such a bridge unifying modes of rationality:

> The European believes mankind is one because he identifies Europe with mankind; he easily forgets that, so far, there is no unitary mankind; there are only different sets of mankind waiting for some unifying formative action. (Patočka 2007, 59)

Let us examine the case of democratic reason. Democracy is not the privilege of Europe and can never be only reduced to majority-rule ballot. Democracy is also and above all "the exercise of public reason" (Rawls 1999, 579-580) based on deliberation and the participation of citizens in the decisions concerning their public affairs. In that sense, there is a grand tradition of public debate in India, China, Japan, Iran, Turkey and in a lot of Arab and African countries.

To recognize that democratic reason at work in other cultures through going out of its unilateral, ethnocentric democratism has become a compelling necessity for Europe. That is an essential task for Europe in order to give a new life to its care for the other and return to the care for the soul without losing its own soul. To crystallize the recognition of a political globalisation of democratic history, to reform itself and take eastern democratic centres seriously, to symbolize the synergy between different cultural forms of democratic reason, such is the task of Europe.

Jan Patočka's questioning is a topical matter of urgency: "Is it certain", he wonders, "that non-European liberation movements are fundamentally identical to the struggle of underprivileged classes in Europe?" (Patočka 2007, 243) Isn't that another Europeanistic view? For more than forty years, Patočka has been warning us that the different spiritualities of non-European cultures may conflict with our hyper-rationalistic conception, which imposes its sole worldview: that is a form of *Polemos* for now and for the years to come.

Thus, only a refoundation of rationality can save Post-Europe: reviving its fundamental spiritual principle, the care for the soul. Life in the idea must contend with ideology and the open soul must contend with subjectivism enclosed on itself. Reason must conquer human understanding. The spirit of distanciation and critical review must be applied to our spiritual tradition without any Eurocentrism or expansionist rationality. "The spirit in this post-European context", Karel Novotný comments, "is that of the solidarity of the shaken," (Novotný 2012, 149)[6] inasmuch as it constantly rekindles problematicity, the shaking up *(thaumazein)* of the certainty of the already there, of the given. Everybody in quest of life in

---

[6] The translation is ours.

truth can share this renewed mode of the gaze into what is. What Patočka aims at is to give a transcendental foundation to a transcultural spirituality, which could unite humans in solidarity with one another in a new form of Socratism, careful of the problematicity of the world. This spirit is open to what the other can make me discover in myself with his foreign spirituality and to what my spirit can unveil in himself.

***

Such a task requires a heroism of the *logos*, a *métanoia*, a new Socratic heresy, an unprecedented choice *(haïrê)*: to substitute the cosmopolitanism of spiritual Europe for the imperialism of economic Europe (constituting Europeanity through cosmopolitanism and not the opposite)[7], and to substitute the universality of democratic *reason* for the imperialism of technoscientific *rationalisation*. The aim of Post-Europe must set itself is to move from rationalisation back to reason, to make sure, as Patočka puts it, that human "understanding may recover itself in reason." (Patočka 2007, 53)

European reflexion, prompted by the limitations of its technoscientific *ratio,* is destined to "fertilize extra-European reflexion." (Patočka 2007, 241) It should set itself as *telos* a new spiritual conversion of its reason (*métanoia*) in place of its cult of rationality.

Europe has no monopoly on the question of *problematicity*. The problematicity of what is, the shaking up *(thauma)* of the given meaning, the liberty to deny the non-problematic evidence of the world are present in a great many other cultures and find their equivalent in age-long Taoist, Buddhist, or Indian traditions. The only way for Europe to reform itself is to open itself to these other forms of problematicity. From now on, this is the sole condition to build a common language and a common world.[8]

"The waking have one common world, but the sleeping turn aside each into a world of his own,"[9] as Heraclitus put it.

Translated in English by François Monnanteuil

Dr. Philippe Merlier, Académie de Limoges, philippe.merlier[at]ac-limoges.fr

---

[7]I developed this idea in chapter III: "L'Europe de Patočka" of my book *Patočka, le soin de l'âme et l'Europe* (see Merlier 2009, 151-210).
[8]"Today, at a time when all the sets of mankind are becoming one, we have beforehand neither a common world nor a common language and the main task awaiting us will precisely be to create both" (Patočka 2007, 243).
[9]Heraclitus: Fragment LXXXIX, according to Plutarch (see Burnet 1920, 140).

References

Balibar, Etienne. "The Borders of Europe," in *Politics and the Other Scene*. London / New York: Verso, 2002, 87-104.
Burnet, John. *Early Greek Philosophy*. London: A & C Black, 1920.
Delors, Jacques. "Address to the European Parliament", 17 January 1989, online: https://www.cvce.eu/obj/address_given_by_jacques_delors_to_the_european_parliament_17_january_1989-en-b9c06b95-db97-4774-a700-e8aea5172233.html.
Habermas, Jürgen. *The Postnational Constellation,* transl. ed. Max Pensky. Cambridge: Polity Press 2001.
Habermas, Jürgen. *Times of Transition,* ed. and transl. Ciaran Cronin and Max Pensky. Cambridge: Polity Press, 2006.
Hegel, Gottfried Wilhelm Hegel. *Lectures on the Philosophy of World History,* transl. Hugh Barr Nisbet. Cambridge: Cambridge University Press, 1975.
Hugo, Victor. "Inaugural address," in *Report of the proceedings of the second general Peace Congress, held in Paris on the 22nd, 23rd, and 24th of August, 1849*. London, Charles Gilpin, 1849, 10-14.
Merlier, Philip. *Patočka, le soin de l'âme et l'Europe.* Paris: L'Harmattan, 2009.
Novotný Karel. *La Génèse d'une Hérésie. Monde, corps et histoire dans la pensée de Jan Patočka*. Paris: Vrin, 2012.
Patočka Jan. *Socrate: Cours du semestre d'été 1946 suivi de Remarques sur le problème de Socrate,* transl. Erika Abrmas. Fribourg: Academic Press Fribourg, 2017.
Patočka Jan. "Réflexion sur l'Europe", in *Liberté et Sacrifice. Écrits politiques*, transl. Erika Abrams. Grenoble: Jérôme Millon, 1990, 181-213.
Patočka Jan. "L'Europe et après", in *L'Europe après l'Europe,* transl. Erika Abrams. Paris: Verdier, 2007, 44-56.
Rawls John. *Collected papers.* Cambridge, MA: Harvard University Press, 1999.
Schuman Robert. "Declaration at the Ministry of Foreign Affairs of 9 May, 1950", online: https://www.robert-schuman.eu/en/declaration-of-9-may-1950

SUSANNE MOSER (Wien)

Political Correctness oder Tugendterror?

Political Correctness or Virtue Terror?

Abstract

Discussing the different meanings of the concept of political correctness, the author argues that it is a part of a profound change in culture within Western democracies that has led to a differentiation and deepening of human and fundamental rights. At the same time, it is shown that political correctness was adopted by the political right and used as a fight against this differentiation of human and fundamental rights in the Western liberal democracies, in order to defame them by linking the corresponding prohibitions of discrimination and equality measures with virtue terror.

Keywords: Political Correctness, hate speech, discrimination, silencing, liberalism, illiberalism

"Politische Korrektheit ersetzt heute passgenau die religiöse Richtigkeit. Sie ist der Religionsersatz der Akademiker." (Bolz 2009, 30) Wie das Zitat von Norbert Bolz zeigt, haben in den letzten Jahren öffentliche, aber auch philosophische Diskussionen immer mehr den Charakter von Glaubenskriegen angenommen. Insbesondere ist es der Wert Gleichheit, der vermehrt Aggressionen auslöst. So wird von einer "Gleichheits-Religion" (Sarazin 2014, 39) gesprochen und von gewaltsamer Missionierung. Themen über gendergerechte Sprache, Gendermainstreaming und Diversity werden unter dem Sammelbegriff *Political Correctness* immer stärker dem Vorwurf des Tugendterrors ausgesetzt.

Zunächst möchte ich der Frage nachgehen, was denn eigentlich unter *Political Correctness* zu verstehen ist, um mich danach den Vorwürfen zuzuwenden, die von übertriebener Moralisierung bis hin zu Tugendterror sprechen. Dabei werde ich zwei Thesen vertreten:

1. *Political Correctness* ist Teil eines tiefgreifenden Kulturwandels innerhalb der westlichen Demokratien, der zu einer Ausdifferenzierung und Vertiefung der Menschen- und Grundrechte geführt hat.
2. *Political Correctness* wurde von der politisch Rechten übernommen als Kampfbegriff gegen die in den westlichen liberalen Demokratien etablierten Menschen- und Grundrechte.

1. Vom linken Campusphänomen zum rechten Kampfbegriff

Im Zuge der Bürgerrechtsbewegungen wurde der Begriff *Political Correctness* ausgehend von nordamerikanischen Universitäten in den 1960er-Jahren zur moralpolitischen Beurteilung von Sprache und Verhalten geprägt. Dahinter stand die Einschätzung und Hoffnung, dass eine veränderte Sprache Diskriminierung von Minderheiten und Frauen abschaffen könne. Es ging darum, nicht-juristische Normen des richtigen politischen und sprachlichen Verhaltens zu entwickeln, da rechtliche Einschränkungen aufgrund des hohen Stellenwertes der Redefreiheit in den USA umstritten sind. Zunächst handelte es sich um ein Campusphänomen. Mitte der 1980er-Jahre begannen Studierende die Ausweitung des Lehrstoffes zu fordern. Statt ausschließlich Pflichtkurse zu "Western Civilization" verlangten sie unter anderem Kurse über außereuropäische Kulturen und weibliche Autoren. Es entstand ein Sprachkodex, der minderheitengerecht sein sollte. Als dieser Kodex immer rigider wurde, entstand der Begriff "*politically correct*" zunächst als ironisch verwendeter Begriff innerhalb der Linken selbst. Bereits hier wurde also die Gefahr der Übertreibung und der Dogmatisierung erkannt und angesprochen.

In den 1990er Jahren kam es zu einer Aneignung des Begriffes durch die politische Rechte und damit zu einer Umkehr. US-Konservative an Hochschulen und in Medien verwendeten in Auseinandersetzung mit dem politischen Gegner *Political Correctness* nunmehr als Kampfbegriff gegen die ihrer Meinung nach falsch verstandene liberale Multikulti-Gesellschaft. *Political Correctness* wurde für sie zu einem Mittel im Kulturkampf gegen die Erfolge der Frauen, Schwarzen und Homosexuellen. Die Genderstudies wurden zur "Gender-Ideologie" erklärt, Mitmenschlichkeit zum "Gutmenschentum", die Antidiskriminierung von Minderheiten zur "Diskriminierung der Mehrheit".

Verbunden damit ist eine starke Ablehnung jeglicher als Bevormundung verstandener Reglementierung von Sprache bis hin zur Forderung nach Meinungs- und Redefreiheit, auch wenn es um offensichtliche Herabminderung, bis hin zu Hassrede und Verhetzung geht.

2. *Political Correctness* als Teilgebiet verschiedener Maßnahmen zum Schutz vor Hassrede

Die Hassrede ist dadurch gekennzeichnet, dass sie sich nicht einfach gegen einzelne Personen richtet, sondern gegen die Zugehörigkeit zu einer bestimmten Gruppe, die als minderwertig betrachtet wird, sei dies nun aufgrund ihrer Hautfarbe, Nationalität, Herkunft, Religionszugehörigkeit, Geschlecht, sexuellen Orientierung, ihres sozialen Status, ihrer Gesundheit oder ihres Aussehens. Diesen Menschen werden bestimmte Eigenschaften zugeschrieben, die dann zum Ausgangspunkt der Abwertung genommen werden. Es gibt im

Prinzip keine menschliche Eigenschaft, die nicht zum Gegenstand des Hasses gemacht werden kann. Was man dazu benötigt, ist die Kategorisierung von Eigenschaften. Man kann zum Beispiel Ostfriesen, Blondinen, Intellektuelle, alle Bewohner einer bestimmten Stadt, einen Fußballverein, usw. aus Hass als "solche und solche" negativ abstempeln. Nicht in der Kategorisierung an sich besteht hier die Hassrede, sondern, dass es aufgrund von Hass zur Zuschreibung bestimmter negativer Eigenschaften kommt.

Konkrete Beispiele dafür gibt es genügende. Eines der folgenschwersten war sicherlich die Kategorisierung von Menschen aufgrund angeblich rassischer Unterschiede. Obwohl z.B. viele Juden bereits assimiliert und zum christlichen Glauben übergetreten waren, wurden sie als "Juden" stigmatisiert. Daraufhin wurde ihnen das Bürgerrecht in Deutschland und Österreich abgesprochen und zuletzt sogar das Menschsein, was in der Folge zur Katastrophe des Holocaust führte. Es waren Simone de Beauvoir und Jean-Paul Sartre, die bereits früh den Zusammenhang zwischen Judenfrage, Rassendiskriminierung und Unterdrückung der Frauen enthüllten. Simone de Beauvoirs *Das andere Geschlecht* und Sartres *Überlegungen zur Judenfrage* zeigen auf, wie Menschen aufgrund der Zuschreibung bestimmter gruppenspezifischer, negativer Eigenschaften zu "Anderen" gemacht werden. In jüngster Zeit sind es die Hassreden islamischer Prediger, die für Aufregung sorgen, in zunehmendem Maße jedoch auch antisemitische, rassistische, sexistische und ausländerfeindliche Angriffe in den sozialen Medien und im Internet.

2.1. Rechtliche Maßnahmen gegen Hassrede (hate speech)

Generell gesprochen gibt es, – insbesondere in den USA, wo es schon lange eine intensive Auseinandersetzung mit *hate speech* gibt, – drei Schwellen für die Notwendigkeit rechtlich einzugreifen, nämlich die Gefahr der Gewalteskalation, die Verfassungswidrigkeit und die Demokratiegefährdung durch Einschüchterung (*silencing*). Wo direkt zu Gewalt aufgerufen wird, d.h. wenn bestimmte Äußerungen eindeutig die Gefahr in sich tragen zu einem illegalen Akt zu führen, gilt es rechtlich gegen *hate speech* vorzugehen. Wenn die Äußerung in der konkreten Situation den Umschlag vom Wort zur Tat erwarten lässt, d.h. "*clear and present danger*" vorliegt, wird in den USA strafrechtlich eingeschritten. Neben dem Kriterium der konkreten Gefahr, gibt es ein weiteres Kriterium, das der Verfassungswidrigkeit. Durch rassistische und sexistische Sprache wird die Minderwertigkeit einer Rasse oder eines bestimmten Geschlechts behauptet, daher gibt es für die Verfassung keinen Grund, solches Sprechen mit der Redefreiheit zu schützen, denn es ist unvereinbar mit den Prinzipien auf denen die Verfassung beruht. Hier geht es um den Schutz der Demokratie vor Feinden: Die Demokratie muss "wehrhaft" sein, will sie nicht durch ihre Feinde ausgehebelt werden. *Silencing* ist ein drittes Kriterium: Es kann nicht akzeptiert werden, dass die Opfer von *hate speech* durch Einschüchterung und Furcht zum Verstummen gebracht werden und dadurch ihrer demokratischen Mitwirkungsrechte beraubt werden.

In Österreich wird Hassrede als Verhetzung im §283 des Strafrechtsänderungsgesetzes 2015 abgehandelt: Wer öffentlich auf eine Weise, dass es vielen Menschen zugänglich wird, zu Gewalt gegen eine "nach den vorhandenen oder fehlenden Kriterien" der Rasse, der Hautfarbe, der Sprache, der Religion oder Weltanschauung, der Staatsangehörigkeit, der Abstammung oder nationalen oder ethnischen Herkunft, des Geschlechts, einer körperlichen oder geistigen Behinderung, des Alters oder der sexuellen Ausrichtung definierte Gruppe von Personen zu Hass aufstachelt, oder sie in der Absicht, ihre Menschenwürde zu verletzen, beschimpft oder in der öffentlichen Meinung verächtlich macht und herabsetzt, macht sich strafbar. Die Schwelle von der bisher "breiten Öffentlichkeit" (ca. 150 Personen) auf "viele Menschen" (ca. 30 Personen)" wurde in der Gesetzesänderung heruntergesetzt. Mit der Einführung einer qualifizierten Vorsatzkomponente, nämlich "beschimpfen in der Absicht, die Menschenwürde anderer zu verletzen" wurde ein Korrektiv geschaffen, das auch auf die Hetze in den neuen Medien anwendbar ist. Durch Einfügung der Wortfolge "vorhandenen oder fehlenden" wurde nunmehr ausdrücklich festgelegt, dass die geschützte Gruppe sowohl positiv als auch negativ definiert werden kann. In diesem Sinne soll nunmehr auch die Hetze gegen "Ausländer" oder "Ungläubige" dem Anwendungsbereich des § 283 StGB unterliegen.

In der Bundesrepublik Deutschland ist es das Netzwerkdurchsetzungsgesetz, das am 1.1.2018 rechtskräftig wurde, anhand dessen die sozialen Medien und andre Netzwerke gezwungen werden sollen, Hassreden konsequenter zu entfernen, als dies bisher der Fall war.

2.2. Einwände gegen ein rechtliches Vorgehen gegen Hassrede

Liberale Demokratien leben davon, dass möglichst alle Menschen an den politischen Prozessen partizipieren können und nicht an der Teilnahme durch Einschüchterung (*silencing*) gehindert werden. Zugleich stellt die Redefreiheit – insbesondere in den USA – einen sehr hohen Wert dar, was seinen Ausdruck in der amerikanischen Verfassung gefunden hat, und zwar im "*First Amendment*" der *Bill of Rights*, wo es explizit heißt: "*Congress shall make no law [...] abridging the freedom of speech [...]*." Allerdings gibt es eine Ausnahme, dann nämlich, wenn eine klare und gegenwärtige Gefahr von Gewaltakten vorliegt (*clear and present danger*). Es ist also sehr wichtig, die Gefahr richtig einzuschätzen. Dafür ist es notwendig, den Kontext, d.h. die konkrete Situation mit zu berücksichtigen. So muss die Äußerung ein und desselben Inhalts – z.B. "Getreidehändler lassen Arme verhungern" – in verschiedenen Kontexten unterschiedlich bewertet werden. Wenn diese Meinung zum Beispiel gegenüber einem aufgeregten Mob vor dem Haus eines Getreidehändlers geäußert wird, sei es nun in gesprochener Form oder durch das Verteilen von Pamphleten, dann muss sie sanktioniert werden, weil sie unmittelbar zu Gewaltakten anstiftet. Wird dagegen diese Meinung zum Beispiel über die Presse auf eine Weise geäußert, die nicht die unmittelbare Gefahr einer gewaltsamen Tat mit sich bringt, dann darf die Äußerung dieses Inhalts nicht verboten werden.

Nach John Stuart Mill ist es nicht legitim, die Freiheit einzuschränken, um jemanden zu schützen und sei es nur vor sich selbst. In *Über die Freiheit* schließt er paternalistische Begründungen zur Einschränkung der individuellen Freiheit ebenso aus wie moralistische: Ein gesunder Erwachsener sollte weder vor sich selbst geschützt werden, noch sollte ihm eine bestimmte Denk- oder Lebensweise aufgezwungen werden. Man dürfe niemanden dazu zwingen, "etwas zu tun oder zu lassen, weil es besser für ihn wäre." (Mill 1988, 16) Obwohl die Kritik die Kritisierten tief verletzen könne, sollte man sie, so John Stuart Mill, dennoch nicht generell verbieten. Würde man – mit Hinweis auf die damit einhergehenden Verletzungen – Kritik verbieten, dann wäre es schwer möglich, auf Missstände hinzuweisen und notwendige Veränderungen einzuleiten. Folgt man Mill, dann muss eine rechtliche Regulierung von *hate speech* in der Lage sein, diese eindeutig von legitimer Kritik zu unterscheiden.

Die Anwendung des Freiheitsprinzips setzt für Mill allerdings einen gewissen Entwicklungsstand voraus. "Freiheit, als Prinzip, kann man nicht auf einer Entwicklungsstufe anwenden, auf der die Menschheit noch nicht einer freien und gleichberechtigten Erörterung derselben fähig ist." (Mill 1988, 17) Mill betont, dass seine Lehre nur auf Menschen mit "völlig ausgereiften Fähigkeiten" (Mill 1988, 17) anzuwenden sei, sie gelte weder für Kinder noch für "Barbaren". Er setzt voraus, dass die Menschen an ihrer eigenen Vervollkommnung arbeiten und mittels öffentlicher Diskussionen und im Austausch von Überzeugungen sich wechselseitig in ihrer Tugendhaftigkeit förderlich sind. Mill glaubt also an die Kraft der Tugend. Er setzt das voraus, was Sven-Uwe Schmitz in seinem Buch *Homo Democraticus* (Schmitz 2000) einem Demokraten zuschreibt, nämlich eine gehörige Portion Unterscheidungskraft und eine Haltung der Selbstdisziplin, die darin besteht, das eigene Urteil nicht als die alleinige Wahrheit zu absolutieren, sondern vielmehr andere Sichtweisen in die Betrachtung miteinzubeziehen. Selbstvertrauen in die eigenen Fähigkeiten und ein grundsätzliches Fremdvertrauen in die Fähigkeiten der Mitbürger zu Moralität und Verantwortungsübernahme sind für Mill Voraussetzungen dafür, dass eine Demokratie gedeihen kann. All dies schlägt sich in den kommunikativen Tugenden wie Einfühlungsvermögen, Offenheit und Wahrhaftigkeit, sowie der Bereitschaft zum Zuhören nieder.

Was Mill ablehnt, ist jede Einmischung in das Leben Anderer. Entschieden wendet er sich gegen die "Tyrannei des vorherrschenden Meinens und Empfindens" um dadurch

"Lebensregeln denen aufzuerlegen, die eine abweichende Meinung haben." (Mill 1988, 10) Mill unterscheidet somit die Tugend als Vervollkommnung der eigenen Person von einem Tugendterror, der auf das Verhalten anderer gerichtet ist.

2.3 Die Gefahr der Unterdrückung von Minderheitsmeinungen und die Angst vor parteilichen Regulierungen

Mill vertrat vehement die Ansicht, dass jede Meinungsäußerung von Wert für die öffentliche Diskussion sein könnte und folglich keine Meinung – auch wenn sie von Vielen oder den Meisten abgelehnt wird – durch Zensur von ihr ausgeschlossen werden dürfe. Er befürchtete, dass in einer Demokratie die Vertreter einer Mehrheitsmeinung dazu neigen, Minderheitsmeinungen zu unterdrücken. Diese Neigung müsse nicht einer Bösartigkeit geschuldet sein, sondern sei in den meisten Fällen darauf zurückzuführen, dass sich die Vertreter der Mehrheitsmeinung sicher seien, die richtige Meinung zu vertreten. Die Gesellschaft müsse vor der "Tyrannei der Mehrheit" auf der Hut sein. (Mill 1988, 9)

Die Ablehnung von inhaltsbasierten Regulierungen der Meinungsfreiheit hat ihren Ursprung also in der Angst vor parteilichen Regulierungen. Im Falle von *hate speech* kann uns eine parteiliche Regulierung zwar als wünschenswert erscheinen, aber nur weil uns eine bestimmte Position missfällt, sollten wir – Mill folgend – noch keine Reglementierung vornehmen. Würden alle Äußerungen, die Gruppen herabwürdigen, verboten, dann würden sie aus der öffentlichen Diskussion ausgeschlossen. Auch diese unmoralischen Aussagen müssten – Mill folgend – in die öffentliche Diskussion eingehen, um in der Auseinandersetzung als solche entlarvt zu werden. Nur so könne man "Irrtümer korrigieren" und richtigstellen: "Diskussion tut not, um zu zeigen, wie die Erfahrung zu deuten ist. Falsche Urteile und Bräuche geben allmählich den Tatsachen und Überlegungen Raum." (Mill 1988, 30) Auch hier zeigt sich wie sehr Mill auf die demokratischen und kommunikativen Tugenden des Menschen setzte.

2.4. Misstrauen gegenüber staatlichen Verboten und Interventionen, Widerstand durch Verschiebung, Untergrabung, Parodierung

Die Sorge, dass juristische Bemühungen zur Wiederholung und Vervielfältigung des verletzenden Sprechens führen, liegt am Ursprung von Judith Butlers Überlegungen zur *hate speech*. In ihrem 1998 auf Deutsch erschienen Buch *Hass spricht* (*Excitable Speech. A Politics of the Performative* 1997) schlägt sie andere als juristische Möglichkeiten vor. Man könne den Widerstand performativ herstellen über Verschiebung, Untergrabung und Parodierung des Gesagten. Generell stellt sie die Frage, wie es überhaupt möglich sei, dass

Sprache uns verletzen könne und ob eine notwendige Beziehung zwischen Sprache und Verletzung bestehe, d.h. ob der jeweilige "Sprechakt die Verletzung als Effekt vollziehen *muß*." (Butler 1998, 28) Da Butler hier keine notwendige Verbindung sieht, ergeben sich für sie Möglichkeiten, die über das Rechtliche hinausgehen und das Feld des performativen Widerstandes eröffnen. "Anstelle einer staatlich gestützten Zensur geht es um einen gesellschaftlichen und kulturellen Sprachkampf, in dem sich die Handlungsmacht von der Verletzung herleitet und ihr gerade dadurch entgegentritt." (ebenda, 64)

Netzwerke wie *no hate speech, belltower.news,* oder *organisierteliebe* versuchen neue kreative Zugänge. So berichtet Kübra Gümüsay, dass sie zunächst versucht hatte, auf die Hasspostings zu reagieren, bis sie es satt hatte nur "hintendrein zu putzen". Wenn sich Menschen für ihre rassistischen Äußerungen nicht mehr schämen, seien wir mit unserer Empörung zu spät dran. Deshalb wolle sie dem Hass nun aktiv mit Liebe begegnen. Wie kann ich meine Liebe zeigen? Teilen, kommentieren, den Kontakt suchen zu Leuten: Belohne ihre Bemühungen, mach ihnen Komplimente! Vielen Bemühungen liegt der Gedanke einer Haltungsänderung zugrunde, die durch persönliche Kontaktaufnahme ermöglicht werden könnte. So stellt sich Ali Can als "Asylant Ihres Vertrauens" in der von ihm gegründeten Hotline-für-besorgte-Bürger den Sorgen und Ängsten der Bürger, weil er davon überzeugt ist, dass man mit den Leuten mehr reden muss, wenn man etwas bewirken möchte.

3. Political Correctness und die Gefahr des Tugendterrors

Unter dem Titel "Wir Tugendterroristen" schreibt Bernhard Pörksen in *Die Zeit* vom 8. November 2012, dass man eine Moralisierung aller Lebensbereiche beobachten könne, eine Neigung zum Tugendterror, die Maß und Mitte verloren habe. (Pörksen 2012) Moralische Empörung liefere die Möglichkeit, sich über den Anderen zu erheben und im Moment der kollektiven Wut Gemeinschaft zu finden. Wer "Skandal" schreie, wolle vor allem eines, nämlich Aufmerksamkeit. In der massenmedial geprägten Mediendemokratie hätten einst publizistische Großmächte darüber entscheiden, was als wichtig zu gelten habe. Es gab räumlich einigermaßen eingrenzbare Wirkungsfelder, klar erkennbare, physisch fassbare Machtzentren. In der digitalen Empörungsdemokratie der Gegenwart seien räumliche, zeitliche und kulturelle Grenzen leicht passierbar geworden. Hier werde die Deutungsmacht der Wenigen zum erbittert ausgefochtenen Meinungskampf der Vielen.

Moderne liberale Demokratien zeichnen sich nicht nur durch eine Trennung von Recht und Moral aus, sondern auch durch einen Pluralismus an Weltbildern und Lebensformen. Dies ist nicht zuletzt die Folge eines langen Kampfes um Anerkennung der gleichen Würde und Freiheit aller Menschen, sowie einer entsprechenden Bildung für alle Menschen, um an den demokratischen Prozessen teilhaben zu können. In seinem Werk

Demokratie und Erziehung (Dewey 1916) weist Dewey darauf hin, wie stark Erziehung und Demokratie miteinander verwoben sind. Für Dewey ist Demokratie mehr als eine Regierungsform, sie ist eine Lebensform, die sich dadurch auszeichnet, dass sie alle Glieder einer Gruppe an den Interessen derselben teilhaben lässt und sich durch die Fülle und Freiheit des Zusammenwirkens dieser Gruppe mit anderen Gruppen auszeichnet. Diese demokratische Lebensform grenzt er von einer "unerwünschten" Gesellschaft ab, "die durch Schranken, die sie innerhalb ihrer selbst und um sich herum aufrichtet, den freien Verkehr und den Austausch der Erfahrung hemmt. Eine Gesellschaft dagegen, die für die gleichmäßige Teilnahme aller ihrer Glieder an ihren Gütern und für immer erneute biegsame Anpassung ihrer Einrichtungen durch Wechselwirkung zwischen den verschiedenen Formen des Gemeinschaftslebens sorgt, ist insoweit demokratisch. Eine solche Gesellschaft braucht eine Form der Erziehung, die in den einzelnen ein persönliches Interesse an sozialen Beziehungen und am Einfluß der Gruppen weckt und diejenigen geistigen Gewöhnungen schafft, die soziale Umgestaltungen sichern, ohne Unordnung herbeizuführen." (Dewey 1916, 136) Dewey schreibt Demokraten also die Fähigkeit zu, neuen Herausforderungen im Rahmen des sozialen Wandels gerecht zu werden, da sie durch unterschiedliche Interaktionen sich stets neu anzupassen in der Lage sind.

3.1. Policital Correctness als Überkompensation?

Neben rechtlichen Maßnahmen der Gleichstellung sind daher immer schon bildungspolitische Maßnahmen notwendig, um den Demokratisierungsprozess voranzutreiben. Insbesondere gegen diese Gleichstellungsmaßnahmen, wird nunmehr der Vorwurf des Tugendterrors erhoben. So spricht Norbert Bolz von *Political Correctness* als einer Überkompensation: "Bei Lichte betrachtet ist die Politische Korrektheit also nur die Inversion des Vorurteils. Es handelt sich um eine Überkompensation, die diejenigen, die früher zu schlecht behandelt wurden, nun zu gut behandelt." (Bolz 2009, 34) Zuerst habe man gegen den Rassismus in den USA gekämpft, danach habe man die Kampfzone auf den Sexismus ausgeweitet und jetzt habe man auch noch die Schwulen- und die Altersdiskriminierung dazu genommen. Der Sensibilisierung für Benachteiligungen seien keine Grenzen mehr gesetzt. (Bolz 2009, 32) Im Namen von Fairness und Gleichstellung propagiere man die "Privilegierung der Unterprivilegierten." (Bolz 2010, 99) Der Stein des Anstoßes liegt für Bolz darin, dass dem Einzelnen durch den Tugendterror dieses "Akademikerglaubens" (ebd. 2009, 5) "sein Recht auf Diskriminierung" (Bolz 2010, 92) genommen worden sei. Es gehe nun darum dem "gesunden Menschenverstand" des "Stammtisches" (Bolz 2009, 31) wieder zu seinem Recht zu verhelfen.

Beim philosophischen Stammtisch des Schweizer Rundfunk diskutierten 14. Mai 2017 unter der Leitung von Barbara Bleisch, Catherine Newmark, Konrad Paul Liessmann und Norbert Bolz über das Thema: *Das Ende der Political Correctness?* Auf die Videoeinspielung von Trumps Feststellung: "Wir können es uns nicht mehr leisten, dermaßen politisch korrekt zu sein!" antwortete Nobert Bolz: "Wir hätten gar nie mit *Political Correctness* anfangen sollen! Dies habe nur zu einer Kultur der Überempfindlichkeit geführt." Auf die Gegenfrage der Moderatorin, ob es wirklich das sei, was wir jetzt brauchen, nämlich, jemanden, der sich wie Trump grob, unhöflich, verletzend und abwertend agiere, wurde der Beitrag einer Hörerin eingespielt: *Political Correctness* sei unentbehrlich in ihrem Kern, wenn wir so etwas wie einen gepflegten Umgang miteinander haben wollen. Ein weiterer Hörer bezeichnete *Political Correctness* hingegen als einen Tugendterror, der zur Ausschaltung kritisch Andersdenkender führe. *Political Correctness* sei eine Einschüchterungs- und Sprachpolitik, die kritisch Andersdenkende dämonisiere, als rechtspopulistisch stigmatisiere und sie dank medialem Pranger zum Schweigen bringe. Schon vor der Silversternacht des Jahres 2015/16, die in Deutschland als die Geburtsstunde der Kampfansage an *Political Correctness* angesehen werde, weil der Migrationshintergrund der Täter verschwiegen worden war, sei Tilo Sarazin niedergemacht worden. Das sei kein Zeichen für Meinungsfreiheit und nicht der Ausdruck einer liberalen Kultur. *Political Correctness* heiße doch schon lange nur mehr, dass man die Wahrheit nicht mehr sagen dürfe.

3.2. Fallstudie Tugendterror

Seine persönlichen Erfahrungen der Ausgrenzung und der Hetzkampagnen, verbunden mit falschen Behauptungen und Verleumdungen seit dem Erscheinen seines Buches *Deutschland schafft sich ab,* stellt Thilo Sarazin als Fallstudie für den neuen Tugendterror an den Beginn seines 2014 erschienen Buches *Der neue Tugendterror. Über die Grenzen der Meinungsfreiheit in Deutschland*. Sarazin positioniert sich selbst als Aufklärer im Sinne Kants, für den die Freiheit des Denkens und die Freiheit der Meinungsäußerung untrennbar miteinander verbunden gewesen sei. Er bedauert, dass die Jahrzehnte des Wohlstandes und der freiheitlichen Demokratie weniger den Mut, als die Anpassungsbereitschaft im Sinne der *Political Correctness* gefördert habe, die sich aus einer "Gleichheits-Religion" (Sarazin 2014, 39) speise, welche den Kern des Tugendterrors ausmache. Als Axiome des Tugendwahns nennt Sarazin unter anderem folgende Punkte: Ungleichheit ist schlecht, Gleichheit ist gut. Männer und Frauen haben bis auf ihre physischen Geschlechtsunterschiede keine angeborenen Unterschiede. Das traditionelle Familienbild hat sich überlebt. Kinder brauchen nicht Vater und Mutter. Kinder sind Privatsache, Einwanderung löst alle wesentlichen demographischen Probleme. Die menschlichen Fähigkeiten hängen im Wesentlichen von

Bildung und Erziehung ab, angeborene Unterscheide spielen keine Rolle. Völker und Ethnien haben keine Unterschiede, die über die rein physische Erscheinung hinausgehen. Wer arm ist, ist ein Opfer von Ungerechtigkeit und mangelnder Chancengleichheit. Alle Kulturen sind gleichwertig, insbesondere gebührt den Werten und Lebensformen des christlichen Abendlandes und der westlichen Industriestaaten keine besondere Präferenz. Der Nationalstaat hat sich überlebt. Die Zukunft gehört der Weltgesellschaft.

Sarazin schränkt seine Kritik an der Gleichheit jedoch wesentlich ein: die Gleichheit vor dem Gesetz und die Chancengleichheit seien ihm sehr wohl wichtig. Auch betont er, dass in all diesen Aussagen ein richtiger politischer Kern und ein ehrenwerter moralischer Impuls liege. "Es ist sogar grundsätzlich richtig, dass die Gesellschaft bestimmte Werthaltungen, etwa die Meinung, dass die Frau dem Mann nicht ebenbürtig sei, mit einem negativen Werturteil versieht. (…) Gleichzeitig verzerren solche Werturteile aber auch das Bild, das sich in der Gesellschaft über die vorherrschenden Meinungen bildet. Menschen scheuen sich nämlich zumeist, Meinungen zu äußern, die nach ihrer Einschätzung nicht der gesellschaftlichen Norm entsprechen. In jedem Fall verzerre jedoch die oben beschriebene Tugendbrille die Wahrnehmung der Welt nahezu ins Groteske." (Sarazin 2014, 42) Er schließt damit, dass er sich mehr Leidenschaft für die Wirklichkeit wünscht und dazu müsse man die Menschen so nehmen wie sie sind: als mit gleichen Rechten, aber mit ungleichen Antrieben und Eigenschaften Geborene, deren Streben nach Glück sie auf ungleiche Wege führen könne.

4. Political Correctness als Kampfplatz zwischen liberalen und illiberalen Kräften

Letztendlich zielt alles auf die Frage ab, ob man es liberalen Demokratie zutraut, die anstehenden Probleme in den Griff zu bekommen. Wenn es um die Verteidigung von Werten wie Familie und Nation geht, werden von der politische Rechten immer wieder Allianzen mit illiberalen und antiliberalen Kräften eingegangen. Mit Donald Trump kommt es für Viele zur Rückkehr eines starken weißen Mannes nach der "Schande" eines schwarzen Präsidenten. Amerika soll seine frühere Größe wiedergewinnen und die Bedrohungen durch die Globalisierung abgewehrt werden. Dass in immer mehr Bereiche der Gesellschaft Frauen vordringen, dass klassische Rollenbilder ins Schwanken kommen, dass Frauen sprachlich mitgedacht werden sollen, geht Vielen an die Substanz. Ein konkretes Beispiel sind die Morddrohungen an die Frauenministerin anlässlich der Änderung der österreichischen Bundeshymne, wo nunmehr neben den "Söhnen" auch die "Töchter" vorkommen, oder die Aufregung freiheitlicher Politiker in Österreich über die neue Bibelübersetzung, in der nun neben den "Brüdern" stellenweise auch "Schwestern" vorkommen.

Wie passt das aber damit zusammen, dass gerade diejenigen, welche die Minderheitenrechte und damit die "Privilegien der Unpriviligierten" (Bolz 2010, 99) rückgängig machen wollen, größter Wert auf die Freiheit legen, insbesondere auf die Meinungs- und Gedankenfreiheit? In seinem Buch *Die ungeliebte Freiheit. Ein Lagebericht*, schreibt Norbert Bolz: "Dass man die Freiheit hat, zu sagen, was man denkt, besagt nicht viel, wenn man nicht mehr zu denken wagt, was man nicht sagen darf". (Bolz 2010, 88) Geht es also darum, für die Wiederherstellung der Meinungsfreiheit und für eine liberale Kultur im Sinne John Stuart Mills zu kämpfen? Gegen Tabuisierung und Ausgrenzung von Meinungen einzutreten, gegen Moralisierung und unter Druck setzen von Menschen, die andere Ansichten vertreten? Gegen einen Tugendterror im Sinne einer Gleichheits- oder sonstigen Religion, die sich berufen fühlt, zu missionieren und sich für eine Rückkehr zu einer liberalen Demokratie in welcher die Vielfalt der Meinungsäußerung im Sinne eines Marktplatzes an Ideen wieder Platz hat, einzusetzen?

Warum dann so viel Hass und so viele Emotionen? Ist es vielleicht doch gar nicht so leicht, andere Sichtweisen, Weltanschauungen und Ideen auszuhalten? Ist man vielleicht allzu schnell bereit, die Augen vor Situationen zu verschließen, die nicht ins eigene Weltbild passen? In seinem kürzlich erschienen Buch *Was gesagt werden muss, aber nicht gesagt werden darf*, spricht Hans Rauscher davon, dass man sich das Thema Zuwanderung und ihre Folgen genauer ansehen müsse. Bisher sei dies nicht mit dem nötigen Realismus und der nötigen Tiefe bedacht worden. Vielleicht sind doch nicht alle Migranten und Migrantinnen so pluralistisch eingestellt wie wir? Vielleicht wollen aber auch viele von "uns" gar keine liberale Demokratie und keinen Pluralismus der Lebensformen und Weltanschauungen? Sind vielleicht doch nicht alle Menschen so sehr daran interessiert friedlich miteinander zusammen zu leben? Vielleicht brauchen wir sogar Feindbilder. Die Position von Norbert Bolz ist in diesem Zusammenhang eindeutig: das Politische zeichnet sich für ihn durch Unterscheidungen in Freund-Feind aus. *Political Correctness* untergrabe jedoch diese Tendenz des Menschen Feindbilder zur eigenen Identitätsbildung herzustellen. (Bolz 2009, 31)

Bereits John Stuart Mill hat in *Über die Freiheit* gezeigt, dass Mehrheitsmeinungen die Tendenz in sich tragen, alle andere Positionen in den Hintergrund zu drängen und sich als die einzige Wahrheit zu setzen. Deshalb gibt es in den liberalen Demokratien die in der Verfassung verankerten Menschrechte, welche als Grundrechte den Schutz sowohl des Einzelnen, als auch von Minderheiten gewährleisten. Im Gegensatz dazu findet in illiberalen Demokratien eine Einschränkung bis hin zu Abschaffung von Grundrechten in der Verfassung statt. In seiner Rede vom 30. Juli 2014 beschreibt Ministerpräsident Viktor Orbán die künftige Staatsform Ungarns als die einer illiberalen Demokratie: "We want to organise our national state to replace the liberal state. (...) In this sense the new state that we are constructing in Hungary is an illiberal state, a non-liberal state." Er lehne die Werte der Freiheit nicht grundsätzlich ab, ordne sie jedoch dem Wert der Nation unter.

Es stellt sich also die Hauptfrage: Welche Einschränkungen der Grundrechte wollen wir hinnehmen? Könnte es sein, dass gerade diejenigen, welche die Meinungsfreiheit aufgrund der *Political Correctness* in Gefahr sehen, weil es sich ihrer Ansicht nach um einen Tugendterror der Mehrheit handelt, daran interessiert sind die Grundrechte, insbesondere die Minderheitenrechte, einzuschränken? Warum soll man bestimmte rassistische, sexistische und ausländerfeindlich Aussagen nicht tätigen dürfen? Warum sollte ein bestimmtes Gedankengut nicht gesagt, ja nicht einmal gedacht werden dürfen? In Österreich verbietet das Gesetz jede Betätigung im Sinne einer nationalsozialistischen Wiederbetätigung, inklusive des Leugnens des Holocaust. Der Holocaust-Leugner David Irving wurde daher in Österreich strafrechtlich verurteilt und inhaftiert. Im Rahmen des von ihm gegen die Historikern Deborah Lipstadt angestrengten Gerichtsverfahrens – sie hatte ihm in ihrem Buch *Denying the Holocaust* Fälschung vorgeworfen – wurde sichtbar, dass Irving nicht nur ein Antisemit ist, sondern ein Rassist und Sexist, der sich darin gefällt öffentlich Menschen herabzusetzen und zu entwerten.

Einmal mehr zeigt sich, dass Sexismus, Rassismus, Antisemitismus und Nationalismus sehr oft zusammengehören. Die Unterdrückung und Zurückhaltung einer abwertenden Sprache gegenüber Frauen, Schwarzen, Juden und Ausländern scheint über die Wirtshaus-Stammtische hinaus immer mehr als Bevormundung, als unerträglicher Paternalismus verstanden zu werden. Im Sinne der Meinungsfreiheit fordert man "Pro und Kontra" als Gegenmittel gegen das Gift der politischen Korrektheit. So wird z.B. an der *Simon Langton School* in der Stadt Canterbury in England ein Kurs angeboten, an dem die These des Ex-Google-Mitarbeiters James Damore diskutiert wird, dass Frauen aus biologischen Gründen für die Arbeit in der IT-Branche weniger geeignet seien als Männer. Auch Thesen aus Hitlers mein Kampf werden in Form von "pro und kontra" zur Diskussion gestellt.

Schlussfolgerungen

Das Thema *Political Correctness* führt direkt ins Zentrum eines Kulturkampfes, der sich entlang der Bruchlinie Nation, Geschlecht, Rasse und sexueller Orientierung bewegt – und dies alles vor dem Hintergrund der Bedrohung durch den Islamismus. Die als Übeltäterin entlarvte "Gleichheits-Religion" wird für die mit Unbehagen wahrgenommenen Umwälzungen verantwortlich gemacht und als Tugendterroristin abgestempelt. Demgegenüber wird mehr Freiheit einfordert, insbesondere freie Meinungsäußerung. Diese richtet sich zumeist gegen den als Gutmenschentum abqualifizierten "liberalen Multikulturalismus" und gegen den als gefährlich abgestempelten "Genderwahn". Ob es sich nun um die "Ehe für Alle", um die Stellung der Frau in der Gesellschaft, um neue Reproduktionstechnologien, oder um die Auseinandersetzung mit Religion im Allgemeinen handelt, sehr bald befinden sich diejenigen, welche von Tugendterror sprechen, in der Nähe derer, die sich selbst als illiberal oder anti-liberal bezeichnen. Und nicht nur das. Es ergibt sich eine auffallende Nähe zu denjenigen Vorstellungen, die in islamischen Ländern und einigen osteuropäischen Ländern mit der Stellung der Frau, der Bedeutung der Familie und der Ablehnung der Homosexualität verbunden sind.

Die Argumentationslinie verläuft dabei entlang eines liberalen Gedankengutes, das für eine möglichst weitgehende und uneingeschränkte Meinungsfreiheit plädiert. Für John Stuart Mill war es wichtig, dass alle, auch noch so widersprüchliche Positionen Gehör erhalten, da sie einen Aspekt enthalten könnten, der für die Weiterentwicklung der Gesellschaft wichtig sein könnte und daher nicht übersehen werden darf.

Welche Stimmen sind es nun, die bisher zu wenig Gehör bekommen haben? Zunächst sicherlich einmal diejenigen, die vor einem politischen Islam in Europa gewarnt haben. Der weltweite islamische Terror, in Verbindung mit einem ungeordneten Zuzug einer großen Anzahl von zumeist islamischen Flüchtlingen über offene Grenzen hinweg, hat zu der Sorge beigetragen, dass es zu einem "Untergang des Abendlandes" kommen könnte. Darüber hinaus sind es diejenigen Stimmen, die vor den Gefahren einer Zerstörung der Familie warnen, vor der Emanzipation der Frau, einer Senkung der Fertilitätsrate und der Zulassung eines dritten Geschlechts.

Mill würde betonen, dass es notwendig sei, diese Positionen in einer öffentlichen Diskussion zur Sprache zu bringen. Denn nur auf diese Weise könne es gelingen, Gefahren rechtzeitig zu erkennen und gemeinsam zu meistern. So gesehen ist es sehr wichtig, jeglichem Tugendterror im Sinne eines "mundtot Machens" von Positionen, die nicht in das eigene Weltbild passen, entschieden entgegen zu treten. Jede Weltanschauung kann durch Übertreibung und Absolutierung zu einem Dogmatismus entarten. So wurde der Begriff *politically correct* – wie schon erwähnt – von Beginn an innerhalb der Linken ironisch verwendet, weil es zu einem immer rigider werdenden Kodex der Sprachregulierung an den amerikanischen Unis kam.

Jede Position trägt die Gefahr der Übertreibung in sich. So hat z.B. die Übernahme des Begriffes der *Political Correctness* als Kampfbegriff durch die politische Rechte dazu geführt, dass alte Gräben aufgerissen und längst überwunden geglaubte Feindbilder wieder zum Leben erweckt werden. Die Geschichte hat jedoch gezeigt, dass das Aufbauen von Feindbildern und die damit einhergehende Kriegsbereitschaft, sowie der Abbau demokratischer Strukturen zu Katastrophen geführt hat. Dies soll nicht heißen, dass man Gefahren, die auf uns zukommen nicht ins Auge sieht, wie z.B. die ungeregelte Zuwanderung. Was heute jedoch mehr denn je gefährdet ist, ist die liberale Demokratie selbst und der damit verbundene Verlust der bereits erreichten Menschen- und Grundrechte.

Es erfüllt mich mit großem Unbehagen, dass gerade diejenigen, die sich auf die Meinungsfreiheit berufen und gegen den Tugendterror der *Political Correctness* mobilmachen, davon ausgehen, dass die Freiheiten, welche in den letzten Jahrzehnten errungen wurden, einen "Werteverfall" darstellen, dem es durch das Wiederstarken antiliberaler Kräfte entgegenzutreten gelte. Schon einmal hat uns die Geschichte schmerzlich gezeigt, dass die liberale Demokratie mit demokratischen Mitteln aus der Welt geschafft werden kann. So gesehen sollten wir mit unserer Freiheit verantwortungsvoll umgehen, damit es nicht wieder im Namen der Freiheit zu einem Terror der "Gleichen" kommt, die jegliche "Andersheit" im Keim ersticken.

Literaturangaben

Beauvoir, Simone de. *Das andere Geschlecht*. Hamburg: Rowohlt 1992.

Bolz, Norbert. *Diskurs über die Ungleichheit*. Paderborn: Wilhelm Fink Verlag 2009.

Bolz, Nobert. *Die ungeliebte Freiheit. Ein Lagebericht*. München: Wilhelm Fink Verlag 2010.

Butler, Judith. *Excitable Speech. A Politics of the Performative*. New York: Routledge 1997.

Butler, Judith. *Hass spricht*. Berlin: Berlin Verlag 1998.

Dewey, John. *Demokratie und Erziehung. Eine Einleitung in die philosophische Pädagogik*. Basel/ Weinheim: Beltz 1993.

Mill, John Stuart. *Über die Freiheit*. Stuttgart: Reclam 1988.

Pörksen, Bernhard, Wir Tugendterroristen, Die Zeit, 8.11.2012

Sarazin, Thilo. *Der neue Tugendterror. Über die Grenzen der Meinungsfreiheit in Deutschland*. München: Deutsche Verlagsanstalt 2014.

Sartre, Jean-Paul. *Überlegungen zur Judenfrage*. Hamburg: Rowohlt 1994.

INTREVIEW

KLAUS NELLEN (Wien)
JAKUB HOMOLKA (Prag)

"Patočka ist gestorben. Wir müssen etwas tun!"[1]

Einleitung: Jan Patočka und das IWM

In den Erinnerungen an den tschechischen Philosophen Jan Patočka (1907–1977) wird häufig auf die Bedeutung des Samisdat und die damit verbundenen Tätigkeiten und Initiativen hingewiesen. In Prag war es eine Gruppe um Ivan Chvatík, den heutigen Leiter des Archivs, die nach Patočkas Tod am 13. März 1977 damit begann, diese Arbeiten zu organisieren, deren Resultat u.a. die 27-bändige Samisdat-Ausgabe von ausgewählten Schriften war. Weniger bekannt sind die parallel verlaufenden Aktivitäten der sog. "Wiener Gruppe".

Jene "Wiener Gruppe" formierte sich Anfang der 80er Jahre am Institut für die Wissenschaften vom Menschen (IWM). Eines der ersten großen Projekte des damals jungen Instituts war eine deutschsprachige Ausgabe von Ausgewählten Schriften Patočkas. Unter dieser Zielsetzung konnte in den 80er Jahren in Wien ein bis heute bestehendes Archiv mit Kopien von Patočkas Schriften aufgebaut werden und in der Folgezeit, in den Jahren 1987–1992, beim deutschen Verlag Klett-Cotta eine Auswahl seiner wichtigsten Schriften in einer Ausgabe von fünf umfangreichen Bänden erscheinen. Außer den Forschern vor Ort beteiligten sich an dieser Ausgabe maßgeblich auch tschechische Dissidenten, die in den 80er Jahren im Wiener Exil lebten.

Das Interesse am Nachlass Patočkas beschränkte sich aber keineswegs auf diese Edition. Der seit dieser Anfangszeit etablierte Forschungsschwerpunkt besteht am IWM bis heute fort und hat mit Forschungs- und Editionsprojekten zur europäischen Moderne, zur

---

[1] Interview mit Klaus Nellen über die Geschichte des Nachlasses von Jan Patočka, die Gründung des Instituts für die Wissenschaften vom Menschen und die klandestine Zusammenarbeit mit den Schülern des tschechischen Philosophen in den 80er Jahren. Das Interview erschien auf Tschechisch am 14. März 2015 in der Zeitung *Lidové Noviny*. Hier wird der integrale Text erstmals auf Deutsch veröffentlicht.

politischen Philosophie und zur Säkularismusdebatte das Archiv weiter entwickelt. All diese Projekte wurden mitinitiert und maßgeblich getragen von Ludger Hagedorn, der im Jahr 2015 die Leitung des Archivs übernommen hat. Neben den Aufgaben einer weiteren Erschließung und Edition von Patočkas Werk ist das Archiv über die Jahre immer mehr zu einem Ort für vielfältige philosophische und phänomenologische Forschung geworden. Ein besonderes Augenmerk galt und gilt dabei politischen und zivilisationstheoretischen Fragen, die in Zukunft mit Blick auf die leitende Thematik Europa – Nacheuropa weiter verstärkt werden sollen. Im Werk Patočkas ist die Frage nach den inneren Antinomien der modernen (europäischen) Zivilisation eindrücklich thematisiert, ihre volle Bedeutung entwickelt sie aber vielleicht erst im Kontext der gegenwärtigen postkolonialistischen Diskurse und der drängenden Fragen der Globalisierung.

Die ursprüngliche Idee zur Gründung des Instituts und zur Realisierung des Wiener Patočka-Projekts hatte der polnische Philosoph Krzysztof Michalski (1948–2013), ein Schüler Patočkas und später Rektor des IWM. An seiner Seite stand von Beginn an Klaus Nellen (*1948), studierter Philosoph und ehemaliger Mitarbeiter des Kölner Husserl-Archivs. Er spielte eine Schlüsselrolle bei der Realisierung des ersten Editionsprojekts und legte die Basis für die weitere Arbeit. Ihm ist maßgeblich zu verdanken, dass Patočkas Vermächtnis in Wien und darüber hinaus bis heute seine Bedeutung entfaltet. Für seine Verdienste wurde Nellen im Jahr 2007 die Jan Patočka Gedächtnismedaile (Pamětní medaile Jana Patočky) der Tschechischen Akademie der Wissenschaften verliehen.

***

Homolka: Nach Patočkas Tod im Jahre 1977 begannen die Bemühungen um die Rettung und Erhaltung von Patočkas Nachlass. Wie kam es dazu, dass Sie sich daran beteiligten?

Nellen: Fangen wir nicht mit 1977 an, sondern mit der Zeit davor, denn alles hängt mit dem polnischen Philosophen Krzysztof Michalski zusammen. Ich habe ihn Mitte der 70er Jahre im *Husserl Archiv der Universität zu Köln* kennengelernt, wo er Humboldt-Stipendiat und ich wissenschaftlicher Mitarbeiter war. Er war seit 1973 in Kontakt mit Patočka und hatte mir auch ab und zu davon erzählt. Ich weiß noch, wie er am 13. März 1977 zu mir kam und sagte: "Patočka ist gestorben. Wir müssen etwas tun!" Viel konnten wir damals allerdings nicht tun. Ich glaube mich zu erinnern, dass wir im Husserl-Archiv eine kleine Gedenkveranstaltung abhielten. Es sollte noch einige Jahre dauern, bis eine Möglichkeit geschaffen werden konnte, etwas für das Denken und den Nachlass von Patočka zu tun – und das hängt mit der Gründung des Instituts für die Wissenschaften vom Menschen in Wien zusammen.

Homolka: Wann genau wurde das Wiener Institut gegründet?

Nellen: Die Idee hatte Michalski 1980 im Inter-University Zentrum (IUC) in Dubrovnik, wo er zusammen mit Hans-Georg Gadamer und Gottfried Böhm ein Seminar veranstaltete. Dieses Zentrum war damals einer der wenigen Orte, wo sich Wissenschaftler aus Ost und West zwanglos treffen konnten. Gegründet hat er das IWM dann 1982. Eines der ersten Projekte hier am Institut war der Forschungsschwerpunkt "Das philosophische Werk Jan Patočkas", den es bis heute gibt, und der der Erforschung und Verbreitung des Denkens dieses bedeutenden mitteleuropäischen Philosophen gilt.

Homolka: Krzysztof Michalski kennen vielleicht nicht alle. Könnten Sie sein Verhältnis zu Patočka erläutern?

Nellen: Er war ein Schüler Patočkas. Michalski hatte Patočka in den 1970er Jahren dazu angeregt, sich mit der Philosophie der Geschichte zu beschäftigen. Herausgekommen sind die Ketzerischen Essays, das vielleicht wichtigste Werk Patočkas. So hat sich Michalski schon früh seinem Mentor verpflichtet gefühlt. Aber er hat ihn auch bewundert als Bürgerrechtler: das politische Ethos von Patočka war für ihn ein großes Vorbild. Man kann wohl sagen, dass er diesem Vorbild sein ganzes Leben lang nachgeeifert hat. Wie Patočka war Michalski nicht nur ein anerkannter akademischer Philosoph, sondern immer auch ein engagierter Bürger und Europäer. Das hat das Institut tief geprägt – es versteht sich eben auch als eine Institution der Zivilgesellschaft, als ein Ort, an dem man sich nicht nur um die Reflexion der Wirklichkeit bemüht, sondern auch um ihre Veränderung. Diesen Geist hat Jan Patočka verkörpert, der von Anbeginn eine Leitfigur für uns war und es bis heute ist, jedenfalls für die Gründergeneration.

Homolka: Aber warum wurde das Institut in Wien gegründet? Warum nicht z.B. in Köln oder irgendwo in Deutschland, wo Sie beide sich in den 1970er Jahren aufhielten?

Nellen: Es war eine pragmatische Wahl. Sie hatte zunächst wenig mit der Idee Mitteleuropas zu tun, hatte also keine philosophischen oder ideologischen Gründe. Der Grund war ganz einfach und hängt mit der praktischen Idee des Instituts zusammen: wir wollten die besten Intellektuellen und Wissenschaftler aus Osteuropa einladen und sie mit Kollegen aus dem Westen zusammenbringen. Einfach deshalb, weil die politische Teilung Europas zu einer sich immer weiter vertiefenden geistige Teilung Europas geführt hat. Die Folge war,

dass im Osten die Intellektuellen weitgehend abgeschnitten waren von der Diskussion im Westen, und umgekehrt. Im Westen war das geistige Interesse an Osteuropa fast vollständig erloschen: in unseren Köpfen war Osteuropa ein grauer Monolith. Welche Arroganz!
Michalski hatte mich schon in den siebziger Jahren nach Polen eingeladen, und ich war fasziniert von der lebendigen intellektuellen Szene in Warschau. Kurz und gut, die Idee war, mit unseren bescheidenen Kräften dazu beizutragen, die Intellektuellen und Wissenschaftler aus diesen beiden Welten, in die Europa zerfallen war, wieder zusammenzubringen. Und dafür mussten wir einen Ort finden, der es unseren Gästen aus Osteuropa nicht zu schwer machen würde, eine Ausreiseerlaubnis zu erhalten. Österreich ist bis heute neutral, also war es z.B. für einen Polen viel leichter, nach Wien zu kommen als nach Köln oder Berlin. So war es im Kalten Krieg. Es ist übrigens eine Schande für den Westen, dass es nach dem Fall des Eisernen Vorhangs für die Osteuropäer jenseits der EU-Grenze keineswegs leichter geworden ist, zu uns zu kommen: Früher machte man ihnen die Ausreise schwer, heute die Einreise.

Homolka: War es für Sie schwierig, unter den Bedingungen des Kalten Krieges ein Institut mit einer solchen Mission zu gründen?

Nellen: Ja, denn damals folgte die sogenannte "Ostpolitik" – d.h. die politische Haltung nicht nur der Bundesrepublik Deutschland zu den osteuropäischen Staaten – der Doktrin der Entspannung: man glaubte, die ideologischen Gegensätze abbauen zu können, und setzte auf friedliche Koexistenz und Konvergenz. Während also die Regierungen in Deutschland und Österreich sich in ihren Gesprächen mit den Regimen im Osten um Entspannung bemühten, gab es im Osten Entwicklungen, die diese Gespräche empfindlich störten: Das waren die Dissidenten, und in Polen hatten sie einen alarmierenden Erfolg, nämlich in Gestalt der Solidarność. Hier war der Widerstand gegen das kommunistische Regime auf die Gesellschaft übergesprungen und mündete in eine Bewegung mit Millionen von Mitgliedern. Das führte bekanntlich dazu, dass General Jaruzelski im Dezember 1981 den Kriegszustand verhängte, um – so seine Begründung – der notorischen brüderlichen Hilfe zuvorzukommen. Ich erinnere mich noch gut, wie Helmut Schmidt, der Bundeskanzler der Bundesrepublik Deutschland, damals die Solidarność ermahnte, nicht den Weltfrieden zu gefährden. Ähnlich dachte man auch in Österreich. Allerdings gab es eine bemerkenswerte Ausnahme, und das war Erhard Busek, damals Vizebürgermeister von Wien, der schon länger Kontakte zu Dissidenten pflegte und das Institut in seiner Gründungsphase tatkräftig unterstützte.

Es war also damals nicht opportun oder populär, Kontakte zu Dissidenten zu haben. Von daher war es nicht so leicht, für die Idee des Instituts Unterstützung zu finden, denn wir haben von Anfang an klar gemacht, welche Leute wir einladen wollen: Wir wollten den zahllosen Anstrengungen um einen Dialog mit Regime-Vertretern keine weiteren hinzufügen, wir wollten aber auch nicht das Gegenteil tun und eine Zuflucht für Dissidenten werden. Vielmehr wollten wir Menschen aus Osteuropa einladen, die selbständig denken. Selbst zu denken war unter den damaligen Bedingungen vielleicht das Schwierigste und konnte einen hohen Preis haben.

Homolka: Kann man sagen, dass Patočka für die Gründer des Instituts ein Symbol für die Vermittlung zwischen West und Ost war?

Nellen: Ja, Patočka war sein ganzes Leben lang ein Vermittler: er hat in Freiburg bei Husserl und Heidegger studiert, er hat die Phänomenologie nach Prag gebracht und dort weiterentwickelt. Und umgekehrt hat er den Beitrag Mitteleuropas zur Moderne erforscht; ebenso war er davon überzeugt, dass die Tschechen eine besondere Verantwortung für Europa tragen. Patočkas Denken in den westlichen Kontext einzubringen, war daher ein wichtiger Teil unserer Aufgabe.

Homolka: Wie sah das praktisch aus?

Nellen: Gleich zu Anfang, in den Jahren 1984/1985, organisierten wir zwei kleine Konferenzen, zu denen wir alle Leute eingeladen hatten, die etwas zum Werk von Patočka zu sagen hatten. Dort waren zum Beispiel zwei alte Freunde Patočkas: Walter Biemel, der bei Martin Heidegger studiert hatte, und Ludwig Landgrebe, ein Schüler Husserls, mit dem Patočka schon im Prag der 1930er Jahre zusammengearbeitet hatte. Es kamen, neben anderen, auch der britische Philosoph Roger Scruton oder der Komeniologe Klaus Schaller, und natürlich tschechische Philosophen wie Ilja Šrubař, Erazim Kohák und Václav Bělohradský. Patočkas Kollegen und Studenten, die damals in der Tschechoslowakei lebten, konnten allerdings nicht kommen.
Auf diesen Konferenzen haben wir die Konzeption der "Ausgewählten Schriften", einer fünfbändigen Ausgabe in deutscher Sprache, diskutiert. Zu deren Realisierung brauchten wir dann einen Verlag und natürlich Leute, die an der Ausgabe arbeiten würden. Michalski konnte den Verleger Michael Klett gewinnen, und der Österreichische Wissenschaftsfond (FWF) hat die Mittel für die Übersetzung und Herausgabe der Bände zur Verfügung gestellt.

Homolka: Wie ging dann die Arbeit an den "Ausgewählten Schriften" weiter?

Die Voraussetzung war natürlich, dass man Zugang zu einem möglichst vollständigen Korpus der Schriften des Philosophen hat, sonst kann ja man nicht vernünftig auswählen. Daher habe ich schon sehr früh zur Familie von Patočka in Prag und zu seinen Schülern Kontakt aufgenommen, um schließlich in Wien ein Archiv aufzubauen.

Homolka: Das bedeutet, dass Sie persönlich nach Prag reisten?

Nellen: Ja, ich war oft dort.

Homolka: Mit wem hatten Sie den ersten Kontakt?

Nellen: Soweit ich mich erinnere, habe ich zuerst Jan Sokol kennengelernt – wohl über Empfehlung von Walter Biemel –, und Sokol hat mich dann mit Schülern Patočkas in Verbindung gebracht. Der erste war natürlich Ivan Chvatík, aber auch Pavel Kouba und Petr Rezek gehörten zu der Gruppe, die ich dann immer wieder getroffen habe, später kam Petr Pithart hinzu.

Homolka: Patočkas Schüler haben Ihnen dann die Schriften übergeben?

Nellen: Nach Patočkas Tod hatte Ivan Chvatik den Nachlass aus Patočkas Haus an einen sicheren Ort gebracht und angefangen, ihn systematisch im Samisdat herauszugeben; gleichzeitig begann er, ihn zu kopieren, natürlich heimlich. Sie müssen wissen, dass damals die wenigen Kopierer, die es gab, einer strengen Reglementierung unterlagen, um die Verbreitung unbotmäßiger Schriften zu unterbinden. Ein Satz Kopien war für Wien bestimmt. Nach und nach wurden alle Schriften, die damals bekannt waren, kopiert und nach Wien gebracht.

Homolka: Wie genau wurden die Kopien von Patočkas Schriften aus Prag nach Wien gebracht?

Nellen: Auf zwei Wegen: Zum einen bin ich zwischen Prag und Wien gependelt. Ich war immer sehr gerne in Prag, und es waren aufregende Zeiten für mich. Die Manuskripte transportierte ich in meinem Koffer. Natürlich wurde man an der Grenze überprüft. Auf die einschlägigen Fragen des tschechoslowakischen Zolls hin sagte ich immer, dass es sich um meine persönlichen Manuskripte handele. Die Grenzbeamten schienen nicht besonders interessiert, sie sich genauer anzuschauen. Bis heute weiß ich nicht, wie stark sich das Regime in den 1980er Jahren noch für die Schriften Patočkas interessierte.

Der andere Weg war der diplomatische: Wir hatten Freunde unter den deutschen und österreichischen Diplomaten, die Manuskripte im Diplomatengepäck nach Wien brachten. Auf diese Weise konnten wir in relativ kurzer Zeit ein Spiegel-Archiv in Wien aufbauen, das den Prager Bestand in Kopie reflektierte. Und so konnten wir bald mit der Herausgabe der Schriften beginnen.

Homolka: Und haben Sie umgekehrt auch etwas von Wien mit nach Prag genommen?

Nellen: Auf jedem Weg von hier nach dort habe ich wissenschaftliche Fachliteratur mitgenommen, meistenteils für Peter Rezek. Die Jan Hus Foundation finanzierte damals Bücher für Kollegen in Osteuropa, damit sie nicht von der westlichen Literatur abgeschnitten blieben. Peter schickte mir regelmäßig Wunschlisten, ich habe die Bücher dann gekauft und nach Prag geschleppt. Bei diesen Wegen wandte ich prophylaktisch einen simplen Trick an: es lag immer ein Playboy-Heft bei den Büchern, das sofort die Aufmerksamkeit absorbierte. Die Zöllner schauten mich dann vorwurfsvoll an und beschlagnahmten das subversive Produkt, nicht ohne mir eine Quittung auszuhändigen. Die Bücher durfte ich behalten. Am Ende hatte Peter eine wunderbare Bibliothek zuhause, die aber für alle zugänglich war. Auf dem Rückweg habe ich dann wieder Papiere mitgenommen – eine kleine, fleißige Ameise zwischen West und Ost.

Homolka: Zurück zu Patočkas Schriften: Sie sind der Mitherausgeber aller 5 Bände – was war genau Ihre Rolle?

Nellen: Eine prekäre Rolle eigentlich. Ich war in der Tat Mitherausgeber aller 5 Bände, ohne aber das Tschechische zu beherrschen. Es fand sich damals kein anderer Herausgeber mit Deutsch als Muttersprache, der gleichzeitig Tschechisch gelesen hätte und philosophisch gebildet gewesen wäre. Mit dieser Situation mussten wir zurechtkommen. Wir haben daher für alle Bände tschechische Kollegen als Mitherausgeber herangezogen – Jiří Němec war der wichtigste, weil vor Ort, sowie Ilja Šrubař, Petr Pithart und Miroslav Pojar. Němec lebte als Flüchtling in Wien, und wir trafen uns fast täglich.

Homolka: Und wie sah die praktische Arbeit an den Bänden aus?

Nellen: Als erstes haben wir eine Auswahl der Texte getroffen. Dann haben wir die Übersetzungen in Auftrag gegeben. Das Problem war wiederum, dass es damals praktisch keine Übersetzer gab, die Sprachkompetenz mit Fachkompetenz vereinigten. Ilja Šrubař und seine Frau waren die Ausnahme, aber sie konnten wegen ihrer anderen Verpflichtungen nur einen Teil übersetzen. Wir haben also mit den besten Literatur-Übersetzern gearbeitet, die sicher ihr Bestes gegeben haben. Die Aufgabe von Jiří und mir war es dann, die philosophische Terminologie zu überprüfen. Das war auch deshalb eine schwierige Aufgabe, weil Patočka die deutsche Terminologie im Tschechischen weiter entwickelt hat und sie nun zurück ins Deutsche gebracht werden musste.

Meine Aufgabe war, die Übersetzungen als erster zu lesen, um zu sie auf Konsistenz zu prüfen bzw. Unklarheiten zu identifizieren. Danach bin ich mit den Mitherausgebern Satz für Satz durch die Texte gegangen. Das war eine mühsame Arbeit, das Ergebnis liegt seit 1992 in den 5 Bänden vor.

Homolka: Sie haben mit einer ganzen Reihe von tschechischen Kollegen zusammengearbeitet, doch – wie Sie selbst erwähnten – war Jiří Němec wohl der wichtigste für Sie. Stimmt das?

Ja, er lebte als politischer Flüchtling hier in Wien und wurde uns von den Kollegen in Prag als Mitherausgeber empfohlen. Jiřís Mitarbeit war entscheidend für das ganze Unternehmen. In den späten 1980er Jahren hat Erhard Busek geholfen, ihm ein Forschungsprojekt zu verschaffen, mit dem er sich über Wasser halten konnte. Natürlich war Jiří von Anfang an unglücklich, dass er in Wien sitzen musste und nicht mehr nach Prag konnte. Er war kein glücklicher Mensch, ich glaube, er litt unter Depressionen. In Prag war er ein Guru gewesen, ein intellektueller Star, aber in Wien interessierte sich so gut wie niemand für ihn. Das war wohl sehr bitter für ihn. Die Mitarbeit an unserem Projekt verband ihn wieder mit Prag und war vielleicht eine kleine Kompensation.

Homolka: Eine andere Person, die in den 1980er Jahren als Visiting Fellow am IWM arbeitete, war der Philosoph Erazim Kohák.

Nellen: Kohák, der damals in Boston lehrte, spielte für unser Projekt eine wichtige Rolle. Er hat sich durch den gesamten Bestand des Archivs gearbeitet und versucht, ihn zu systematisieren. Das hat uns geholfen, uns einen Überblick zu verschaffen, wobei Kohák einen ganz bestimmten Zugang zu Patočka hatte. Später arbeitete er dann mit einem Schüler von Krzysztof Michalski, James Dodd, an englischen Übersetzungen der Werke Patočkas.

Homolka: Sie haben die Kooperation zwischen Wien und der Gruppe im Prag beschrieben. Wie änderte sich die Arbeit nach 1989, als das klandestine Jan Patočka-Archiv in Prag endlich eine offizielle Institution wurde?

Nellen: Das Wiener Archiv war inzwischen zu einem Ort geworden, an dem zahlreiche Wissenschaftler zu Patočka arbeiteten. Zu den Visiting Fellows gehörte auch Erika Abrams, die als ausgezeichnete Übersetzerin der französischen Ausgabe von Patočkas Schriften bekannt ist und für ihre Verdienste das Ehredoktorat der Prager Karls-Universität erhielt. In Kooperation mit Prag haben wir das Archiv fortlaufend ausgebaut und aktualisiert, so war z.B. in den 1990er Jahren der sog. Strahov-Nachlass hinzugekommen. Zugleich folgten dem ersten Projekt – der Edition der 5-bändigen Ausgabe – weitere mehrjährige Forschungsprojekte zum Werk des tschechischen Philosophen. Und in der Zwischenzeit war eine neue Generation von Patočka-Forschern herangewachsen. Hier will ich vor allem Ludger Hagedorn nennen, der Slawistik und Philosophie studiert hatte und bald zu einer tragenden Säule der Patočka-Forschung am IWM werden sollte.

Homolka: Das internationale Interesse an Patočka hält also bis heute an. Aber der Kontext für dieses Interesse hat sich verändert – es ist nicht dasselbe wie vor 1989. Wie würden Sie den Unterschied beschreiben?

Nellen: Ja, es ist sicher anderes als früher. Insbesondere hat das Interesse für die Generation der Dissidenten, das Interesse an den Dissidenten als Leitfiguren und öffentliche Intellektuelle, nachgelassen. Václav Havel ist dafür nur das prominenteste Beispiel. Entsprechend wurde Patočka damals eher als mutiger Bürgerrechtler wahrgenommen, denn als Philosoph, natürlich auch weil man sein philosophisches Werk noch nicht so gut kannte. Ich glaube, hier müssen wir einfach geduldig sein – Patočkas Zeit kommt erst noch.

Homolka: Trotzdem – kann man diesen Idealismus der damaligen Zeit, der auch in Patočkas Nachlass zu finden ist, heute noch spüren, oder ist das alles vergangen?

Nellen: Havel ist im Pantheon, wird also eine wichtige historische Figur bleiben. Ob aber die Menschen sich heute noch von ihm inspirieren lassen, das weiß ich nicht. Die Postmoderne hat die von den Dissidenten verkörperten Werte plötzlich altmodisch aussehen lassen. Doch wenn man an den Maidan in der Ukraine denkt, sind eben unsere Grundwerte und die Idee Europas, die für Patočka so zentral waren und die wir hier im Westen fast schon vergessen haben, plötzlich wieder da und entfalten eine große Kraft. Ich hoffe, dass die Ukrainer ihren Enthusiasmus trotz des Kriegs in ihrem Land bewahren können und dass etwas davon auf uns überspringt. Ich bin sicher, Patočka hätte das nicht anders gesehen.

Nachwort: Die Edition von Patočkas Werk

Der schriftliche Nachlass Jan Patočkas zeichnet sich durch einige Besonderheiten aus. Zum einen ist dies die Tatsache, dass es sich bei einem großen Teil davon um Manuskripte handelt, die zu Lebzeiten des Autors nicht veröffentlicht wurden; darunter finden sich sowohl umfangreiche Studien wie auch kürzere Texte, Anmerkungen oder Entwürfe. Zum zweiten ist Patočkas Oeuvre besonders im Hinblick auf seine breite thematische Ausrichtung: Beiträge zur Phänomenologie, Geschichtsphilosophie oder antiken Philosophie sind ebenso präsent wie Studien etwa zu Kunst, tschechischer Kultur und Geschichte oder zur Komeniologie. Die verschiedenen Editionen seines Werkes folgen in der Regel diesen Themenbereichen.

Nicht anders verhält es sich auch im Fall der deutschsprachigen Ausgabe, die unter der Leitung von Klaus Nellen mit seinen tschechischen Mitarbeitern Jiří Němec, Ilja Šrubař, Petr Pithart und Miroslav Pojar am Wiener IWM ausgearbeitet und im Verlag Klett-Cotta publiziert wurde. Als erstes erschien ein Band, der sich Patočkas Arbeiten zu Fragen der Kunst und Kultur widmete (Kunst und Zeit, 1987), es folgten die Beiträge zur Geschichtsphilosophie (Ketzerische Essais zur Philosophie der Geschichte und ergänzende Schriften, 1988), welche u.a. das berühmte Hauptwerk enthalten, das dem Band seinen Titel gab, sowie auch die Reflexion zur "nach-europäischen" Epoche. Im weiteren erschienen zwei Bände mit phänomenologischen Schriften (Die natürliche Welt als philosophisches Problem, 1990, und Die Bewegung der menschlichen Existenz, 1991). Die Reihe wurde dann abgeschlossen mit den Schriften zur tschechischen Kultur und Geschichte (1992), die u.a. den Essay "Was sind die Tschechen?" sowie die Texte zur Charta 77 enthielten.

Ins Deutsche wurden in der Folgezeit natürlich noch eine ganze Reihe weiterer Texte übersetzt. Wenn von Übersetzung die Rede ist, sollte aber auch die Vielzahl der Übersetzungen ins Französische erwähnt werden, die insbesondere dem Einsatz der Übersetzerin Erika Abrams zu verdanken sind. Vergleichsweise bescheiden sind hingegen die englischsprachigen Übersetzungen, um die sich vor allem Erazim Kohák verdient machte. Weiterhin wurden verschiedene Texte Patočkas in eine Reihe von anderen Sprachen übertragen.

Den systematischsten und umfangreichsten Versuch zur Strukturierung von Patočkas Nachlass stellt natürlich die tschechische Werkausgabe der Sebrané spisy Jana Patočky (Gesammelte Schriften) dar, welche die frühere Samisdat-Ausgabe ersetzt. Verantwortlich dafür zeichnet das Patočka-Archiv am Center for Theoretical Study (Centrum pro teoretická studia, CTS), einer gemeinsamen Arbeitsstelle der Karls-Universität Prag und der Tschechischen Akademie der Wissenschaften. Unter der Leitung von Ivan Chvatík und Pavel Kouba, früheren Studenten Patočkas, wird eben hier die Herausgabe der philosophischen Schriften systematisch betreut. Seit 1996 sind im Verlag OIKOYMENH bereits 17 Bände dieser Werkausgabe erschienen. Der vorerst letzte waren die Phänomenologischen Schriften III/1, eine ganze Reihe weiterer Bände steht aber noch aus.

Klaus Nellen, Institut für die Wissenschaften vom Menschen, Wien, nellen[at]iwm.at

Dr. Jakub Homolka, Charles University, Faculty of Human Studies, Prague, jakub.homolka[at]fhs.cuni.cz

BOOK REVIEW

SUSANNE MOSER (Wien)

Jan Assmann: *Totale Religion. Ursprünge und Formen puritanischer Verschärfung*. Wien: Picus Verlag, 2016, 184 S.

"Die 'Wiederkehr der Religion', die wir seit einigen Jahrzehnten erleben, ist auf beängstigende Weise mit Gewalt, Bedrohungsszenarien, Hass, Angst und der Produktion von Feindbildern verbunden." (Assmann 2016, 25) Deshalb müssen wir, so Assmann, die Frage nach einem Zusammenhang zwischen Monotheismus und Gewalt auch immer wieder neu stellen. In seinem 2016 erschienen Buch *Totale Religion. Ursprünge und Formen puritanischer Verschärfung* greift Assmann auf Carl Schmitts Konzept des totalen Staates zurück, um das Zustandekommens einer totalen Religion und deren Gewaltexzesse zu erklären: In seiner Schrift von 1932 plädiere Carl Schmitt für den totalen Staat: "Er will den *ganzen* Menschen, das *einige* Volk, den *totalen* Staat." (ibid., 117). Schmitt wolle damit die Ausdifferenzierung der Moderne in verschiedene Wertsphären, wie Recht, Kunst, Wissenschaft, Wirtschaft usw. überwinden und alle Bereiche des Lebens unter die Hegemonie des Politischen bringen. Schmitt verstehe das Politische als eine polarisierende Kraft, die zwischen Freund und Feind unterscheide, was allerdings erst im Ernstfall, nämlich demjenigen des Krieges, zum Tragen komme. (ibid., 117) Diese Verbindung von "Ausdifferenzierung und Hegemonialisierung" im Sinne der Unterwerfung aller anderen Bereiche, sieht Assmann in der totalen Religion am Werk, indem diese alle Lebensbereiche zu kontrollieren beansprucht und sich selbst das Politische unterordnet. (116) Unter totaler Religion sei nicht eine bestimmte Religion, sondern deren Aggregatzustand oder Intensitätsgrad zu verstehen. Sowohl im Judentum als auch im Christentum, habe es immer wieder solche Phasen gegeben. Heute konfrontiere uns jedoch insbesondere der Islamismus "mit Erscheinungsformen der totalen Religion." (ibid., 131)

Als paradigmatischen religiösen Ernstfall nimmt Assmann den durch menschliches Vergehen verschuldeten Gotteszorn über den Bundesbruch an: "Der Gotteszorn, der sich entweder bereits in einer furchtbaren Katastrophe manifestiert hat oder nach vorgefallenem Gottesfrevel als unmittelbar bevorstehend zu befürchten ist, lässt sich ähnlich wie der Krieg in Carl Schmitts politischer Theorie als ein Ernstfall verstehen." (ibid., 119) Als Urszene des Ernstfalles sieht Assmann die Geschichte vom Goldenen Kalb, infolge derer Moses unter den Treulosen durch die Leviten ein Blutbad anrichten lässt, um Gottes Zorn abzuwenden. Zwei Dinge sind für Assmann hier ausschlaggebend: Die Verletzung der Bündnistreue einerseits, die Wiederherstellung der Treue durch den Einsatz menschlicher Gewalt gegenüber den Bündnisbrechern andererseits. Sei bis dahin Gott selbst es gewesen, der gewalttätig war, so seien es nunmehr die Zeloten, die Eiferer, die im Namen des eifersüchtigen Gottes Gewalt ausübten. (ibid., 120)

Assmann fügt noch einen weiteren Aspekt hinzu, der für das Zustandekommen einer totalen Religion notwendig ist, nämlich die puritanische Übersteigerung. Die radikalpuritanische Opposition des Propheten Hosea habe der herrschenden Praxis einen Begriff von Religion in ‚Reinkultur' entgegengesetzt: "So wie Carl Schmitt im Blick auf den theoretischen Ernstfall des Krieges den totalen Staat, fordert der deuteronomistische Puritanismus die totale Religion." (ibid., 122) Während Hosea die Untreue des jüdischen Volkes gegenüber seinem Gott anprangere, gehe es Josia um die Reinheit des Kultes, Esra und Nehemia hingegen bei der Scheidung der Mischehen um die Reinheit des Blutes. Als Metapher für den Verstoß gegen das Reinheitsgebot diene oft das Geschlechterverhältnis, insbesondere das Verhalten der Frau: Jerusalem werde als untreues Weib dargestellt, Ephraim als eine Hure und Israel als unrein. (ibid., 16) Puritanismus als ein Streben nach Reinheit in Lehre und Praxis finde sich zwar in vielen Religionen – so sei im Alten Ägypten der "Reine" der allgemeinste Priestertitel – der radikale Puritanismus zeichne sich jedoch dahingehend aus, dass nicht allein der Kult, sondern das ganze Leben ein Gottesdienst sein solle, wodurch ein totalisierendes Element in die Kultur komme. (ibid.) Religion transzendiere damit den Bereich des Kultes und bestimme in Formen geltenden Rechtes das ganze Leben. In diesem Sinne sei sie weder Kult noch Weltanschauung oder Glaubenssystem, "sondern vor allem Lebensform." (ibid., 147) Dies treffe nicht nur für die Josianische Kultreform zu, sondern auch für den englischen Puritanismus, der auf der reinen Lehre Calvins aufbaue, ebenso wie auf den heutigen radikal-puritanischen Wahhabismus des Saudischen Königshauses. Typisch für den radikalen Puritanismus in seinen verschiedenen Erscheinungsformen sei die Forderung nach Abkehr und Rückkehr zur Reinheit des Ursprungs (*salaf* im Arabischen). "Dieser innere Nachvollzug der Unterscheidung von Reinheit und Profanität und der Entscheidung für ein Leben im Zeichen der Reinheit erfordert eine Anstrengung, die im Islam *djihad* heißt." (ibid., 19) Assmann sieht eine Parallele zwischen heutigen fundamentalistischen Strömungen und den Entwicklungen des Zelotismus im hellenistischen Palästina: So wie der Eifer der Reformjuden gegen das Gesetz und für eine "allgemeine" Lebensform den makkabäischen Zelotismus als den Eifer für das Gesetz ausgelöst habe (ibid., 148), so sei der Zelotismus der iranischen Mullahs "unter anderem auch eine Reaktionsbildung gegen die Zwangsmodernisierung des Iran. Die Öffnung, um die es den jüdischen Reformern ging, ähnelt in ihren Aspekten der Modernisierung, der Aufklärung und der religiösen Reform dem, was die modernen islamischen Staaten als ‚Verwestlichung' brandmarken." (ibid., 150)

Assmann hebt hervor, dass es sich bei all diesen Formen von Gewalt um eine schriftgestützte Gewalt handle, die im Sinne einer heiligen Verpflichtung vollzogen werde. (ibid., 130) "Der radikale Puritanimsus – von Josia bis zum saudischen Wahhabismus – ist besonders anfällig für die tätliche Umsetzung sprachlicher Gewalt, wie sie in den kanonischen Texten kodifiziert sind." (ibid., 128) Assmann weist in seinem Vorwort darauf hin, dass der erste Teil seines Buches auf eine 2004 gehaltene Vorlesung über *Monotheismus und die Sprache der Gewalt* (Assmann 2006) zurückgeht und im Lichte neuer Forschungen von ihm ergänzt wurde. (Assmann 2016, 9) Für die Leserin und den Leser bietet sich in diesem Kapitel die Möglichkeit, einen Überblick zu erhalten über die intensiv geführten Diskussionen rund um das Thema Monotheismus und Gewalt im Allgemeinen und Assmann Thesen im Besonderen.[1] Denn Assmann geht es um eine besondere Gewalt, nämlich die durch kanonisierte Texte *motivierte* Gewalt.[2] Warum erzählt man sich immer noch solche Geschichten? Das "semantische Dynamit", das in den heiligen Texten der monotheistischen Religionen stecke, werde in den Händen der Fundamentalisten zur Zündung gebracht.[3] Man müsse die Texte daher auf ihren Ursprungskontext zurückführen. "Es gilt, ihre Genese aufzudecken, um sie in ihrer Geltung einzuschränken." (ibid., 76)

Die Lektüre von Assmanns Buch spricht wahrscheinlich vielen Leserinnen und Lesern aus der Seele: Wie kann man heute noch – auch als gläubiger Mensch – Texten folgen, die auf Feindbildern aufbauen, Ausschlüsse produzieren und Gewalt verherrlichen? Assmann spricht von einer "im Zeichen der Katastrophe entwickelten Theologie". (ibid., 107) Die einzige Möglichkeit, dem Scheitern und Verlust von Staat, Königtum, Land und Tempel einen Sinn abzugewinnen, sei darin gelegen eine Strafe Gottes aufgrund von Verfehlun-

---

[1] Siehe dazu insbesondere die rege Diskussionstätigkeit, die sich im Anschluss an sein Buch *Moses der Ägypter* (Assmann 1998) entwickelt hat. Assmann hat verschiedene Kritikpunkte aus diesen Diskussionen zum Teil aufgenommen und weiterentwickelt: https://www.perlentaucher.de/blog/2013/01/29/ die-monotheismusdebatte-editorial.html
[2] Assmann weist darauf hin, dass es nicht immer leicht ist zwischen religiös motivierter und religiös legitimierter Gewalt zu unterscheiden. "Die Form religiöser Gewalt, von der dieses Buch handelt, ist allein religiös *motivierte* Gewalt." (Assmann 2016, 57)
[3] So könne man mit Recht bezweifeln, ob der harte Kern des "Islamischen Staates", der sich aus marodierenden Soldaten des gestürzten Präsidenten Saddam Hussein zusammensetzt, religiös motiviert ist. Die jungen Leute, die sich dem IS anschlossen, könnten jedoch sehr wohl von salafistischen, d.h. radikal-puritanischen Motiven geleitet worden sein. (Assmann 2016, 57)

gen in Sachen kultischer Reinheit und Untreue zu sehen. Um dieser zuvorzukommen, seien immer wieder Gewalthandlungen gesetzt worden, um Gottes Zorn zu besänftigen. Assmanns Unterscheidung zwischen einem Monotheismus der Treue, d.h. einer Theologie des Gottesbundes, wie sie heute noch im rabbinischem Judentum, im protestantischen Christentum, sowie Teilen des Islam vorzufinden sei (ibid., 69) und einem Monotheismus der Wahrheit, der sich erst im babylonischen Exil entwickelt habe und einen einzigen und wahren Gott annehme, sei hier nur am Rande erwähnt. Assmann spricht beim Monotheismus der Wahrheit von einer "mosaischen Unterscheidung" von wahr und falsch im religiösen Sinn, also zwischen wahrem Gott und falschem Götzen. (ibid., 32) Als ein Beispiel unter vielen führt er die Scheidung der "Mischehen" zwischen jüdischen Männern und kanaanäischen Frauen und die Verstoßung der Kinder nach der Rückkehr aus dem babylonischen Exil an. Hier werde eine "im eigentlichen Sinne ‚mosaische Unterscheidung'" getroffen, die getragen sei von einem "radikalem Puritanismus". (ibid., 128)

Dem Ägyptologen Assmann gelingt es, die verschiedenen antiken Textschichten und Erzählstränge in einen historischen Kontext zu stellen und in einen chronologischen Zusammenhang zu bringen, wodurch sie auch Nicht-Theologen zugänglich werden. Ist es doch sein erklärtes Ziel, "uns über die mosaischen Grundlagen unserer westlichen Welt Rechenschaft abzulegen." (ibid., 76) Es sei wichtig, sich klarzumachen, dass die Gewalt dem Monotheismus nicht als eine notwendige Konsequenz eingeschrieben ist. "Warum sollte die Unterscheidung zwischen Wahr und Falsch gewalttätig sein?" (ibid., 76) Die Sprache der Gewalt entstamme dem politischen Druck, aus dem der Monotheismus gerade befreien wolle. Sie gehöre in die revolutionäre Rhetorik der Konversion, der Abkehr, des kulturellen Sprunges aus dem Alten ins Neue. Das postmoderne Bewusstsein, sei über die Schwelle schon längst geschritten und bedürfe keiner eifernden Einschärfung mehr.

Assmann tritt hier seinen Kritikern entgegen, die ihm vorwerfen, einen notwendigen Zusammenhang zwischen Monotheismus der Wahrheit und Gewalt gegen all diejenigen, die diesen "wahren Gott" nicht kennen oder anerkennen, anzunehmen. Mit seiner Rede vom "semantischen Dynamit", das in den monotheistischen Schriften stecke, entschärft und verschärft er die Situation jedoch zugleich. Natürlich muss dieses Dynamit nicht notwendig gezündet werden, dennoch ist es vorhanden und kann im Ernstfall zur Explosion kommen. Oft reiche es, so Assmann, Bedrohungsszenarien zu konstruieren, wie dies die USA im Fall der "Massenvernichtungswaffen" Saddam Husseins taten. Die Ankündigung der Apokalypse stelle die äußerste Form des Bedrohungsszenarios dar: "Das Besondere der Apokalyptik aber ist die Verbindung von Weltende und Weltgericht. Diese Ideenverbindung und die sich daraus herleitende Disposition zu dualistischen Polarisierungen ('Armageddon', 'Achse des Bösen') scheint mir eine Eigenart des Monotheismus." (ibid., 156) Die Apokalypse, so

Assmann, verkörpere die schärfste Waffe in der Strategie der Gewalt und bilde "zugleich den gemeinsamen Nenner von westlichem und östlichem, christlichem und islamischem Fundamentalismus." (ibid.)

Man würde nun erwarten, dass Assmann in seinem Schlusskapitel, das den Titel "Ausgänge aus der Sprache der Gewalt" trägt, für eine Vermeidung der Rhetorik des Ernstfalles plädiert. Umso verwunderlicher erscheint, dass Assmann nunmehr den Ernstfall im staatlichen Totalitarismus verortet: "Was dagegen im Raum der Religion wirklich als ‚Ernstfall' gelten kann, ist der staatliche Totalitarismus mit seinem Anspruch, alle Lebensbereiche und damit auch die Religion zu regulieren und kontrollieren." (ibid., 158) Der Religion komme daher die positive Aufgabe zu, dem Totalanspruch des Staates einen ganz anderen Anspruch entgegenzusetzen, nämlich denjenigen des Reiches Gottes, das von Jesus neben das weltliche Reich gestellt worden sei. "Die Unterscheidung der beiden Reiche, die Augustinus dann auf die Formel von den beiden *civitates* brachte, der *civitas Dei* und der *civitas terrena*, läuft auf eine Entpolitisierung der Religion und eine Entsakralisierung der Politik hinaus." (ibid., 159) Was will Assmann damit sagen? Geht es jetzt nicht mehr um die Gefahr einer totalen Religion, so wie er sie im derzeitigen Islamismus am Werk sieht, sondern um die eines neu entstehenden totalen Staates? Kann man in der abendländischen Geschichte wirklich von einer prinzipiellen Entsakralisierung der Politik und einer Entpolitisierung der Religion sprechen, oder findet diese nicht erst in der Moderne statt? Auch stellt sich die Frage, ob moderne Formen totaler staatlicher Gewalt, wie der Faschismus, wirklich so ohne Weiteres mit vormodernen Herrschaftsformen in Eins gesetzt und durch diese erklärt werden dürfen. Desweiteren vermisst man bei Assmann die Frage nach der Verflechtung zwischen totaler Religion und totalem Staat, sowie möglichen Formen der Überschneidung in ihrem Kampf gegen die Moderne. Hier einige Beispiele: In seinem Buch Hitlers Theologie (Bucher 2008) zeigt Rainer Bucher, dass Hitler an einen Schöpfergott glaubte, der das deutsche Volk zur Weltherrschaft und ihn zum Führer bestimmt habe. Im Christentum wie im heidnischen Germanenkult habe Hitler Mythen für das einfache Volk gesehen. In "Der islamische Faschismus" (Abdel-Samad 2014) zieht Abdel-Samad Parallelen zwischen Islamismus und Faschismus. Beide seien zeitgleich in den 1920er-Jahren stark geworden. Beide würden die Welt in Freund und Feind einteilen und ihre Anhänger mit Ressentiments und Hass vergiften. Beide Ideologien richteten sich gegen die Moderne, gegen den Marxismus, gegen die Juden und glorifizierten Militarismus sowie Opferbereitschaft bis in den Tod.[4]

---

[4] Hitlers "Mein Kampf" sei eines der meistverbreiteten Bücher in der islamischen Welt.

Als eine Medizin gegen den religiösen Radikalismus bringt Assmann den Pluralismus der hebräischen Bibel ins Spiel: "Die beste Gegenwehr gegen religiösen Radikalismus bleibt immer der Pluralismus, wie ihn die hebräische Bibel in ihrer Vierstimmigkeit verkörpert." (Assmann 2016, 159) Diese Bezugnahme auf die jüdische Weisheitsliteratur scheint zweifach motiviert zu sein. Einerseits entkräftet er damit den Vorwurf, die Juden in seinem Verständnis der jüdischen Religion als einer Theologie der Katastrophe selbst für den Holocaust verantwortlich gemacht zu haben, indem er die Weisheit der Mischna als ureigene Kraft des rabbinischen Judentums hervorhebt, andererseits sieht er hier den Grund zu einer "*religio duplex*" angelegt. Bereits in seinem 2010 erschienen Buch *Religio Duplex* hatte Assmann eine Verbindung zwischen den Ägyptischen Mysterien und der europäischen Aufklärung hergestellt. (Assmann 2010) Nunmehr bezieht er auch die jüdische Weisheitsliteratur in seine Überlegungen mit ein.

Assmann stellt dem "Entweder/Oder" der radikalen Religion das "Sowohl/Als auch" der "religio duplex", d.h. einer allgemeinen Menschheitsreligion gegenüber, der alle Menschen angehören und die neben der jeweils angestammten Religion für Frieden und wechselseitige Anerkennung sorgt. "Diese Form schafft die Differenz nicht ab, sondern respektiert sie im Hinblick auf etwas Übergreifendes, das man im 18. Jahrhundert ‚natürliche Religion' nannte und das sich heute in erster Linie mit dem Begriff der Menschenrechte verbindet." (ibid., 171) Diese seien jedoch gerade nicht religiös, sondern säkular und zivilgesellschaftlich und würden nicht auf Gott und Offenbarung, sondern auf Vernunft und Einsicht beruhen. (ibid., 167) Zwischen Vernunft und Glaube, Aufklärung und Menschenrechte einerseits sowie Bibel und Religion andererseits bestehe kein Widerspruch, wie Papst Benedikt XVI immer wieder betont habe: "'Sowohl/Als auch' – das Prinzip der *religio duplex* – ist in der katholischen Kirche nach wie vor lebendig." (ibid., 169) Auch wenn man an den wahren Ring der Lessing'schen Ringparabel nicht glaube, müsse man doch erkennen, welch große Kulturleistung die Religionen vollbracht haben. Religion sei das einzige Mittel, "das dem Menschen gegeben wurde, Gewalt – soziale und politische – einzudämmen und ihr nicht Gegengewalt, sondern eine andere Macht entgegenzusetzen." (ibid., 171) Diese große und unverzichtbare Aufgabe könne Religion jedoch nur erfüllen, wenn sie ihrerseits auf jede Art von Gewalt verzichte. Assmann scheint also auch eine positive Wirkungsmacht in den Religionen anzunehmen, denn er schließt sein Buch damit ab, dass es zwar die "wahre Religion" nicht gebe, wohl "aber die heilende, Frieden, Gerechtigkeit und Schönheit stiftende Kraft der Religion." (ibid., 174)

Am Ende angelangt, fragt man sich, welche Schlüsse man aus diesem Buch ziehen soll. Zunächst einmal sicherlich, das "semantische Dynamit" zu entschärfen. Dies wäre eine Aufgabe der Religionen selbst und zwar in doppelter Hinsicht: die kanonischen Texte einer

Überprüfung zu hinterziehen und eine kritische Gesamtausgabe herauszugeben, so wie dies bei Hitlers *Mein Kampf* mittlerweile der Fall ist und darüber hinaus öffentlich jegliche Rhetorik der Gewalt und Angst in Politik und Medien entschieden zurückzuweisen. Diese Schlussfolgerung vermisst man jedoch leider bei Assmann. Sein Vorschlag einer "*religio duplex*", eines "sowohl als auch" greift meines Erachtens zu kurz. Denn was nützt die Einzäunung durch die Menschenrechte, wenn das "semantische Dynamit" im Bereich der angestammten Religion immer noch nicht entschärft ist. Die Geschichte zeigt, dass im Ernstfall Gewalt immer wieder mit schriftgestützter Gewalt legitimiert wird. Jüngstes Beispiel dafür ist der Irakkrieg, in dem Verteidigungsminister Rumsfeld den streng gläubigen Präsidenten George W. Bush mit Bibelzitaten in seinem täglichen Report zu motivieren und dessen Entscheidungen zu rechtfertigen suchte.[5] Wieso fällt es Assmann so schwer, die Forderung nach einer generellen Entschärfung und nachhaltigen Entsorgung des semantischen Dynamits zu stellen? Wieso können sich sowohl jüdische, islamische als auch christliche Verantwortungsträger nicht von den zu Gewalt auffordernden Textstellen distanzieren und den Kanon revidieren?

Desweiteren stellt sich die Frage, wofür man überhaupt noch Religionen braucht, wenn sie durch Menschenrechte "eingezäunt" und entschärft werden müssen, um globalisierungsfähig zu sein. Viele global agierende Menschen- und Frauenrechtler, sowie Umwelt- und Tierschützer ziehen die Kraft ihres Engagements aus Gerechtigkeitsüberlegungen, die sich aus der Forderung nach Überwindung hierarchischer Dualismen und Feindbilder speisen. Möge es sich nun um die patriarchalen Unterdrückungsmechanismen der monotheistischen Schriften handeln, in denen die Frauen in einem Dauerverdacht der Sündigkeit und Unreinheit stehen, oder um die Vorstellung der Notwendigkeit, Andersdenkende, also "Ungläubige" gewaltsam bekehren oder sogar töten zu müssen, für viele Menschen stehen heute angesichts des religiösen Terrors Religionen unter einem Generalverdacht. Assmann möchte dieses Problem durch sein Konzept der "*religio duplex*" lösen, das er in der römisch-katholischen Kirche verwirklicht sieht. Aber ist diese Sichtweise der römisch-katholischen Kirche haltbar? Es kann hier nicht der Ort sein, theologischen Fragen im De-

---

[5] Der Zufall wollte es, dass ich gerade zu dieser Zeit die Exerzitien des Ignatius von Loyola las, in denen dazu aufgefordert wird, sich ein Heerlager in der Gegend von Jerusalem vorzustellen, wo der Befehlshaber der Guten, Christus, weile, während sich in einem anderen Heerlager in der Gegend von Babylon, sich der Häuptling der Feinde, nämlich Luzifer befinde. Man solle "sich vorstellen, wie sich der Anführer aller Feinde in jenem großen Heerlager von Babylon hinsetzt auf einen großmächtigen Thron aus Feuer und Rauch, ein einer Gestalt von Schauer und Schrecken." (Loyola 1993, 47) Besser kann man sich "die Achse der Bösen" gar nicht vorstellen.

tail nachzugehen, eines scheint jedoch auf der Hand zu liegen, dass weder Benedikt XVI, noch die römisch-katholische Kirche so liberal sind, wie Assmann sie darstellt.

Damit komme ich zum dritten Punkt, nämlich zu Assmanns Kennzeichnung der totalen Religion als Lebensform. Die Frage, die sich hier stellt ist, ob dies nicht auf alle Religionen zutrifft. Assmann scheint den generellen Zug der Religionen, alle Bereiche, von der Wiege bis zur Bahre zu bestimmen, zu unterschätzen. Daran ändert auch die christliche Zweiwelten-Lehre nichts, die im Mittelalter zu einer Machtteilung zwischen Kaiser und Papst geführt hat. Seine eigene Lebensform unabhängig von der Religion bestimmen zu können verdankt sich einem langen Ausdifferenzierungsprozess der Menschenrechte, ausgehend von der Gewissensfreiheit über die Glaubensfreiheit bis hin zur Meinungsfreiheit. Die Menschenrechte sind subjektive Rechte. Sie schützen das Individuum vor staatlichen und religiösen Eingriffen und ermächtigen das Individuum zu einer selbstbestimmten Lebensform. Gerade damit hatte die römisch-katholische Kirche jedoch immer schon große Probleme. So wurden im 19. Jahrhundert die Priester unter Eid verpflichtet, der Moderne und damit den Menschenrechten abzuschwören. Erst die Katastrophe des Holocaust hat der Kirche die Augen für die Bedeutung der Menschenrechte geöffnet, was nicht heißt, dass es nicht immer noch Spannungen gibt. Denn die römisch-katholische Kirche greift immer noch weit in die persönlichen Lebensbereiche ein. Katholisch zu sein, bedeutet in diesem Sinne auch heute noch, einer bestimmten, vorgegebenen Lebensform zu entsprechen.[6]

Viele, auch gläubige, Menschen, tragen in sich die Sorge, dass es – mit oder ohne Ernstfall – zu einer religiösen Verschärfung kommen könnte und stehen aus ihrer liberalen Grundverfassung heraus einer allzu großen Stärkung und einem Überhandnehmen der Religionen skeptisch gegenüber. Darüber hinaus steht die Dynamik der Selbstermächtigung in der Moderne in krassem Widerspruch zu einer vormodernen Logik des Verbotes und der Bestrafung. Dadurch wird der wirkliche Kern des christlichen Glaubens – und nur von diesem kann ich persönlich Zeugnis ablegen – vollkommen verstellt. Dieser zeichnet sich nicht nur dadurch aus, wie der "wahre" Ring der Lessing'schen Parabel "bei Gott und den Menschen beliebt zu machen" (ibid., 162), sondern durch eine ganz besondere Liebeskraft, die – wie Paulus sagt – Berge versetzen kann. Dadurch wird ein Versöhnungs- und Vergebungspotential freigelegt, das dazu verhelfen kann, nicht nur selber ein friedvolles, freudiges und vor allem angstfreies Leben zu leben, sondern auch dahingehend auf die Welt einzuwirken. Dass dabei nicht nur kühne Träume am Werk sind, zeigt die Realität: der gewalt-

---

[6] Die Lebensform der Keuschheit vor der Ehe; die Lebensform der Ehe als lebenslange und unauflösliche Lebensform mit dem Verbot der Empfängnisverhütung und der Aufforderung, möglichst viele Kinder zu bekommen; die Ablehnung der gleichgeschlechtlichen Partnerschaft als Lebensform und vieles mehr.

freie Widerstand Mahatma Gandhis, Martin Luther-Kings Nelson Mandelas und Lima Bowees, sowie die Versöhnungsprozesse in Ruanda und Südafrika gehen auf diesen christlichen Kern der Liebe und Gewaltfreiheit zurück. Nur wenn man die Ambivalenz der Religionen aufzeigt, d.h. nicht nur ihr Versöhnungs-, sondern auch ihr Gewaltpotential, kann man dazu beitragen, den Weg frei zu machen für eine Religionsform der Zukunft. Dabei wird es von Nöten sein, sich von jeglicher Form von Gewalt entschieden zu distanzieren.

Dr. Susanne Moser, Institut für Axiologische Forschungen, Wien /
Karl Franzens-Universität Graz, susanne.moser[at]univie.ac.at

Literaturhinweise

Abdel-Samad, Hamid. *Der islamische Faschismus*. München: Droemer Verlag, 2014.
Assmann, Jan. *Totale Religion. Ursprünge und Formen puritanischer Verschärfung*. Wien: Picus Verlag, 2016.
Assmann, Jan. *Religio duplex*. Berlin: Verlag der Weltreligionen, 2010.
Assmann, Jan. *Monotheismus und die Sprache der Gewalt*. Wien: Picus Verlag, 2006.
Assmann, Jan. *Moses der Ägypter: Entzifferung einer Gedächtnisspur*. München: Carl Hanser Varlag, 1998.
Bucher, Rainer. *Hitlers Theologie*. Würzburg: Echter Verlag, 2008.
Loyola, Ignatius. *Exerzitien*. Freiburg: Johannes Verlag Einsiedeln, 1993.

www.ingramcontent.com/pod-product-compliance
Lightning Source LLC
Chambersburg PA
CBHW080806300426
44114CB00020B/2842